| THE POLITICS OF INEQUALITY |

The Politics of Inequality

A POLITICAL HISTORY OF THE IDEA OF
ECONOMIC INEQUALITY IN AMERICA

Michael J. Thompson

COLUMBIA UNIVERSITY PRESS   *New York*

COLUMBIA UNIVERSITY PRESS
Publishers Since 1893
New York   Chichester, West Sussex

A CARAVAN BOOK. For more information visit www.caravanbooks.org

Library of Congress Cataloging-in-Publication Data

Thompson, Michael, 1973–
    The politics of inequality : a political history of the idea of
economic inequality in America / Michael J. Thompson
        p. cm.
    Includes bibliographical references and index.
    ISBN 978-0-231-14074-4 (cloth : alk. paper)—
ISBN 978-0-231-51172-8 (e-book)
        1. United States—Economic policy. 2. Distributive justice—
United States—History. 3. Distribution (Economic theory)—
Political aspects.
    I. Title.

HC103.T56 2007
339.2'20973—DC22

2007012874

∞ Columbia University Press books are printed on permanent and durable acid-free paper.
This book is printed on paper with recycled content.

Printed in the United States of America

c 10 9 8 7 6 5 4 3 2 1

DESIGN BY VIN DANG

FOR MY TEACHERS

ἰσότητα δ᾽ αἱροῦ καὶ πλεονεξίαν φύγε

— MENANDER

| Contents |

| *Acknowledgments* |

Many people helped me think about and develop the ideas in this book. Stephen Eric Bronner, Ruth O'Brien, and Frances Fox Piven read various versions of the manuscript with great care, providing me with critical comments and challenging different aspects of my argument. Others gave comments on the manuscript or helped me through our conversations on the subject matter of this book: Sam Aboelela, Stanley Aronowitz, Marshall Berman, Bob Fitch, Philip Green, Dick Howard, Gareth Stedman Jones, Eliot Katz, Antonia Levy, Elena Mancini, John Mason, Charles Noble, Corey Robin, Anne Routon, Joan Tronto, John Wallach, Debbie Wolf, and Gregory Zucker. I would also like to thank my editor at Columbia University Press, Peter Dimock, for his consistent interest in this project and his deeply insightful comments on the manuscript. I would also like to thank Korey Hughes for compiling the index. Of course, it goes without saying that all errors are my own.

| THE POLITICS OF INEQUALITY |

| *Introduction* | The Political Dimensions of
Economic Inequality

What is the political significance of economic inequality? With what moral wrongs does it resonate? In what ways does the existence of economic divisions in society threaten or put into question our conception, culture, and institutions of democracy? Throughout the history of Western political thought, injunctions against unequal divisions of property, wealth, and power can be found, from the scrolls of ancient Greece to the political philosophy of the mid-twentieth century. The problem of economic inequality has always been tied to the discourse of politics, to the problem of power itself. As the consciousness of political freedom has spread through time, so has the problem of economic inequality been central to this debate. Today, however, even as we witness the ballooning of economic divisions, we are faced with the reality that, as a political concern, economic inequality seems to have lost its place at the center of the debate about democratic life. It is time to remedy this deficiency.

This book seeks to make an argument about economic inequality that has all too often been neglected in contemporary debates; it is an argument that finds its roots deep in the tradition of Western political thought: that economic relations are, in fact, political relations; that the economy is political precisely because it manifests relations of social power. This was taken for granted by thinkers in the past, but it is something that has been sadly lost as we have witnessed the separation of economics from politics in the present age. The existence and the worsening of economic inequality in contemporary America—not to mention globally—therefore constitutes a serious threat to the republican themes that motivated the birth of the American political project from its inception, as well as the democratic themes that broke through to the world during the Enlightenment.

The final decades of the twentieth century witnessed a radical transformation in American economic and political life. The great reaction against the welfare state, which was erected during the New Deal and had its roots in the Progressive Era's philosophy of an expanded state and a skepticism of laissez-faire economic philosophy, has given way to a new, altogether different conceptualization of economy and society. How this happened and what this transformation means are at the heart of the present study. This book examines economic inequality as it was conceived by political thinkers and social critics throughout American political thought for the purpose of shedding light on the nature of contemporary American politics and its relation to the problem of economic inequality. In the first instance, it will trace the historical development of the ideas that American political thinkers and critics held concerning economic inequality. My second aim is to explain the current acceptance and toleration of economic inequality in America; to examine the change in political ideas and values that have led to the acceptance and sometimes legitimation of economic divisions and inequalities that mark the contemporary American political scene.

My basic argument is that liberal and republican themes were wedded in the American mind at the nation's founding. Both viewpoints saw an intimate relation between power and property, if not coevality with each other. Liberalism was a doctrine of individual labor and, by extension, property, and it sought to give independence to individuals, smashing feudal relations of dependency that were predominate before the American Revolution. Republican themes emphasized the need for the institutions of the state to ensure that inequalities in property—and by extension, power—were kept in check. Within the context of an emerging commercial society bent on popular government, the theme of economic inequality was therefore central. Both liberalism and republicanism—two doctrines that have traditionally been seen as oppositional in previous literature on American political history—were actually seen as two sides of the same coin. Both sought to confront inequality of property and political power, and each saw that this was a central concern in eradicating the vestiges of feudalism that were at the heart of the birth of the American republic and modernity more generally. But the real essence of the story is that these two impulses begin to differentiate over the course of American history as the economic context develops. The evolution of capitalism begins to chart a course for liberalism at the expense of republican themes. By the end of the twentieth century, liberalism becomes co-opted by capitalism, and republican themes of the past fade into the background. The result is an overall acceptance or at least toleration of economic inequality and the gross differentials in political and social power it engenders in contemporary American politics and culture. I contend that this has led to a reorientation of democratic life in America and that as long as economic inequality and politics are held separate, a more vibrant democratic culture and consciousness will not be possible.

Indeed, the success of neoconservative and neoliberal thought over the last thirty-five years has had the effect of redrawing the boundaries of American liberalism. Nowhere is this more in evidence than in the loss in mainstream American political discourse of one of the most crucial veins of American political thought, which ran, until quite recently, like a roiling river at the heart of American life. This vein is the politics of economic inequality—a subject this book attempts to reclaim for our present. An intellectual history of the politics of economic inequality in American political thought is necessary, I think, to restore to American political culture its more generous and accurate contours after the assault that has been made upon American liberalism by the forces of American conservatism in recent decades.

How and why has an economy that continues to generate and perpetuate such rigid forms of economic inequality and such disparities of political and social power that spring from it not fostered more resistance and critique from within the American body politic? This book contains an attempt at a partial answer to this crucial question. The answer requires, among other things, an analysis of the developmental changes in the way that the concept of economic inequality has been understood down through American history. That understanding must entail, in turn, the recognition that the way the present economic inequality in both the American nation and the world is understood and justified marks a profound departure from the tradition of egalitarianism that dominated American political thought for most of its history. My aim in this book is to retrace the outlines of that American egalitarian political tradition and to locate it within the long tradition of democratic political thought going all the way back to the Greeks. At the end of this effort, it is my hope that the reader will be in a position to see the American egalitarian tradition's present exhaustion in the national political arena as an argument for—and not against—its resuscitation and rejuvenation as a necessary part of a worldwide democratic politics yet to be realized.

In addition to this, I think that the economic egalitarian tradition that I will present here is so crucial because it is at the heart of the American republican project itself. The American idea of a democratic republic had always been premised on an antipathy toward unequal divisions of property because early American thinkers saw in those unequal shares of economic power echoes of what had been historically overturned: a sociopolitical order of rank and privilege; a static society that sought to crystallize power relationships and hierarchical economic and social relations characterized by corruption and patronage; in short, a feudal order where the exercise of power was arbitrary and the prospect of domination pervaded everyday life. The reason I trace the historical development and inevitable dissolution of the discourse on economic inequality in American political thought is to show that the American republican project was, in fact, deeply tied to the issues of economic inequality as a reaction to feudal social relations. Any political community that suffers from severe imbalances between rich and poor is in danger of losing its democratic character, and I will investigate this theme in detail in the pages that follow.

American political thought has therefore been characterized over the centuries by an overriding concern with the problem of economic inequality, and the reason for this should come as little surprise. Students of American political thought and political theory know the Enlightenment foundations upon which the American political project has always rested. Rooted in the political concern for equality and for democratic republicanism, it has also been marked by a liberal economic ethos and the rapid development of a capitalist economy, class conflict, and competing views of the "public good." The clash between these two impulses in American political history occurs frequently. Perhaps the most salient historical locus for this clash is the subject of economic inequality, and it is one that—at least throughout modern history—has galvanized political movements and social critics to rail against hierarchy, servitude, unfreedom, and the erosion of democratic forms of life. The exhaustion of the once-robust critique of economic inequality therefore coincides with the erosion of political life more broadly and the fate of modern democracies more specifically, since it is within the nexus of economic constraints that most Americans face threats to their well-being, substantive political rights, and a culture of democracy. Even more, the present debates that surround economic inequality need to widen the field of vision, to enlarge the scope of concerns that, in the past, were associated with unequal divisions of property and wealth. The political dimensions of economic inequality can be seen not only in the conditions of the working poor, in urban ghettos, and in the overall stagnation of wages even as corporate profits surge. These debates need to include a discussion of the ways that economic inequality gives undue influence to the business community, transforms the imperatives of education, and fosters a culture of competitiveness and consumerism at the expense of broader political concerns. Any discussion of economic inequality needs to be tied to much more than debates about "fairness" and "opportunity"; it must confront the ways that this inequality shapes the political community as a whole by creating relations of subordination among its members.

Although the concern with economic inequality has hardly faded from the public discourse, it certainly no longer commands the attention it once did. The question, "Should inequality matter?" has become a common one in contemporary debates about American public and economic life. Economic liberalism has provided arguments for justifying inequality just as contemporary political culture also seems to tolerate economic divisions more than at any other time in American history. In the not too distant past, the realities of economic inequality spurred moral outrage. Combating the effects of inequality was the imperative of much of American social policy throughout the twentieth century. Indeed, during the New Deal and through the 1960s, there was great attention paid to the distributional impact of the capitalist economy and its effects on social welfare. Far from seeing markets, as they are seen today, as neutral and natural, the realities of the Great Depression and massive inequalities in wealth and incomes were seen as a detriment to political democracy. The reorientation of government policies has been matched by a similar change in public attitudes toward economic and social inequality. Although Americans still think economic inequality is morally wrong, they have accepted its consequences more than in previous eras in American history. They no longer see the connection between politics and economics, nor do they glimpse the ways that economic constraint interferes with the project of political democracy.

But even more, the problem of economic inequality needs to be looked at afresh in my view because it is no longer an issue that presents itself solely within a national context. Economic inequality is intimately bound up with the global system, with the elaborate networks of markets and capital flows that enmesh the planet. There is no way around the fact that America's economic egalitarian tradition is something that, although it was born out of a national context, in my view can also reinvigorate the global discourse on economic inequality. What this American tradition privileged was the notion that economic relations were, in fact, essentially *political* since they could impede or enhance, depending on the institutional context, political freedom and a more substantive, realistic sense of human equality. Not content with the formalism of political and legal equality, this tradition in American political thought saw that economic life was a counterpart of political life and the ability to live without excessive want or dependency on others and with self-sufficiency was an essential element of human liberty. It was not possible for an individual to be in any way free or possess any kind of substantive liberty if he was dependent upon another person or institution for wages or, in any other way, for the means of his existence; if he was forced into near pauperism while others profited off of his labor. These concerns were at the very center of the egalitarian ethos—it was not an absolute equality of property that was sought, but equality in terms of the power that individuals and groups had over others. This ethos was imbued with a concern for the public good but also with a real concern for the individual and the absence of what those who held it saw to be dependence and servitude. For the thinkers in this tradition, the core object of critique was the existence of domination and the lingering of feudal institutions and social relations, which focused their criticisms of the emerging capitalism and the kind of social and economic relations it was beginning to forge. Economics was therefore seen in political terms.

The essence of this tradition therefore has implications outside of the American context, and this is one of the additional, albeit implicit goals of the present work: to provide an understanding of economic inequality that is capable of moving *beyond* the national context. Concern with economic inequality is grounded in a political tradition that—although firmly based in ideas and values inherited from Western political thought

and shaped by American historical experience—still has a broad relevance
for confronting what today has become a dominant neoliberal ideology
that places markets and economic imperatives over political imperatives
and stresses the need to liberate markets even while enduring some of the
most severe social costs. The thinkers that make up the American egalitarian tradition were not concerned, for the most part, with political economy as we know it today. Rather, their concern was to apply what they
saw as the living pulse of American political culture, what made America's
republican experiment wholly unique, which was that political and social
relations needed to be bereft of all forms of domination in order for any
real sense of freedom to be realized. Their aim was to expose the antidemocratic character of economic life that was emerging as capitalism
developed. Their views changed over time, and so did their language. But I
will argue that there was a consistent concern with economic inequality as
a set of power relations. What made these egalitarian critiques and arguments so morally compelling, in my view, was their insistence on a much
broader, much richer understanding of democratic life and community
than is currently held today. Narrow self-interest and possessive individualism did not pervade this discourse, even though most of the critics in
this tradition did embrace a liberal economic ethic. What they saw was
that economic relations must be prevented from distorting the qualities of
human dignity, equality, and freedom, ideas that they saw embodied in the
republican (i.e., nonfeudal) nature of early American politics.

What I present here is a political history of the *idea* of economic inequality in American thought. The emphasis on ideas is important because it is how political actors think about their material or economic context that has political implications and helps to explain why a once vibrant
egalitarian tradition has, in many senses, exhausted itself. But my emphasis is not on ideas alone—rather, it is in the way that ideas have meshed
with the economic realities of their particular time that is so important.
We cannot simply argue that ideology alone accounts for the changing
pattern of ideas about economic inequality in American thought.[1] Only
by considering the way that egalitarian themes grapple with a particular
economic context—say, from small producers to a large-scale industrial
economy, or from contract labor to wage labor—can we actually have a
fruitful discussion of the mechanism of change in America's egalitarian
tradition. Indeed, when explaining the origins of inequality, Rousseau
frames the problem of the relation between material inequality and ideas

nicely by tying it to the origins of modern civilization itself and the founding of the institution of private property. He does this by highlighting the link between material interests and the values, conventions (*moeres*), or prevailing ideas of society as a whole that accompany them. And this only made sense since for Rousseau, the real essence of the problem of inequality was not simply the fact that it existed materially—something that was empirically obvious to any eighteenth-century observer—but a problem of the ways that the ideas legitimated the material divisions of society.

> The first person who, having enclosed a plot of land, took it into his head to say *this is mine* and found people simple enough to believe him, was the true founder of civil society. What crimes, wars, murders, what miseries and horrors would the human race have been spared had someone pulled up the stakes or filled in the ditch and cried out to his fellow men: "Do not listen to this imposter. You are lost if you forget that the fruits of the earth belong to all and the earth to no one."[2]

Rousseau's insight was that it is not the mere existence of inequality in material terms—e.g., in terms of property, income, or class—that is the essence of the problem but the ways that this inequality was in fact *legitimated*. For Rousseau, the issue is that people were "simple enough" to believe in the legitimacy of the institution of property, which made inequality—and all of its deleterious effects—acceptable and "real" through mere convention and the acceptance of this convention as *natural*. Rousseau's insight highlights what the relationship between economics and political ideas actually is: not a simple, direct scenario where one set of interests wins out over another, but a scheme that requires *legitimation* and therefore a transformation of political culture and values that enables the material forces within society, such as the market or capital, to shape society and its institutions by affecting attitudes, beliefs, and the way that economic institutions are interpreted. The politics of inequality is therefore something that requires a thorough analysis of political ideas and values, those things that frame the ideological field within which politics operates. To do this, I have chosen texts that were highly influential among public intellectuals and the public at large rather than more academic philosophical writings. My choice of texts therefore gets us closer to the broader public mind and the ways that general public conceptions and debates—as exemplified in these writings—transform through time.

There have been other, recent approaches to the problem of economic inequality and its relation to American politics that have focused on the influence of wealth on politics and the subsequent distortion of democratic politics. Kevin Phillips's *Wealth and Democracy* documented the "troubling and crippling side effects" of the "concentration of assets, inequality, and conspicuous consumption."[3] Phillips's work is an attempt to document the way that economic power has outstripped the democratic nature of American politics. But it is also an analysis that fails to take into consideration many of the prevailing ideas that have generated a legitimacy for inequality on a broad scale: the acceptance of inegalitarian market outcomes, the weakening of the sentiment of working people against their sinking economic fortunes, and so on. The economist Edward Wolff documents the expansion of wealth inequality and its long-term effects on quality of life in his book *Top Heavy*. But what has been missing in much of this contemporary literature is a historical approach that seeks to tease out of American political thought and history the political impulse that treated economic inequality with condemnation and dread.

The analysis I present here, by contrast, is meant to shed light not only on the political *implications* of inequality—such as the distortion of democratic politics that Phillips speaks of or the differences in life chances that Wolff does—but on the way that economic inequality itself is a political phenomenon that is embedded in the way individuals relate to one another, the institutions of the society they inhabit, and the ways that they legitimate the social world around them. By speaking of a "politics of inequality," I am arguing that the only way to approach economic inequality in contemporary American life is to revive the egalitarian impulse that was an outgrowth of the desire to eradicate social domination, expand the realm of political and social freedom, encourage a more robust sense of civic life, privilege political life over the narrow imperatives of the market, and check the imperatives of the minority of private interests, which were seen to be a threat to the very idea of a democratic republic that America—as opposed to the feudal institutions of Europe—was supposed to embody.

I will argue that economic inequality was central to the political debates that spurred America's political and social development, that it was a defining strand of American political thought and culture. In addition, I will argue that economic inequality was a central moral and political concern throughout American political history and that American political values of equality lessen in intensity as we follow the discourse on economic inequality throughout American political history. Today it has become customary to exclude class when discussing American political and social history. In its place, the issue of equality has been cast in racial and gendered terms. To be sure, these, too, are central aspects of the development of American political history, culture, and institutions, but the dynamic of class inequality remains a stubborn reality. Clarifying the ways that economic inequality threatened political conceptions of liberty, citizenship, and democracy is therefore a central concern that needs to be probed and explored, for in no other time in American history has the gap between political and economic democracy been so evident than in the present moment.

This analysis does not only make a point about America's past and the trajectory of American politics. It also points toward new avenues in political and democratic theory. Analysis of the history of the idea of economic inequality shows how the political ideals and expectations of American politics were in time corrupted by the intrusion of venal interests and the emergence of economic modernity. The radical critics of the early to mid-nineteenth century were consistent in their attack on economic inequality for forging permanent political inequalities between owners and laborers. But even when Progressive intellectuals, who were still critical of inequality in the late nineteenth and early twentieth centuries, embraced industrial capitalism, they continued to emphasize the atomizing effects of modern capitalism and the erosion of American democracy that resulted from it. In an age where the market once again is promulgating social atomism and intensifying inequalities, this theme from the past requires attention, and what I will later call a "republican modernity" needs to be explored.

What is in fact consistent about the discourse on economic inequality in American political thought is how intimately bound up it is with the distinct political concerns of freedom and democratic republicanism, or a concern for the elimination of social relations that enforce forms of subservience—conscious or otherwise. Divisions between wealthy and poor, not to mention employer and employee, were seen as distinct power relationships and not simply as a matter of class difference. Politics was deeply embedded in the ways that economic relations were interpreted, and it is in the ways that economic inequality were conceptualized, discussed, analyzed, and debated that we can glimpse an alternative way of relating politics and economics. The privileging of politics over economics was a crucial bulwark against excessive economic inequality and was a crucial source of the economic egalitarian impulse. This is something that needs to be revived if any real progress can be made in combating the contemporary phenomenon of excessive economic inequality. Mere facts and figures cannot do the job in convincing the public and political figures to take the issue seriously once again: what is needed is a repoliticizing of the issue, and history can serve as an important resource for this project. And even though talk of American exceptionalism is still vibrant, this should not be taken to mean that American political ideas have no relevance to political groups and traditions outside of the America. Far from being the case, America's egalitarian tradition shows a universal relevance for the themes of equality and a rich, deep conception of democratic social and political life, one that has been eroding even within the American national political context.

This tradition and its unique perspective on the relationship between politics and economics is in distinct contrast to contemporary approaches to economic inequality, those dominated by empirical economists and sociologists or moral philosophers. This study wants to show that politics has its own distinct perspective on the problem of economic inequality and a claim on the debate in both its historical and contemporary manifestations. The key to understanding economic inequality as it was viewed by thinkers throughout the development of American political thought is to see it in political terms, and this view retains its salience. Inequalities in the economic sphere are also distinct asymmetrical power relationships that dictate many aspects of everyday life in addition to structuring inequalities in quality of life and access to basic economic goods that enable, or disable, social mobility. Economic hierarchies are not simply the result of differentials in talent and skill between different individuals. They are the result of the activity of markets and the operation of capital, itself a distinct social institution. But in the end, this is not really the issue; rather, what needs to be emphasized is that any movement toward economic equality has been historically achieved by political pressure in the form of social movements that have sought some measure of economic rights, whether in the form of unionization or direct redistribution. The importance of political ideas, of the ways that political actors interpret the material context within which they live, is of primary importance.

Historically speaking, economic divisions within society were a primary lens through which Americans viewed social power in everyday life because these divisions provided the structure of power relations. Central to this argument is the notion that American political ideas about individualism, liberty, and equality—which we broadly term liberalism—have different meanings in different historical-economic contexts. Liberalism was a radical doctrine when it was faced with the encrusted, aristocratic power relationships that characterized social relations during the eighteenth century. The concern with the right of each individual to be paid according to his labor—and not to profit off of the labor of others—was a radical interpretation of the liberal doctrine that wanes in the late nineteenth, twentieth, and twenty-first centuries. With the reconciliation of working people to the wage system and to a broad liberal-capitalist consensus, liberalism would lose its radical edge in arguing for economic equality and become more of an implicit defense of the prevailing system. This becomes a major theme of this study: namely, that as the nature of the economic system changes and becomes more "naturalized," there is a consequent acceptance of economic divisions in American politics and culture. It is not the fact that political ideas have changed—Americans still embrace economic liberalism, for example—but that the economic context within which those ideas operate changed over time.

This leads me to a second, not unrelated argument: that the contemporary tolerance of economic inequality is actually the result of liberalism and liberal thought itself. Although the liberal economic ethic was central in combating feudal forms of political and social life, liberalism—defined here as the political philosophy that emphasizes individualism and property rights—has become ascendant at the expense of republican themes in American political culture. Economic inequality needs to be seen not simply in terms of different economic outcomes; I argue that—keeping with the majority of American political thought on this topic—economic inequality must also be seen in political terms: in the ways that it creates new forms of hierarchy, social fragmentation, and constraints on individual liberty. American political thought was, at least through the beginnings of the twentieth century, a mixture of liberal and republican themes. Politically, the emphasis on individual liberty was matched by a concern for a community of equals. Republican themes emphasized the need for the absence of domination, which was itself understood as the ability of one person to arbitrarily interfere with another. This was a more robust understanding of freedom than liberalism offers since it was sensitive to the ways that institutions bound working people to conditions that eroded their substantive freedom and rights.

I highlight the various ways that economic inequality was either problematized or praised (there was, and still is, an inegalitarian tradition in American political thought as well). What writers and thinkers within the economic egalitarian tradition sought to emphasize was the way that the growing disparity of economic power would form the groundwork for distortions in political and social power. New forms of economic life would foster not individual liberty and independence but a new form of economic dependence of working people on others (namely owners) and the erosion of social and political freedom. At the root of the American economic egalitarian tradition is the notion that economic divisions lead inexorably to political and social inequalities of power; that the essence of any real sense of political equality could only be guaranteed by a sensibly equal distribution of property and wealth. This meant that political and economic life were in fact inseparable and that social power was a function not only of political power but of the ways that individuals had the power over their own economic life and the ability to direct their lives independently of others—whether political tyrants or factory owners. Historically, Americans were reacting against the memories and vestiges of aristocracy and feudalism. This formed part of a political-historical consciousness that militated against class divisions. The fear of the aristocracy and the destruction of America's republican experiment were therefore at the core of early American ideas about inequality. The political moment was therefore always explicit, and this is something that has been lost in contemporary American attitudes toward economic power and class inequality.

Late-nineteenth- and twentieth-century American political history saw the expansion of the role of the state in the economy and the market. For many intellectual elites of the time, the inegalitarian effects of industrial capitalism were in growing opposition to newer ideas and conceptions of democracy that were becoming current at the time. But more important, what the New Deal and the rise of the American welfare state ushered in was a new interpretation of democracy, one that saw, both implicitly and explicitly, that political democracy was untenable without a substantial degree of economic equality as well. The redistributional character of the welfare state was a result of this overall reconceptualization of democracy, but it was precipitated by the reaction against the massive economic divisions of the late nineteenth and early twentieth centuries, as well as a response to the overall crisis of capitalism. New Deal liberalism would eventually evolve into Great Society liberalism, and it would not be until the late 1970s that a successful neoconservative assault on the welfare state and on the doctrine of economic equality began to redirect this political project.

But different historical periods possess different ideas about how equality could be achieved and how inequality was in fact generated. It is usually assumed that eighteenth-century American political ideas about inequality were largely concerned with the problem of *political* inequality—with the rights of different citizens to participate in the political sphere—more than with the problems of a lack or inequality of property. Politics was the nexus where the dimensions of social power clashed, and, as a result, economic inequalities were seen as bound up with political inequalities in two ways. First, there was an assumption that inequalities in the economic sphere derived from political privilege. With the abolition of this privilege, it was largely presumed, the bulk of oppressive economic inequality would also vanish. But once capitalism began to develop more intensely, it soon became obvious that the political ideals of liberal republicanism were being called into question by the institutional constraints of economic modernity. The central point therefore became the nexus between the economic and the political: the reality of economic inequality itself and its various implications.

But second and, indeed, more important, economic inequalities were seen to have political effects on the political community as a whole. This was a view that began to take distinct shape in the early nineteenth century. Economic inequality did not only deny certain segments of the political community the material means for adequate survival—something that had sparked anger and revolts for centuries on end—it also dispossessed them of their autonomy and robbed them of substantive social and political liberty in the sense that they would be subject to domination, live according to the interests and the power of others, and cease to be self-sufficient—and therefore cease to be free. In this sense, and in contradistinction to today, economic inequality was always seen as a distinctly political concern; it touched on broader themes and ideas deriving from a robust anti-aristocratic sentiment and also a political impulse toward individual self-sufficiency in economic and political terms as a central aspect of what was seen to be America's "republican civilization."

This is no idealization of the past. The writings of the overwhelming majority of those who were critics of economic inequality are imbued with these themes, and they constitute a distinct tradition within American political thought. Thus, the analysis of economic inequality in American political thought needs to be seen as a *politics of inequality*, as the way that the mechanisms of the market and the developmental logic of the American economy and its effects were countered by a concern with unequal relations of power and how they constituted an assault on prevailing conceptions of democratic community as well as social and individual liberty. Central to this discourse was the problem of servitude and its opposition to liberty; the ways in which economic relations—not simply the differentials in the amount of property that was accumulated—translated themselves into the broader relations of political and social life. For in the end, economic inequality also meant the decline of self-sufficiency and legal and political equality, as well as the re-creation of the barbarity of feudal institutions.[4] This had its roots in the commonwealth tradition in England in the seventeenth and eighteenth centuries—itself derived from republican themes—which was then transposed into the American context.[5] Economic inequality was not only viewed as dangerous to broader conceptions of the public good and to moral ideas of fairness; the drive to abolish it was also heavily tempered by a political imperative to enhance individual and social freedom.

Today the legitimation of economic inequality has acquired a position of influence as in no other time in American political thought. Of course, America has its inegalitarian tradition as well, beginning with thinkers such as Alexander Hamilton and continuing on through thinkers such as Milton Friedman. Well over twenty years ago the political theorist Philip Green could write that "special advantages for economic elites, as in the United States tax code, are introduced *sub rosa*, never proclaimed out loud. No one defends legislation by suggesting that the better class should be rewarded more and the inferior less." This is no longer strictly the case.[6] To understand this transition in American political life requires a multilayered analysis of American political ideas. And such an analysis also needs to take into account how ideas about equality and inequality have operated as ideologies with respect to the prevailing economic system that, by its very nature, produces inequalities of wealth.

The historical development of ideas about economic inequality in American political thought has witnessed a transformation from radical criticism to relatively passive acceptance. As the liberal doctrine of competitive individualism became more dominant, calls for equality of condition were replaced with calls for equality of opportunity. As inequality began to worsen during the later decades of the twentieth century, it was these same liberal ideas that were in effect co-opted by a renewed economic libertarianism, which gave justification to inequality not only on the basis of "fairness" but on the basis of the neoliberal argument that inequalities were the product of an efficiently operating economy that would also produce an enhancement in economic incentives, prodding the economy to continuous growth and prosperity.[7] The study of political ideas should not be seen as simply an academic enterprise; the way we think has much to do with the various ways that institutions are legitimated and an impact on the future evolution of those institutions and on the ways that political actors respond to and shape political realities.

From the very beginning, issues of economic inequality factored into the debates of the framers of the Constitution, as well as theorists of American republican democracy. To be sure, America's democratic development has been a result of a confrontation with multiple forms of inequality. The problems of racial and ethnic inequality and issues of gender have been at the forefront of the American democratic project. But the reality and persistence of economic divisions has been a consistent theme of opposition throughout American political history. Even though the problem was persistent, the ways that thinkers approached the problem varied, and it is this history of ideas that requires analysis in order for us to derive political meaning from them. These thinkers generally confronted the problem of inequality from a political and moral position that has been eroded by modern liberalism. But even though this is the case, one of the central themes that runs through this study is that the closer we look at the ideas and writings of the critics of economic inequality, the clearer it becomes that their concern was not for a utopian conception of absolute economic equality. They were critics of the effects of inequality, but they did pragmatically accept the idea that some inequalities would need to exist. Unquestionably, there were utopians among them, but the overwhelming tenor of this tradition was the elimination of inequalities that would create unequal relations of social and political power and that would also lead to social and political fragmentation and the subordination of the public good to the interests of the few.

These ideas were radical to be sure. They rejected the emerging economic order in the early decades of the nineteenth century, and many of them rejected the entire structure of economic modernity itself, seeing smaller economic communities as superior to the trends that were moving toward a nationalized market economy. But as capitalism continued to develop, these themes began to lose their radical edge. The Progressive Era and its thinkers were hardly egalitarians, but they saw that the excesses of capitalism required the state's intervention and a reconceptualization of the goals of the national economy. They knew that the massive inequalities of the Gilded Age had to be counteracted and a sense of public life needed to be reinvigorated. Alleviating economic inequality and gaining some degree of control over laissez-faire capitalism was therefore one of the key aspects of Progressive philosophy and policy. At the same time, this led to a liberal-capitalist consensus that would reduce inequalities for the sake of preserving the broader economic system as a whole.

THE "NEW INEQUALITY"

The concern with economic inequality in American political thought and history therefore relates directly to the political concerns of the present. What has come to be known as the "new inequality" has been characterized by the specific pattern in which economic inequality has manifested itself in late-twentieth-century and early-twenty-first-century America. Beginning in the early 1980s, there was a massive increase in income inequality due to "the unprecedented abysmal earnings experience of low-paid Americans, income stagnation covering about eighty percent of all families, and an increase in upper-end incomes."[8] The divergence of incomes was largely attributable to the increase in real incomes for high-income earners and a sharp decline in wages for those at the bottom. Pay differentials increased along the lines of education, age, and experience, the only real exception being gender, which saw a decrease in income dispersion.[9] A key aspect of the "new inequality" is a result of the restructuring of American capitalism, that is, its integration into a more competitive world market for production and consumption.[10] Indeed, this is the most common explanation behind the rise in income dispersion that has been at the center of the recent surge in social inequality in America. Wages have grown more unequal as a result of macroeconomic causes such as unemployment, inflation, rapid economic growth and stagnation of the minimum wage, the decline in the power of unions and their influence, as well as the exchange rate of the dollar.[11] In addition, the emergence of segmented labor markets—which accompanied and was exacerbated by the process of deindustrialization—has also created a situation of spatial and racial/ethnic exclusion as affluent, white suburbs become more economically and socially distant from decayed urban areas. The segmentation of labor markets is therefore accompanied by a segmentation of housing, public goods such as education and environmental standards, and therefore life chances and opportunities, creating an "American apartheid" where separation of racial and class groups becomes all but insurmountable.[12]

Although this is clearly true, there is also another side to the "new inequality," one that is decidedly more pernicious in the sense that what we see happening is a change not only in the structure of work and income in a postindustrial order but also the deepening of class divisions along the lines of wealth inequality. Edward Wolff has argued that when discussing inequality we should focus on the inequality of wealth since wealth inequality between households means a disparity in the ability to buy a home, and the wealthier family is more "likely to be better able to provide for its children's educational and health needs, live in a neighborhood characterized by more amenities and lower levels of crime, have greater resources that can be called upon in times of economic hardship, and have more influence in political life."[13] This trend in wealth inequality is a directional change from the broad secular trend since 1929, which featured was a pronounced decline in the concentration of wealth in America through the 1970s.[14]

What the economic literature points to is the emergence of patterns of inequality that are both enduring and worsening. These inequalities are also complex in nature, since they are relationships between social classes that affect different dimensions of social life in terms of wealth, income, quality of life, housing quality, and access to public goods such as education, many times in spatial or regional terms as well. They endure partly because of the transition of American capitalism from an industrial to a postindustrial kind, but also because of the pullback of government services throughout the last two decades of the twentieth century. Of course, these are both partly the results of changing economic factors, but the politics behind this new upsurge in inequality needs to be located and analyzed. It is true that many economists have done an excellent job of parsing the mechanisms of the "new inequality," but what needs to be assessed is the way that political ideas have come to legitimize these economic relations. It is one of the primary assumptions of my analysis that political ideas act as a legitimating force on economic realities. Shedding light on the political assumptions and implications of economic inequality will therefore reveal deeper relations between economic inequality and democracy and pull the current discourse around economic inequality away from mere empirical concerns, placing politics at the center of the debate.

INEQUALITY AT THE END OF HISTORY

Neoliberalism and neoconservatism have occupied a central place in American politics over the past two and a half decades and, in so doing, have radically reoriented American politics and the discourse about democracy more broadly. Whereas politics had always taken precedence over economics throughout American political and social thought, neoliberal ideas represent the reversal of this tradition. The need to foster "free" markets at the expense of their social and political effects, as well as the optimism that characterizes such institutional forms, is spreading beyond America itself. The embrace of the market by so much of mainstream American thought and culture is at odds with the desires of most Americans to have a welfare state that protects their economic interests. One of the defining aspects of neoconservative thought has been its emphasis on the market as an institution that allows for the expression of individual liberty. In this view, politics and economics are linked, but in the most superficial and abstract way. What is ignored is that what actually generates inequality in economic terms is not the market itself but *capital*, and this is something that was seen from the beginning of the American egalitarian tradition. The critics of economic inequality in America before the Civil War all saw the political-economic relationship between capital and labor, and they saw it as impervious to reform. Today, neoconservative (or neoliberal) ideas and policies have been able to wed American liberalism to the notions of individuality, liberty, and efficiency that markets supposedly embody. By doing this, they are able to draw attention away from what has problematized the relationship between capital and labor for the entirety of American political history: that the interests of these two classes are inherently opposed to each other and generate inequalities in economic and political terms that distort democratic life and re-create class hierarchies that are at odds with what was at the heart of the American political project from the beginning.

At the core of neoconservative and neoliberal philosophy is the notion that equality has extended as far as it will ever be able to extend without endangering individual liberty. Equality is to be realized and contained exclusively in the legal and political sphere, and even then, only in the abstract or formal sense. This differs strongly from the insight that was offered and acted upon by Progressive and New Deal thinkers who saw the role of the state expanding into the economy as necessary for a more substantive conception of democracy to flourish. These thinkers were reacting against the massive inequalities of the late nineteenth century, but, even more, they were reacting against the entire social theory upon which it had been based: laissez-faire individualism. And it is precisely this theory of society and government that has made a triumphant return in contemporary American politics.

Tracing the history of the politics of economic inequality therefore can shed light on the present political situation and the assumptions that currently dominate economic and political life. Freedom has reached its culmination in the institutional matrix of liberal democratic capitalism, and any movement outside of this system is bound to end up in a situation of unfreedom. Taking its cue from Hegel's notion of the end of history as the speculative realization that human freedom is at the very core of the development of history, this argument—first penned by Francis Fukuyama as a characterization of a post-1989 world with an ascendant liberal capitalism—has had the effect of redefining much of American liberalism. Now, the liberal idea of political equality has been realized, and the true nature of human liberty has manifested itself. This "end of history" thesis in many ways has defended the structure of the politics behind the "new inequality." The persistence of economic inequality has much to do with the structural transformation of work and the transition to postindustrialism as it does with the new transformation of political ideology. Nevertheless, the ascendance of libertarian ideas about economy and society has not only influenced the elites responsible for public policy but also has affected public sentiment on a whole range of economic issues as well as the way that the public conceives of contemporary economic life. The inverse relation between the rise of inequality and the amount of political aversion to it requires explanation, and I think it can be found in the way that the idea of liberalism, with its emphasis on individualism and its conception of labor and property, has triumphed over broader conceptions of the common good that were espoused by republican-minded thinkers. Bled of its older political implications, a narrow sense of liberalism can no longer provide a robust critique of economic divisions, even among those who suffer most from them.

But if what I have been arguing here is at all true, then an analysis of the developmental changes in how the concept of economic inequality has been understood—as a concept but also as a condition—is required, as is an analysis of the political concerns that served as the backdrop for those ideas. Indeed, contemporary American sentiment on these issues has been shaped not by objective truths or historical experience but by an ideological shift that views economic inequality as valid in pursuit of larger social and political goals. The neoliberal mantra of the rising tide that raises all boats is only marginally seen as a justification for the reduction of the public sphere and the growth of the market as the solution for social problems. There is also the ideology of self-improvement and social mobility that accompanies the liberal economic ethic. This renewed conception of liberalism traces its foundations back to thinkers like Ludwig von Mises, Friedrich Hayek, and Milton Friedman. But today it has become hegemonic in the way that economic life is understood and economic inequality justified, and it marks a reorientation away from the tradition of egalitarianism that had dominated much of American political thought and its emphasis on egalitarian conditions and a broader notion of social solidarity, rather than atomistic individualism.

This can, and should, also be seen as a reorientation of American democracy away from the more substantive ideas about equality that were privileged by the thinkers of the early twentieth century. In this sense, the discussion of economic inequality therefore resonates much more deeply with other dimensions of American political and cultural life. It is, indeed, first and foremost an empirical question of how people respond to unequal divisions of power, but it also brings into question the nature of American democratic culture itself. If Western political thought, from the writings of Plato on through those of John Dewey, saw economic inequality as dangerous, it did so not out of a liberal concern for "fairness" or opportunity but because it marked divisions that threatened a culture of equality and freedom. Conceiving individual liberty outside of the context of economic constraint—as is so fashionable with neoconservative thought and libertarian apologists—is so narrow an understanding of social life that it becomes an absurd theoretical abstraction.

Even more, the rise of neoconservative thought on this topic should be seen as a grave turn against the American egalitarian tradition that railed against economic inequality for its effects on political and social power. There is no denying that the impulse toward equality among Americans has lost its political power to mobilize people against those economic institutions and policies that continue, at least by all statistical measures, to make them more and more unequal to the wealthiest Americans. The consequences have been drastic. This is at core a political problem, and it raises the question of which political ideas, which traditions are being embraced. Investigating the lineage of these ideas is therefore essential, for it will tell us much about the American pursuit of economic equality, social justice, and the realization of a fuller, more robust understanding of democratic life. This is where the ideological, institutional, and political levels of the analysis converge, since ideas are used to justify and to legitimize certain institutions and interests. This story begins at the very heart of American political thought in its earliest generations—from thinkers as diverse as Thomas Jefferson and John C. Calhoun—and stretches through the modern attack on the welfare state. Unearthing the political traditions of inegalitarianism and egalitarianism will enable us to see how politics was always central to the concerns over economic inequality and that it was the issue of politics, of power, that dominated the various debates. For it is only when we begin to move away from the purely moral or empirical understandings of inequality and embrace the political dimensions of the problem that a revival of a more robust debate over the serious problems of economic inequality can be realized.

By seeing economic inequality through the lens of politics, we are confronted with profound questions about the nature and culture of American democratic life and politics. If inequality is seen merely in economistic terms and simply as a debate about "fairness," then the political implications of inequality have indeed been lost. The critics of inequality that make up the American egalitarian tradition interpreted economic inequality as not only pernicious in and of itself but also as a threat to social and individual freedom. The overwhelming majority of these critics saw that the political institutions of America's republican democracy could only function once there was a relative absence of unequal wealth. They emphasized an aversion toward plutocracy and neo-aristocratic institutions over plans of social fantasy. Rejuvenating deeper nuances of American democracy therefore hinges upon breathing life once again into this egalitarian tradition, the particular way that it connected social power and economic inequality, its anti-hierarchical stance, and its emphasis on a richer conception of social and individual freedom. Only once political imperatives are placed over the imperatives of the marketplace and the antidemocratic nature of contemporary social stratification is exposed for what it is will it again become possible to expand and enrich American democratic politics.

I

The Critique of Economic Inequality in Western Political Thought
The Continuity of an Idea

An imbalance between rich and poor is the oldest and most fatal ailment of all republics.
|PLUTARCH|

━━━

The contours of the Western political tradition show a deep and enduring concern with the problem of economic inequality. The critique of economic inequality seems to be a fairly consistent theme because it was always bound to the discussion of how to govern with justice, or at least with some degree of order. This motivation is interesting because, unlike the approach of many scholars to the question of the emergence of equality as a political ideal in Western political thought, it indicates that economic inequality was not critiqued simply because it was seen as morally wrong but because it was viewed as a concrete social ill that would, more often than not, erode social cohesion, create political fragmentation, and even, in its worst instances, lead to the dissolution of the political community itself. Over time, this becomes a consistent critique that can be seen throughout Western political thought and, I think, constitutes a coherent intellectual tradition. It is a tradition that stretches back to the classical world, receives ample treatment from radical Christian thought, and was given renewed vigor during the seventeenth and eighteenth centuries, when the discourse of antimonarchism and antifeudal ideology began to bloom.

Roughly speaking, there exist two broad conceptions of economic equality in Western political thought. The first, which we can call the utopian or strict form of equality, argues that only a communal sharing of social wealth and property—usually an elimination of private property—will result in true social justice. The other type of equality argues that a toleration of small gaps of inequality between social groups or classes is permissible to the extent that the political and social power between those groups does not diverge to a significant degree. The importance of this distinction should not be overlooked or underemphasized since the two types are frequently in conflict. Therefore, the core axis around which the discourse on economic inequality rotates is not, in fact, competing conceptions of economic or social equality but the adverse effects of inequality itself. Thinkers throughout the Western political tradition have seen in economic inequality the seeds for the unraveling of society; the creation of social divisions and dissension; the corruption of ideas of the public good; and, finally, the erosion of any conception of political or individual freedom through the creation of unequal relations of power such as oligarchy and aristocracy.

The importance of sketching the continuity of the critique of economic inequality throughout Western political thought lies in its power to illuminate the way that this tradition saw that economic divisions of power were intimately tied to political imbalances of power; to show how an integrated political life was an outgrowth of some degree of economic equality; and finally to demonstrate how the critics of economic inequality were able to identify the link between economic disparities and social justice. These critics were aware that unequal property led to unequal power—and those concerned with justice and freedom throughout Western political thought confronted these issues on a regular basis. Consistently, the Western political tradition has shown a concern for lessening economic inequalities and promoting social and political harmony and integration at the expense of economic divisions of power, and this forms a crucial part of the tradition itself. In contrast to modern ideas on the subject, the economy was seen as subordinate to the political; and it was for this reason that the anti-aristocratic impulse that emerged with the Enlightenment could also find affinity with the republican impulses of Greek and Roman political thought.[1] The relation between economic equality and political stability, the enhancement of human liberty, and the desire to prevent the excess of political power in the hands of the few and construct republican institutions that were in agreement with these broad political aims are all therefore informed by this long egalitarian tradition in Western political thought.

Since the rise of market societies in the Mediterranean world, inequalities of wealth and property have been the cause of endless strife and social and political fragmentation. In the Bible, injunctions against inequality of wealth and property are numerous. The Jewish and Christian traditions warned specifically against advocating for the rich at the expense of the poor, and this inevitably translated into many ethical notions and values in Western political thought. However, it was in classical philosophy, in Greece primarily, that the discourse on economic inequality became paramount and concerns with its effects on political life and social cohesion became central. Thinkers as diverse as Hegel and Matthew Arnold, as well as David Hume and John Stuart Mill, were steeped in the political philosophy of Greek thinkers, and it was the notion of the *polis* that informed many of their ideas about social solidarity in the face of political and economic fragmentation. Their aversion to inequality arose from a conception—although admittedly sometimes vague—of public good, which was put in danger by the reality of political fragmentation and strife caused by the excesses of economic inequality.

But what is central to the discourse on economic inequality in Western political thought emerged in the ancient world and its concern with restraining what its thinkers saw as "perverted" forms of government—that is, those forms of political life where the few ruled over the many and the public good was trampled by the wealthy, powerful, and elite. This "classical republican" tradition consistently saw that inequality in economic terms would lead toward such perversions of government. They saw that what was required was not a utopian form of equality but a set of institutions and laws—and hopefully a civic culture as well—that would limit the excesses of wealth and poverty. This tradition necessarily begins with the Greeks and their concern for the relationship between inequality in property and the existence of stable political communities.[2] What is so important in Greek thought over the Jewish and Christian traditions and their moralistic injunctions against inequality is the fact that the Greeks attempted to understand unequal distinctions between human beings in a material and sociological context.[3] What Greek thought made evident was that economic inequality was a distinctly *political* concern, that it had deep social implications, not to mention moral ones, and that material inequities between different classes and individuals would erode the possibility of a community of free citizens and even, in the most extreme cases, effect a weakening of social solidarity and the dissolution of the political community itself. Economic power was tied with political and social power, and it is this aspect of the Greek discourse on economic inequality that serves as a foundation for later European and American understandings of inequality and its effects.

An examination of the historical continuity of the idea of inequality is important, first of all, to show how much of a deviation the modern turn against equality is from the Western political tradition as a whole. It is, of course, true that very few thinkers within the tradition ever advocated a radical form of equality—an absolute equality in property, for instance— but what is also true and essential to see is that there is a consistent notion that the sphere of politics must protect against extreme forms of inequality not simply because of ethics but for reasons more fundamental: that economic inequalities lead ineluctably toward social and political fragmentation and that, even for thinkers such as Plato who were not democratic, the very cohesion and even the possibility of the existence of society was threatened by exacerbated inequalities, which cause social divisions and threaten the harmonious relations among individuals within the political community. The coherence of this position extends from the political philosophy of the Greeks through the Enlightenment and modern liberalism, even though there are changes to the doctrine in each of these periods.

Most important among these various changes has been how modern ways of thinking about political life tend to exclude more and more the impact of the market. A crucial dimension in the recent transformation of the discourse on economic inequality in Western political thought has been the shift from what one could call *political society* to *economic society*. In the past, economics was seen as a corollary to political life, subordinate to the needs of society and therefore, as Max Weber remarked, a branch of *political* science. We tend to see things differently today: the economy is no longer viewed as a component of political life; it is seen as a separate system altogether. The result has been a violent tearing of *homo politicus* from *homo oeconomicus*; a depoliticization of economic life has emerged; and economic inequality has escaped the critiques that were leveled against it throughout Western political thought. Having lost touch with this tradition, we have become less trenchant in our critiques of economic inequality, less able to see the ways it leads inevitably to inequalities in social and political power, and blind to the ways that it can, and indeed has, diluted civil society and civic virtue. The insight that economic inequality can fray a republic based on equality no longer lingers in the air—and it is for this reason that the Western discourse on economic inequality needs to be seen for its concrete contributions.

The trajectory and development of the discourse on economic inequality throughout ancient and early-modern political thought sets the stage for the way that the discourse of economic ideas was framed in the American political consciousness. One of the most important issues in understanding the relation of economic inequality to politics is the way that the economy was interpreted as an institution. Today, it is customary to approach the economy simply as a formal system of exchange, prices, production, and distribution, an amoral institution working according to its own internal logic. This is the result of the distinction between what was known as the "natural economy" and the "moral economy," a distinction that stretches back to antiquity and to the Aristotelian emphasis on the insight that the economy was subordinate to political and moral concerns of the broader community rather than to self-interest and accumulation.[4] Karl Polanyi makes the important distinction between a formal and substantive understanding of the meaning of the word "economic":

> The term economic is a compound of two meanings that have independent roots. We will call them the substantive and the formal meaning. The substantive meaning of economic derives from man's dependence for his living upon nature and his fellows. It refers to the interchange with his natural and social environment, in so far as this results in supplying him with material want satisfaction. The formal meaning of economic derives from the logical character of the means-ends relationship, as apparent in such words as "economical" or "economizing."[5]

Morality and politics were therefore both deeply entwined in older conceptions of the economy and the distribution of its fruits. More important, the idea of property and its "proper use" was a discourse that began in classical thought where economics, politics, and morality were inseparable. Polanyi also makes this point by pointing to the fact that the ancient economy was one that was "embedded in non-economic institutions."[6] The concept of economic inequality as a danger—both morally and politically—to the unity of society as a whole and as a matter of justice itself was first lucidly raised in Greek thought. Greek political and moral thought had to wrestle with the implications of a market society that, especially in a place such as Athens in the fifth century B.C., had become highly successful economically as well as extremely unequal with respect to the distribution of wealth.

When early American thinkers began to write and think about the meaning of the economy and its function and purpose, they, too, would need to confront the moral aspects of the economic system that the new nation would encourage. Indeed, one aspect of justifying inequality in American thought has been achieved by transforming the relation between morality and economics. Whereas the early American political thinkers were concerned with the moral and political consequences of property and its distribution—although there was no consensus on this—from the era of industrialism well on to the present, there has been a dissociation of economics, property, and markets from morality and politics. Whether it was Thomas Jefferson's critical views of an incipient industrial capitalism, John Adams's belief that inequality would surely rise with the economic development of the nation, or Alexander Hamilton's promotion of industry and manufacturing as a means to higher social progress and civilization, these early American thinkers were all attempting to redefine the proper moral structure for American economic life. For this reason, all discussions of economic inequality in American political thought need to see it as embedded in a much broader discourse, not only because this was the intellectual background for these debates and the formulation of American political ideas but also because it is crucial to see how drastic a change has occurred over time in the development of America's political and economic ideas.

INEQUALITY AND THE FRAGMENTATION OF THE GREEK POLIS

In book 8 of his *Republic*, Plato has Socrates recount a mythic tale of a city containing two distinct groups who, as a result of their different attitudes toward money and wealth, undergo a period of strife that threatens the entire political community. The first group, the "iron and bronze," were drawn toward "money-making and the acquisition of land and houses and gold and silver." The other group, made up the people of gold and silver, who were "not poor, but by nature rich in their souls, were trying to draw them back to virtue."[7] The people of gold and silver, unable to curb the appetite of the people of iron and bronze, are forced to enslave them as serfs, perpetually watching over them since their appetitive nature had been forever transformed by their lust for riches and wealth. The central fear of the thinkers of antiquity was that the moral character of individuals would become corrupted by excessive desire for the accumulation of property and material goods since this would lead them away from social concerns and a life of virtue—by which they meant an ethical orientation toward the political community—and toward self-interest, thereby creating factions, internal strife and competition, and the erosion of the harmony and order that a just political society was supposed to possess.

In this sense, the mythic tale buried in Plato's *Republic* was not meant as a justification for oligarchy but rather as an illustration of how the Greeks viewed the problem of economic inequality: not simply as an issue of economics but as a symptom of perverted souls bent on avarice and the love of acquisition for the sake of acquisition (*philochrēmaton*). Political and indeed moral virtue were therefore crucial categories for Greek thinkers and their particular approach to the problem of economic inequality. The roots of their arguments place political virtue over economic acquisition, value the public good over private interest, and see the problem of justice and social cohesion as fundamental to judging economic transactions and activity.

The philosophical and ethical backdrop for the entire discourse on inequality in classical Greek thought is the idea of a cohesive, harmonized political community, one whose very viability was at risk once social classes became more stratified and the animosity among the poor toward the rich became increasingly disruptive or the power of wealthy oligarchs began to erode any sense of social solidarity among citizens in the community. Economic inequalities therefore posed a threat to the communitarian basis of Greek political society and what was at stake in the discussion of inequality was therefore the preservation of society itself at the expense of political and, even more serious, social fragmentation and the unraveling of the polis, the central form of political life.

This discourse begins in the first decades of the fourth century B.C. in Greece and continues until the Roman conquest in the middle of the second century B.C. New economic processes began to have a severe impact on the economic life of ordinary people. First, there was a decline in small and medium landholding as property began to agglomerate into fewer and fewer hands, resulting in large agricultural properties owned by a small but powerful elite. Second, there was the emergence, through the growth of trade and small-scale manufactures, of a quasi-capitalist economic system, especially in cities such as Athens and Sparta. This meant the decline of the agricultural middle class, something that had been a constant in Greek economic life from the Persian Wars through the end of the Peloponnesian War.

|32|

These structural economic changes led to a new awareness by philosophers, writers and poets of what has been called the "social problem" of classical Greece, defined essentially by what was commonly discussed at the time as "poverty and riches" (*penia kai ploutos*).[8] Economic inequality was such a serious problem that much of the literature of the time is replete with this theme.[9] Aristophanes' final two plays, *Ecclesiazusae* and *Ploutos*, are both about the elimination of economic polarities and the foundation of wholly new and utopian economic systems where absolute equality reigns and private property is eliminated.[10] Economic equality is seen as a panacea, the solution for all of the "sore evils" (*anakesta kakon*) of society, and even though Aristophanes clearly intended his egalitarian utopias as comic, the idea that such a theme would have appealed at all to Athenians shows how much the problem of material inequalities was of major importance. It is a theme that is also present in other literature of the time. *The Holy Writing* by Euphemeros envisions an imaginary city, "Panachia," where there is no private property outside of one's home and a small plot of land surrounding it and everyone works according to his abilities and receives according to his needs (although the class of priests are given twice their share). Utopian visions of absolute economic equality are also seen in Iambolous' *Island of the Sun*, where a communistic society exists in a state of complete equality and brotherhood and without competition and social strife.[11]

This theme also emerges in Plato's *Republic*, where he observes that the nature of the modern city consists of "not one, but two states, the one of the poor and the other of rich men; and they live on the same spot and are always conspiring against one another."[12] The problem with inequality is raised in the *Republic* where the very conception of justice and the just city is taken up, in part, in relation to the distribution of property. The idea of economic equality arises explicitly in response to what many thinkers saw at the time as the increasing fragmentation of the polis—especially in Athens—as wealth disparities grew and society was fundamentally divided between an ever richer mercantile class and large-scale agricultural prop-

erty owners, on the one hand, and workers, slaves, and small-scale farmers, on the other.[13] Plato's views on the problem of economic inequality
are grounded in his broader view of the just polis. This ideal of justice
emphasizes the importance of privileging the whole over its constituent
parts and the promotion of harmony among the different social segments
of the political community and its various classes, and it is in this that we
begin to see the birth of the classical republican tradition with respect to
economic inequality. When discussing the ideal city in book 4 of the *Republic*, Plato has Socrates say:

> What we had in mind when we founded the city was not how to make one
> class happy above the rest, but how to make the city as a whole as happy
> as it could be. For we believed that in such a city we were most likely to
> find justice, and injustice again in the worst managed city; then we might
> examine them and decide the matter which we have been searching all this
> time. Well then, now, as we believe, we are molding the happy city; we are
> not separating a few in it and putting them down as happy, but we take it
> as a whole.[14]

Justice is not to be found in good acts or in the mere existence of "just"
laws and virtuous rulers. More important, justice is found in the arrangement of *social structure* itself; it is manifest in the specific way that the polis
is organized, with all having equal shares because each class depends on
the activities of all others. The promotion of economic equality is therefore part and parcel of the project of building a just city. Plato's *Republic*
therefore privileges economic equality in the light of a broader political
and moral concern for social solidarity and the desire to prevent the fragmentation of community and the dissolution of political society itself.
Economic inequality is not viewed simply in the light of justice or fairness,
it is also, and to a certain extent more essentially, seen as crucial to the very
survival of the political community itself.

The general view of social harmony and wholeness informs the classical republican idea, and it is central in understanding the basic foundations for the discourse of economic equality in Western thought. Plato, as
well as other Greek thinkers of the period, saw that the institution of the
polis was something that was *naturally formed* not something that *existed
naturally*. The difference is crucial: individuals come together for mutual
support and to take advantage of the different abilities that each individual, family, or class has to offer. Society flourishes only when it is efficient

and each person is able to dedicate himself to his task and therefore enrich the totality of the polis—individual self-sufficiency is dependent on the maintenance of the social totality, a theme that would also emerge in American political thought on the subject of inequality. The ethical-political ideas that Plato advocates in the *Republic* are therefore not metaphysical concepts; they are a function of the vision of the material operation of a just society and the specific type of harmony that he valued. The necessity for economic equality flows from the realization that for justice to be made real in the world, people ought not to be treated differently but with equality, since each in his own way contributes to the good of the whole. This was not only a moral concern; since the economic foundation of the state lies in the cooperative nature of citizens, this, in turn, means that the state found its very legitimacy and binding force in human need itself: in the idea that man is a political animal, as Aristotle would later articulate it.[15] Hence, economic disparities did not simply spell injustice; they were a prelude to the breakdown of the cohesion that held society together.[16] But even more, there was a growing sense that the emerging principles of equality and freedom that were developing in the Greek city-states were coming into opposition with the economic life of the time.[17] Throughout the fourth century B.C. in many of the Greek city-states, as well as Greek islands such as Syracuse, Cos, Lesbos, and Naxos, among others, there were political revolutions that had as their underlying justification the redistribution of property as well as economic and social equality and the abolition of debts.[18]

The problem of the fragmentation of the polis as a result of increasing economic polarity is one of the key messages behind Isocrates' attack on inequality and the degeneration of the Athenian polis in his orations. In his *Areopagiticus* he recalls a golden age of Athens, when "the wealthy were better pleased to see men borrowing money than paying it back. For they therefore experienced the double satisfaction, which should appeal to all right-minded men, of helping their fellow citizens and at the same time making their property productive for themselves."[19] For Isocrates, the key was a sharing by the wealthy with the poor, on a voluntary basis motivated by an ethical impulse for social solidarity. The great social problem of ancient Greece, "poverty versus wealth," was therefore to be solved not by a radical egalitarianism—as advocated in the literature of the time and in Plato's *Republic*—but through a voluntary sharing of property by the rich with the poor through the impulse of their (the wealthy's) morality and their devotion to the polis itself. It was a political concern with the public good that would motivate all citizens to lessen inequality, promote social solidarity, and leave egoism and greed behind. Isocrates saw the tendency to ease social and material inequalities as the moral basis for the polis, and he saw that the growth and expansion of markets and inequalities in wealth and property created a lapse in both public and private morality. Economic inequality was therefore dangerous to the moral fabric of society and the individual, and it implied a much wider form of social breakdown than "mere" political injustice. It was therefore not the case that the argument for economic equalities existed from the start only in utopian form, one that saw the leveling of all distinctions and abilities. Rather, some saw the solution to the social fragmentation and political disintegration that arose from the resentment of economic polarity as the pursuit of a middle path between the excesses of property and wealth and the utopian visions of absolute equality and communal ownership.[20]

Plato, too, saw this to be the case about twenty years after writing his *Republic*. Rigorous forms of equality were, as Kurt Raaflaub has argued, "not a serious issue, and belonged in the sphere of comic surrealism and abstract theoretical schemes,"[21] which meant that more pragmatic solutions needed to be found, as Isocrates himself had hinted in his orations. In his *Laws*, Plato argues that inequalities of wealth may in fact be unavoidable and it is therefore necessary to concentrate on narrowing the gap between rich and poor rather than seeking to eliminate it completely.[22] He argues that this can be done through state laws that would not allow the level of inequality between its richest and poorest members to exceed a factor of four. As John Wallach has observed, Plato's intention was the minimization of social conflict through the narrowing of economic disparities: "This relatively small gap in the material conditions of rich and poor is necessary to facilitate political action, prevent disputes from arising among citizens, and achieve the greatest possible unity of the *polis*."[23] Unlike in the *Republic*, Plato is not trying to argue here for some utopian schema that will be the blueprint for the ideal state; rather, he is attempting to deal pragmatically with the seemingly natural inequalities that spring up within market society and mandate a form of equality that, although not strict and absolute in nature, can still mollify the social and political disintegration that economic inequities necessarily cause.

Isocrates, then, initiates a new perspective on the discourse on inequality: that of "moderation" (or what the Greeks themselves termed *metriotēs*). For both Isocrates and the later Plato, the concern becomes how we can narrow and then manage inequalities rather than trying to eradicate them completely. Both insist not on a strict and absolute communistic form of economic equality, as advanced in the *Republic* and the utopian literature of the period, but on the revival of a civic morality where the rich voluntarily help the poor (Isocrates) or on laws, implemented by the state, that will not tolerate class inequalities beyond a certain, fixed measure (Plato's *Laws*).

Both of these concerns merge in Aristotle's treatment of the problem of economic inequality. Aristotle's take on the issue of material equality is most developed in his discussion of political science in the *Politics*, but it has roots in his discussion of justice in the *Nicomachean Ethics*. In his ethical formulation of justice, Aristotle argues that the unjust man is one who "breaks the law and the man who takes more than his share, the unfair man. Hence it is clear that the law abiding man and the fair man will both be just."[24] For Aristotle, the terms for "taking more than one's share" (*pleonektes*) and the "unfair" (*anisos*) are important categories in discussing the problem of justice. The concept of *pleonexia* is central to the moral dimensions of economics for the Greeks since it is more equivalent to greed and rapacity than to the more polite rendering—and the one preferred by John Stuart Mill—of taking more than one's share.[25] But the key insight that the *Nicomachean Ethics* puts forth is the notion that there is some kind of median amount of possessions, which one can exceed and therefore become unfair (*anisos*) and then unjust (*adikos*).[26] The dynamics of the economy were not to be seen simply in individualistic terms. Grounded in broader concerns of moral life and community (*koinonia*), the economy was to be "subordinate to the broader communal and political needs of the *polis*."[27]

Although Aristotle is typically seen as the political antidote to the theory of the Platonic state, in the sense that he advocated private property over that of common property, his notion of equality—although not as radical in its impulses as the ideas of Plato and Isocrates and other thinkers of the time—is that there be a manageable inequality between classes and that the rule be a moderate equality rather than extremes of wealth and poverty, like Plato's mandate in the *Laws*.[28] Aristotle's distinction in the *Politics* among three classes, the wealthy (*euoroi*), the poor (*aporoi*), and the middle class (*mesoi*) was made not only in an attempt to solve the problem of internal social conflict and the instability that would result but also a means of producing a political regime where social relations were not characterized by master-slave relations. In this sense, the problem of political subjugation (*douleuein*) emerges when either extreme—the wealthy or the poor—obtains power since they then rule in their own interests at the expense of the rest of the community.[29] Aristotle sees political societies as tending toward two kinds of institutions, both of which arise from unequal property relations. First, there is oligarchy, which arises from the concentration of property and wealth among the few, and the second is democracy, where all are relatively equal in terms of property and political power. The problem, as Aristotle sees it, is that both forms of organization are imperfect since they both lead to social instability. Oligarchy is the worst of the two, since "in oligarchies two sorts of faction arise: one among the oligarchs themselves and another against the people."[30] Democracies are also prone to social unrest since "the only faction is against the oligarchs since there is none worth mentioning among the people themselves."[31] This leads Aristotle to his basic position on equality and its political implications: "a constitution based on the middle classes is closer to a democracy than to an oligarchy, and it is the most secure constitution of its kind."[32] This is clearly not the equality of Plato's *Republic*; it is specifically defined in opposition to that form of communistic equality (*koinonesantes*) that, according to Aristotle, Plato advocates. Aristotle offers a justification for moderation; an argument for the attenuation of material inequalities of property and political-power differentials to which they give rise; and the creation and maintenance of a more secure, and therefore more just, political society based on an approximate equality grounded in the middle class.

Aristotle's fear of social and political faction (*stasis*) is not unlike that of James Madison in his "Federalist 10," where he predicts that social divisions based on competing and clashing economic interests will cause political fragmentation and even the possibility of social breakdown or some other kind of political domination such as tyranny or oligarchy. But even more than this, what Aristotle opens up—as did Plato and Isocrates before him—is the way that economic inequality can pervert political life. All these writers are specific about the ways that economic imbalances of wealth and property lead to ambition, injustice, and the impossibility of what was for them the true aim of government: the maintenance of "*eudaimonia*," the "good life." This is the real essence of the contribution of classical thought to the problem of economic inequality and the need for some form of egalitarianism with respect to the attenuation of excessive disparities of wealth. The problem of unevenly distributed power and wealth is not simply ethical in nature; it is, as we saw in Isocrates and Plato, a central concern for what Aristotle himself terms a "secure constitution." This arises from his discussion of revolution in book 5 of his *Politics*. The secure constitution guards against political divisions, economic factions, and the disintegration of the community. And at its base lies the need for preserving some degree of economic equality, "to make all attempts to mix together the multitude of the poor and that of the wealthy or to increase the middle class (for this dissolves party factions arising from inequality.)"[33] This constitutional idea is more just in the sense that "justice is the common benefit," which is the guiding principle in Aristotle's conception of political justice. Aristotle's conception of politics is anthropological in nature: he sees the polis as the institution that defines the human subject. Unlike later liberal theories of the prepolitical nature of man, Greek thought—and Aristotle in particular—saw that it is in the mutuality of man's existence that politics and justice were created.

But even more, Aristotle's discussion of the problem of the imbalance of wealth was meant to connect more closely to his theory of constitutions. Aristotle is clear that the polis as an institution was one created by people themselves as a free association of citizens. Economic inequality would lead to a clear imbalance of political power resulting in the destruction of the free association of citizens through the imposition of relations of servitude.[34] The essence of Aristotle's argument was to prevent what he called "deviations" (*parekbasis*) from "right constitutions" (*orthai politeiai*). What distinguished right from "perverted" (*hēmartēmenai*) constitutions was the fact that they were framed with the aim of the common interest; deviant constitutions contained elements of despotism where certain groups or individuals ruled for their own benefit at the expense of the common interest of the polis. This ethical-political vantage point was one that informed the problem of economic inequality since disparities in wealth would lead to corruption and to deviant constitutions.

Roman thought differed in many respects from the Greek conception of economic inequality. Central to the Romans was the problem of legal relationships and the protection of private property.[35] Cicero makes it clear that one of the primary duties of anyone serving in government office is to "make it his first care that everyone has what belongs to him and that the right of private citizens' property rights is not violated by the state."[36] His remarks on the issue of the equal distribution of property are clear in the same passage, several lines later, when, commenting on the speech by Philippus[37] advocating such a policy, he says that "this speech deserves unqualified condemnation, for it favored an equal distribution of wealth of property; and what more ruinous policy than that can be conceived? For the chief purpose in establishing a constitutional state and municipal governments was so that individual property rights would be secured."[38] But it would be misleading to leave the discussion here. Cicero, as well as other Roman thinkers on the subject, saw that the relationship between economic life and political life was a precarious one. To have a secure set of property rights was, of course, crucial, but at the same time, the worshiping of wealth would surely lead to moral corruption.[39]

In his *De re publica*, Cicero provides a more nuanced analysis of the problem of wealth inequality and its relation to political and social power. His main concern is not simply with preventing social fragmentation and preserving order but with the maintenance of a free nation (*libero populo*), by which he means the ability of citizens to possess full control over the laws and administration of justice within the republic. Cicero's republicanism is therefore explicitly concerned with the issue of social power that can be derived through wealth since he points to the ways that private wealth can distort the laws and workings of republican government. "When one person or a few stand out from the crowd as richer and more prosperous, then, as a result of their haughty and arrogant behavior, there arises [a government of one or a few], the cowardly and weak giving way and bowing down to the pride of wealth."[40] Cicero is able to point to the deformation of republican government under the influence of wealth and the imbalance it creates. It is not that he advocates the redistribution of property by the state, but rather that laws are to be made so that the possession of wealth remains a private affair, never becoming a public one. Laws are therefore to be crafted to treat all citizens equally, irrespective of their economic status:

> Since law is the bond which unites the civic association, and the justice enforced by law is the same for all [*ius autem legis aequale*], by what justice can an association of citizens be held together when there is no equality among citizens? For if we cannot agree to equalize men's wealth, and equality of

innate ability is impossible, the legal rights of those who are citizens of the same commonwealth ought to be equal. For what is a state except an association or partnership in justice?[41]

Despite this, Cicero was unable to see that the private wealth of citizens could in effect still distort the principles and practice of republican government. But he was able to see the ways that economic inequality was antithetical to republican government and political life. It is true that his ideas were still directed against the interests of the poor, seeing them as a potential danger to the stability of the republic. Rome was divided between defenders of the republic and oligarchic rule (*optimates*) and those that sought reform through land redistribution (*populares*). Cicero's republicanism was opposed to the reformist tendencies of the *populares* but also to the rule of the wealthy. His opposition to the *populares* was not completely ill founded: no Roman of Cicero's time would have been able to forget the tumult caused when Tiberius Gracchus sought to institute his agrarian land law (*lex Sempronia agraria*), which was meant to dissolve control by a small group of wealthy land owners and redistribute land held by the state to the populace. These reforms were opposed by the *optimates* and led to the downfall and murder of Gracchus amid a riot between his supporters and the supporters of the senate. The opposition populist reformers who aimed at land redistribution were a genuine concern in Rome, but attempts at legislating these reforms rarely succeeded in changing social structure.

What we must look at is not simply the way that thinkers such as Cicero came down on the issue of economic inequality but rather the way that they articulated the relation between wealth seeking and the sphere of politics. The broader aim of political life for classical thinkers, of whom Cicero is only one of the more articulate exemplars, was the protection of the public good in the face of private interests so that citizens could live a life bereft of subjugation and domination and free from the interference of others. They saw economic inequality not simply as an empirical reality produced naturally by competing interests but more likely as a result of moral corruption itself. Plato refers to it as *philochrēmaton*, the "love of wealth"; both Plato and Aristotle also use the term *chrēmatistikon*, or the "art of wealth seeking"; and Cicero refers to the "worshiping of wealth" (*admiratione divitiarum*). But irrespective of the name, they saw the ascendance of economic life over political life as fatal for republican government. By seeing that economic inequality was a crucial problem for such a form of political association, classical thinkers were able to point to the ability of economic life to be effectively political, and this itself constitutes a distinct contribution to the way that the concept of economic inequality would be viewed by later thinkers, especially in the formative years of the American republic.

The idea of economic equality therefore lies at the heart of classical political and social thought. By seeing that the economy was not a separate sphere of human activity but one thoroughly embedded in the social, moral, and political life of all citizens, inequality and its relationship to social and political stability were taken seriously. It is around the concept of a moderate distribution of property that the political arguments for economic equality will be organized in the modern world. Although communism and anarchism—among other utopian political ideologies—put forth radical forms of equality, this was not what most thinkers and reformers argued for when they sought economic equality. The two broad strands of argument on economic equality—utopian or communistic, on the one hand, and practical or moderate, on the other—will therefore dominate the political and economic debate in the modern era as capitalism and a new market society emerges to shape new social divisions and new social struggles.

INEQUALITY AND THE MODERN CONTEXT: THE ENLIGHTENMENT AND MODERNITY

The modern discourse of economic inequality began to take shape after the idea of equality became a concern again. If the Reformation initiated the realization in political history of the necessity for political equality, it was merely the birth of a *political* conception of equality and one that did not extend—by its own logic—into the economic sphere. It was with this concern for political equality, the rise of an anticlerical impulse, and the movement against feudal institutions that were at the center of political thought in the early modern period, and these would immediately awaken concern for divisions of power and wealth and the effects of these divisions on forms of government and society that were meant to produce equality and freedom. Later, the Enlightenment would expand the critique to the economy and put forward the notion that political power and property were inherently linked. With the Enlightenment, the notion of equality takes on more radical depth and wider scope, and the problem of politics and economics is dealt with for the first time in a modern context. The concern for equality would be tied to the concern for mitigating political and social power. The initial impulse of Enlightenment thought was to cast off the vestiges of feudal society and the forms of social and political hierarchy that they maintained. But political and economic power went hand in hand, and this insight was not lost on Enlightenment thinkers. As the economic situation in Europe and the emerging American states became more capitalist and moved from smaller forms of ownership and manufacture in the older agrarian forms of economic life, economic inequality once again became a pressing issue in politics. This was perhaps made more sensitive because the discourse of political equality was also on the rise, and arguments for equal treatment by the state had grown decisively since the seventeenth century.

When economies began to grow once again in Europe and trade expanded in the later Middle Ages, new concerns over inequality began to emerge. Machiavelli's *Discorsi* argues that the only way to preserve a republic of free citizens is in the limitation of unequal wealth (see book I, chap. 55). The relation between civic equality and economic equality was seen to be inherently linked since extremes of wealth and poverty led to either corruption or the desire for revolution: "Let, then, a republic be constituted where there exists, or can be brought into being, notable equality."[42] But by the eighteenth century, there had already been countless peasant revolts, many of them now seen to be organized around the interests of economic equality and the redistribution of property.[43] Economic inequality was therefore something that, even though it had yet to become a major concern of modern political philosophy, was still a palpable issue at the level of everyday people.

But the modern perspective on economic inequality is not simply the result of a carrying over of the classical republican tradition. It was also given its most important weight at the outset by the theological forces unleashed by the Reformation and the new idea of the political subject that it unleashed. It is crucial to see that the central problem that Reformation thought was able to put forth was a radical antihierarchical ethos. This initially took a theological form with the antiecclesiastical impulse of Luther's ideas, but it took on a broader relevance in the world as a radical notion of egalitarianism that began to transform the way both the reformers and the reformed viewed the political landscape. "A Christian man is the most free lord of all, and subject to none; A Christian man is the most dutiful servant of all, and subject to everyone,"[44] writes Luther, but it is important to interpret this correctly since by not being subject to earthly domination, the Christian man is able to be a servant to public life. In many ways, this was a continuation of the humanism that developed during the Renaissance, but in others, it was a unique turn in the way that secular political power ought to be organized, what was legitimate and what was not.[45] This turn was important since it added a new push toward the idea of political equality. With the more radical separation between society and politics, on the one hand, and the religious subject, on the other, the domain of the political was now severed from the conceptions of order and hierarchy that characterized the feudal world.

Because of this separation, new ideas about equality and inequality began to emerge. Economic life became central once again to the nature of political life, but this time in a different guise: now the idea of salvation was tied to individual effort, to work. This meant that a shift in power to those who earned their living through honest labor from those who did not became a crucial concern for a middle class whose rise was itself propelled by the Price Revolution during the sixteenth century.[46] The significance of this concern was that a new idea about economic inequality—a liberal one—would emerge that was different from, although not incompatible with, the classical republican notion of economic equality. Both individualist and emancipating in their outlook, the new ideas of liberalism that were unleashed by the Reformation gave a religious cast to economic and political life. Instead of the Catholic doctrine of "works," virtue was expressed in industriousness and frugality, and this new thought "condemns as corrupt privileged aristocrats and leisured gentlefolk."[47] The impact of this on ideas about economic inequality was complex and would unfold over a long period of time. But suffice it to say for the context of the present discussion that the main target of dissent was not economic inequality in and of itself—for the Dissenters and other radical Protestant groups (mainly in England, where they were most successful politically), the problem was an outdated feudalism that took wealth and privilege away from those who labored honestly. This would translate into an antifeudal and antiaristocratic radicalism, but it was aimed primarily at feudal institutions and the state. The economy was seen as corrupted by these institutions; if it were to be left alone, unfettered by the distortions of patronage and privilege, it would produce its own form of equality.

The cause of economic inequality was therefore not honest economic activity but the corruption of the idle rich. This new attitude toward political and secular life brought forth the notion that the individual was central in upholding a political order that had shed the hierarchy of man over man. This introduces a crucial twist in the way that the relation between politics and economics would be perceived, for if it is the case that individual economic activity is a source of salvation, then the economic activity of individuals becomes sacred, protected by a natural right, à la Locke. This leads to a situation where private property and the market could be defended on the grounds of human liberty against the excesses of the state and the aristocracy. But despite this, the classical republican idea about economic inequality persisted. American thought would, in the beginning, seek to mesh the republican and liberal ideas—and this synthesis is at the heart of the present study.

The emergence of the idea of natural rights did not diminish the persistence of the classical republican conception of economic equality, however. The problem of the concentration of wealth and property became an explicit cause for reform during the Enlightenment. The discourse on economic inequality during this time was intimately tied to the problem of political power and political inequality. Whereas the discourse on political equality was a more pervasive one in England with the Levellers' "An Agreement of the People" delivered to Parliament in 1649 and the ideas of Hobbes and Locke coming shortly thereafter, these arguments were made largely by an emerging middle class that owned property and sought political rights and equality within an outmoded political and social order.[48] But even for Locke, inequalities in the distribution of property were an essential moral concern—his *Second Treatise of Government* argues that excessive accumulation, to the point where others lack the means to support their own lives, is a violation of natural law, defined as the treatment by each person of every other as equal and fair.

But the classical republican tradition would remain the more vital lens through which the problem of economic inequality would be viewed. Somewhat earlier, James Harrington's *Commonwealth of Oceana* (1656) advocated a largely egalitarian division of property through "agrarian law." This was to be achieved by requiring the owners of large estates to divide their property equally among male heirs. Harrington saw the nature of the political parties that would emerge out of unequal divisions of property and advocated equality to enhance the prosperity of the commonwealth and the liberty of each individual: "equality of estates causes equality of power, and equality of power is the liberty, not only of the commonwealth, but of every man."[49] Harrington's republican model was one that saw the obvious links between economic and political power and sought to construct an argument that would unite the concerns of the liberty of the individual with an equality of political and economic power. Calling for a "balance of property," Harrington believed that this was not only the one possible way to sustain a republican form of government but also that it would form a culture of equality that would be more robust than previous cultures of the servitude of men under men.[50]

But as with the turn in Greek thought on the subject, the pervasive argument for economic equality during the Enlightenment throughout Europe was not one of radical egalitarianism but a critique of inequality and the promotion of social harmony through remedying the excesses of economic disparities. The return of the classical republican notion of economic equality was not seen as utopian. These thinkers were well aware that an exact equality of property and wealth was not possible. But thinkers in the republican tradition would construct an argument for economic equality on the basis that the political power of any polity could never be equal as long as wealth was unequally distributed. This was an equality that would need to be enshrined in law in order to protect the public good from those who would seek to dominate others. "In monarchies and despotic governments," writes Montesquieu, "nobody aims at equality; this does not so much as enter their thoughts; they all aspire to superiority. People of the very lowest condition desire to emerge from their obscurity, only to lord it over their fellow-subjects."[51] Montesquieu's republican argument hinged on the substantive notion of equality—not simply equality under the law but also laws that would regulate economic affairs toward the end of equality. Even though this could never be accomplished with exactness, it was still necessary for republican government:

> Though real equality be the very soul of a democracy, it is so difficult to establish, that an extreme exactness in this respect would not always be convenient. Sufficient is it to establish a census, which shall reduce or fix the differences to a certain point: it is afterwards the business of particular laws to level, as it were, the inequalities, by the duties laid upon the rich, and by the ease afforded to the poor. It is moderate riches alone that can give or suffer this sort of compensation; for as to men of overgrown estates, everything

which does not contribute to advance their power and honor is considered by them as an injury.[52]

|46| The classical republican critique of extreme inequalities of wealth or property remains one of the most important, long-standing traditions in Western political thought on the subject of economic equality. Indeed, as were the Greeks, Enlightenment thinkers were concerned with the social and political repercussions of economic divisions since their overall concern was the ways that a republic could be formed and the excesses of oligarchy, monarchy, and aristocracy avoided. They saw that such inequalities would not only threaten the viability of a republic but also that their eradication was the only way out of the problem of human servitude and subjection that had characterized previous history. Their aim was to promote human liberty, and this could not be achieved where economic divisions left the opportunity open for an elite to make citizens into subjects. Unequal wealth and property would lead to this servitude—republicanism, on the other hand, would ensure that these divisions would be kept in check so as to prevent the concentration of power in a few hands and the inevitable descent into subjection for the many. Even as Enlightenment thinkers clearly celebrated the newly created market system of the emerging bourgeoisie—which many of them saw tied to an ethos of modern freedom and human progress through economic development and growth—they were also consistently skeptical about the different political interests that the middle classes produced and the problems of social division that resulted from the operations of the market and the accumulation of wealth and property. The idea that the expansion of the market and commerce would refine the sentiments of man and, in Albert Hirschman's words, "restrain the arbitrary actions and excessive power plays of the sovereign"[53] was one adopted by many Enlightenment thinkers, and it is this tension between the market and the notions of republican equality that has become central in American ideas about economic inequality.

This was the case even for Adam Smith. Although he does not argue for a radical form of equality, his position is that economic interest comes at the expense of public interest:

There are three orders in society—those who live by rent, by labour and by profits. Employers constitute the third order. . . . The proposal of any new law by or regulation which comes from this order ought always to be listened to with the greatest precaution and ought never to be adopted till after having been long and carefully examined, not only with the most scrupulous but with the most suspicious attention. It comes from an order of men whose interest is never exactly the same with that of the public, who have generally an interest to deceive and even oppress the public.[54]

Smith was hardly naïve as to the relationship among economic power, property, and civil government. He follows this general trend of arguing against the inequality of wealth and property in defense of civil harmony: "Wherever there is great property there is great inequality. Civil government, so far as it is instituted for the security of property, is in reality, instituted for the defence of the rich against the poor, or of those who have some property against those who have none at all."[55] This was a common concern of many who saw the ills of inequality; it was not always the weak and the poor they were seeking to protect. But despite Smith's fear of social dissension arising from the propertyless—a fear shared by Aristotle as well as Plato—Smith does end up arguing something similar to the Greeks' concern that extreme inequalities can only have a detrimental impact on society as a whole and its "happiness":

> Servants, laborers, and workmen of different kinds, make up the far greater part of every great political society. But what improves the circumstances of the greater part can never be regarded as an inconveniency to the whole. No society can surely be flourishing and happy, of which the far greater part of the members are poor and miserable. It is but equity, besides, that they who feed, clothe, and lodge the whole body of the people, should have such a share of the produce of their own labor as to be themselves tolerably well fed, clothed and lodged.[56]

Inequality is therefore something that Smith, too, sees as generally problematic and tied to a certain civic morality that needs to be the ultimate end of both economy and polity alike.[57]

Aside from the issue of civic morality there was also a concern with the implications of inequality on the operation of the state. In his essay "Of Commerce," David Hume argues that an equality of incomes is not only preferable as a result of the maximization of happiness but also of primary interest from the larger viewpoint of the political community itself.

|48|

> No one can doubt, but such an equality is most suitable to human nature, and diminishes much less from the *happiness* of the rich than it adds to that of the poor. It also augments the power of the state, and makes any extraordinary taxes or impositions be paid with more cheerfulness. Where the riches are engrossed by a few, these must contribute very largely to the supplying of public necessities. But when the riches are dispersed among multitudes, the burthen feels light on every shoulder, and the taxes make not a very sensible difference on any one's way of living.[58]

For Hume, there was also the element of power and interest. Economic inequality did not simply diminish benefits for the entirety of the political community through decreasing the incentive to pay as wealth accrued in smaller and smaller shares of the population; he also saw that there was a general interest in the rich to oppress the poor by laying an increasing burden on them—by which he meant tax burdens—and the protection of their own wealth and power. "Where the riches are in few hands, these must enjoy all the power, and will readily conspire to lay the whole burthen on the poor, and oppress them still farther, to the discouragement of all industry."[59]

What is interesting in the views of Smith and Hume is the way that they see the realities of economic inequality as inherently political in nature. They seem to have presaged—based on their readings of history—that economic inequalities were inevitable and that there were certain ways that the state could deal with them. But even more, there is the interesting fact that both Smith and Hume knew of the benefits of industry and modern economic thinking. They make a point of showing that even within the new economic system, the old problems of inequality and their effects would retain their power. Their understanding was far more realistic than many have assumed, and it is only with the rise of an ideology that would legitimize these same inequalities that a politics of inequality would begin.

In France, during the later phase of what some have called the radical Enlightenment, figures such as Denis Diderot, Jean-Jacques Rousseau, and Baron d'Holbach, among many others, argued explicitly against the concentration of wealth and property on the basis of the political inequality that was its consequence. Others, such as the Italian Count Alberto Radicati or the German plebians Matthias Knutzen and Johann Christian Edelmann argued for the erasure of social hierarchies and inequalities of all kinds through a massive redistribution of property.[60] What they railed against was the way that an outdated aristocracy was suppressing the emerging rights of individuals to live and work as equals.

Economic inequality and the quality of citizens' lives became important topics before the French Revolution since they were seen as contrib-
uting fundamentally to social hierarchy and oppression.[61] This was the
radical strain of the Enlightenment, and its connection and focus on the
problem of economic inequality will become important when discussing
the way in which this same discourse develops in American political and
social thought. But it should be remarked here that this is a deviation from
the tradition of moderation, a turn toward the radical abolition, or leveling, of all forms of hierarchy. And this is important because the view was
emerging that economic inequalities were reproducing hierarchies of social power that were the heritage of the feudal past. This was a salient
theme in the early years of the American republic, but the concern with
economic inequality continued through the nineteenth and early twentieth centuries as a dialogue about the problem of political divisions and
social fragmentation.

Rousseau was also concerned with the problem of how economics
must relate to political life. In his *Discours sur l'économie politique* he saw
that if economics was not constrained by political principles—namely the
power of the "general will" (*volonté générale*), or public good, over the interests of particular individuals (*volonté particulière*)—than only injustice
or the dissolution of society would result. The function of a "public economy" (*l'economie publique*) was to reflect in economic terms the political
principles of a true republicanism: both were to exist for the purposes of
the mutual needs of individuals (*par leurs besoins mutuels*) and promote and
maintain a sense of reciprocity (*sensibilité réciproque*).[62] Rousseau was able
to mirror his concerns for political wholeness and totality in economic
terms, further arguing against economic fragmentation and the way that
economic inequality would lead to the erosion of the totality by placing
the interests of particular individuals and groups over those of the whole.
The Greek themes return once again to invigorate a discourse against
economic inequality.[63] Rousseau's radicalism was therefore inspired by his
hope for a return of classical republican themes, and it was driven most
of all to combat what he saw as the central problem of modernity: the
sanctioning of human servitude through law and habits of mind (*moeurs*).
Rousseau's concern was for the elimination of *amour-propre*—the vanity

and self-directedness of modern life that turned people away from their communal essence, destroying not only civic life in general but the humanity of the individual in the process. Wealth creates distance between the wealthy and poor; it dehumanizes both the rich and the rest of the community.

|50|

As the nineteenth century progressed, it was quickly becoming apparent that the primary problem with modernity was how to preserve some kind of social integration in the midst of a market-based society. The concern with the state and its relation to the economy became paramount along with the problems that inequality and property posed to very idea of modern politics. This is first seen in Hegel's account of the relation between the state and the economy in his political philosophy and his account of ethical life (*Sittlichkeit*) and civil society (*bürgerliche Gesellschaft*). Although Hegel's remarks on inequality are generally seen as a criticism of the doctrine of any kind of equality of property, he did, in fact, see the emergence of complex modern civil society, with its different social classes (*Stände*), as having adverse effects on the political community. Hegel is very specific about the notion of "natural inequality," something that Aristotle himself—and other ancient thinkers as well—saw as the foundation of all inequalities. But Hegel's argument against equality of property ought to be seen as an argument against the utopian aspirations toward absolute equality, which he dismissed because of their impracticality. In this sense, he argues for a distinction between political and ethical equality, which is absolute, on the one hand, but not in terms of the equal possession of property: "Men are equal, it is true, but only as persons, that is, only with reference to the source of possession."[64] Which means that "the assertion that the property of every man ought in justice to be equal to that of every other is false, since justice demands merely that everyone should have property. Indeed, among persons variously endowed, inequality must occur, and equality would be wrong."[65]

Although some commentators have taken this to be Hegel's final point on the problem of inequality,[66] his discussion ought to be seen in light of the classical discourse on inequality, which was critical of communitarian schemes and notions of absolute equality of property. Hegel fits into the egalitarian tradition in his insistence that the entire political community (*das Allgemeine*) has the responsibility to prevent excesses of poverty and wealth since this can only cause the growth of social dissension and social fragmentation. Hegel's argument against inequality is—like that of

Aristotle and the later Plato in the *Laws*—the fear of the disintegration of the political community: the increase of the poor and those disenfranchised by the new, economic system of modernity, which is replacing the older, traditional forms of agriculture and small-scale production, creates a mass of people, or rabble (*Pöbel*), whose interests are the destabilization of society because of their disenfranchisement. Thus, the complex nature of modernity and of an emerging capitalism need to be attenuated by society and the institutions of the state because injustice, and even the threat of revolution itself, is inevitable:

> In states where the poor are left to fend for themselves, their situation may become miserable in the extreme. . . . It is not possible for them to obtain their right through formal justice—merely appearing in court—owing to the costs involved in the formal process of justice . . . This contingency must be overcome by the whole community. In the first place special provisions must be made for the indigent in a fatherly fashion.[67]

What Hegel sees is the problem of social integration in modern society among various social classes.[68] Inequality is unjust once it becomes a systemic social problem linked less to the moral claims of individuals against one another than to the claims among entire social classes: "whole classes, whole branches of industry can succumb to poverty when the means this sector of the population produces are no longer sold and their business stagnates. The conjunction of the different factors involved goes beyond what the individual can grasp, and here the state must provide."[69] It is the responsibility of society as a whole—and the institutions of the state—to remedy these "contingencies" since it is not possible for individuals to remedy them on their own.[70] A moderate form of economic equity is therefore necessary to enable modern society to be integrated and to have even some trace of the Greek concept of harmony and wholeness, something Hegel specifically wanted to preserve while merging it with the modern conception of autonomous subjectivity.

The rise of the liberal state therefore does complicate the tradition of the discourse on inequality in Western political thought. For Hegel it was a problem of social atomism caused by the maturation of market institutions. Only the state—the true expression of absolute freedom—was able to quell the divisions that liberal atomism had created in the sphere of civil society. Inequality would be rampant once the economic and political spheres were separate; this would become a major theme in Progressive and New Deal thought: the insight that politics had to be placed at the forefront of economic concerns. The movement against laissez-faire individualism would become an important theme in early-twentieth-century political thought in America, and its Hegelian flavor needs to be recognized. What Hegel brought forth was the rekindling of the classical themes of Plato, Aristotle, and Isocrates: an emphasis on the importance of the ideal of political community and social cohesion and the dangers to public life and political institutions that economic inequality posed to the public good.[71]

As the industrial age matured and the nineteenth century wore on, the concern with economic inequality grew in intensity. Indeed, although the insight that political and economic power were inherently related did not diminish as the egalitarian discourse progressed through the nineteenth century, English political and social thinkers began to examine the relationship between "civilization" and economic equality. Matthew Arnold is one of the most lucid thinkers on the privileging the relationship among material inequality, culture, and civilization over the problem of political inequality. For Arnold, the late nineteenth century saw the emergence of what he termed the "religion of inequality." This was largely attributable to the rise of Social Darwinism, which justified economic inequalities between classes as the natural outcomes of social struggle and the Spencerian notion of "survival of the fittest." This was an ideological counterpart to the transition to massive industrial production and urbanization in England and America. But for Arnold, the central problem of economic inequality was the relationship between civilization and the material forms of life that enabled men to acquire it. Central to Arnold's analysis was the way that economic inequality robbed individuals of the capacity to acquire not only the preconditions for their material well-being but also a capacity for education, culture, and humanization itself. His concern was with *l'esprit de société*, which he saw as equivalent to a society of equality between economic classes.

> [A] community having humane manners is a community of equals, and in such a community great social inequalities have really no meaning, while they are at the same time a menace and an embarrassment to perfect ease and social intercourse. A community with the spirit of society is eminently, therefore, a community with the spirit of equality. A nation with a genius for society, like the French or the Athenians, is irresistibly drawn to equality.[72]

Arnold's argument is not unlike that of Marx who, about thirty years earlier, had discussed in his *Economic and Philosophical Manuscripts* the deformity of civilization produced by the inequities of capitalism: "labor produces for the rich wonderful things—but for the worker it produces privation. . . . It replaces labor by machines—but some of the workers it throws back to a barbarous type of labor, and the other workers it turns into machines. It produces intelligence—but for the worker, idiocy, cretinism."[73] The insight shared by Marx and Arnold was that economic inequality is not simply an issue of political power; it also infects the very character of culture as well. Arnold's problem with inequality was not simply that it distorted political arrangements; rather, it was that the effects of inequality were reducing civilization to barbarism. It pitted owners against laborers, the rich against the poor, and in the process reduced culture to a war of economic interests. The brutalization of culture, or civilization was at hand, and economic inequality would be the cause, in his view, of the downfall of the culture and the rise of anarchy. Indeed, for Arnold as well, economic inequalities were increasingly becoming a problem that was expanding beyond the boundaries of social justice; it was a matter of *culture* as well, having permanent effects on the development of civilization and humanity itself:

> Surely it is easy to see that our shortcomings in civilization are due to our inequality; or in other words, that the great inequality of classes and property, which came to us from the Middle Age and which we maintain because we have the religion of inequality, that this constitution of things, I say, has the natural and necessary effect, under present circumstances of materializing our upper class, vulgarizing our middle class, and brutalizing our lower class. And this is to fail in civilization.[74]

This concern with the preconditions for individual livelihood—both in economic and cultural terms—was also central to the thought of John Stuart Mill, who saw that the realities of economic inequality also had a serious effect on political and public life. Unlike Arnold, Mill was deeply familiar with the technicalities of economics, having penned his *Principles of Political Economy* in 1848. But for Mill, as for Arnold, economic inequality posed a problem of morality and culture because it made whole swaths of the population—namely the working class—dependent on another, wealthier class. For Mill, this dependency was nothing less than neofeudal. Even more, Mill argues that property rights and the specific forms of income distribution within any society can and must be interfered with by the political community in order to enhance the cultural and moral life of citizens. Skepticism of the power of the market and its interests to provide for the fully developed well-being of citizens was a primary theme in Mill's writings, and the problem of inequality as destructive of a cohesive, cooperative moral political community was as well. As Nadia Urbinati has insightfully argued:

|54|

> Mill pursued a more interventionist design and gave the political community the right to interfere with property rights and income distribution. He proposed counteracting social inequality both directly, through redistribution, and indirectly, through cultural and social initiatives that would nurture the habit of cooperation.[75]

Mill's arguments against social inequality were therefore grounded not in a discourse of strict egalitarianism but in the preeminence of politics over economics, an emphasis on the erosion of a robust democratic public sphere. Drawing inspiration from the idea of the Greek polis of antiquity, Mill rightly saw that inequality endangered the possibility of a free political life defined along the lines of free human development and a public sphere characterized by conditions of harmonious social interaction. Mill further saw that economic society would emerge at the expense of political society and that the interests of the market would inevitably devalue politics as a consequence of this shift. Economic divisions could not be justified by some natural right to property because property rights are, in the end, *social* rights and therefore not natural. What was natural, Mill argued in the manner of the ancient Greek thinkers, was political society, and whereas markets were an aspect of social progress and the satisfaction of social needs, they were also a sphere of activity that threatened political cohesion on cultural grounds as well as through their effects, especially class divisions and social fragmentation. In many ways, the concerns of Arnold and Mill represent the last gasp of the spirit of the ancients and their vision of a cohesive political life characterized by social solidarity, virtue, liberty, and equality in the face of the atomizing effects of the capitalist market system and its deep class divisions. This was also the concern of their contemporaries such as Marx, Max Weber, and Emile Durkheim, who saw modernity—a crucial aspect of which they diagnosed as the divisive impact of modern economic life on the community as a whole—fragmenting social bonds and eroding political life.[76]

These themes run straight into the twentieth century. R. H. Tawney argues, after Arnold, that the "religion of inequality" has become resurgent and that it dominates modern views of economy and society. Dewey argues that the concerns of the public need to be privileged over those of the individuals or smaller segments of society and that inequality is one of the great threats to society and any kind of thriving democratic community. The erosion of this discourse—which has been clear for the past several decades as the ideology of neoliberalism has increasingly gained ascendancy—has once again meant a return to a religion of inequality, toward a justification of inequality as a means toward social progress and even ideas of liberty and freedom as well.

The Western political tradition possesses a clear and salient egalitarian tradition, one that saw the importance of economic inequalities and inequalities in political power but that also saw that excesses of economic inequality would mean the erosion of public life and of the preconditions for individual and social freedom. When followed historically, this tradition shows a coherent path from classical thought through the modern, even though not all of the various thinkers were of one mind on the problem. The coherence of this tradition lies not in the prescriptions that these various thinkers articulated to diminish economic inequalities but in the way that they all conceptualized inequalities of wealth and property as diminishing the strength of the political community and any kind of democratic or republican political culture. All believed that political life would be threatened by the unequal power relations that the concentration of economic power—wealth and property—created. The discourse also shows a growing response to the emergence and dominance of a market economy, and it shows a consistent concern with the welfare of the public, of society as a whole over its minority interests. Even those thinkers—such as Aristotle, Smith, and Hegel—who argue that there is a "natural inequality" between human beings do not argue that inequalities within society should persist if they lead to the dominance of one class. Indeed, what is consistently argued by both radical and moderate alike is that markets create inequalities that ought not to be tolerated and that require the intervention of society or the state. This concern for some kind of social and economic equity is no strict form of egalitarianism; it represents a concern for political society over the imperatives of markets and therefore the predominance of economic society, a philosophical and ethical perspective that privileges the common weal over that of particu-

larist and venal interests.

American political thought is a crucial offshoot of this tradition. But in many ways, it has complexified it. It was the product of English radicalism, but also of the classical republican tradition that has been outlined above. The American discourse on economic inequality therefore inherits a curious mixture of traditions. Of course, this can only be seen historically because the determining factor of how these two traditions relate—the liberal and the classical republican—is the economic context within which political history itself unfolded. The discourse on economic inequality in American political thought is complex because it was born into the context of market capitalism, but it retained, at least in the beginning, much of the radicalism that was inspired by the liberal movement as a whole. Markets were seen in the eighteenth century as a means of liberating citizens from the burdens of feudal obligation as well as a way of freeing their creativity and ensuring a sense of security; republican themes sought to guarantee a sense of civic cohesion and to prevent the ascendance of unaccountable authority. Individuals could not, the argument went, be safe and free unless there were republican institutions to prevent the excesses of power of any group within the political community—the liberal and the republican therefore meshed in the early American mind, and this is where the story of America's encounter with the idea of economic inequality rightly begins.

2

The Liberal Republic and the Emergence of Capitalism

The Political Theories of Optimism & Radicalism

One might put it this way. The surface of American society is covered with a layer of democratic paint, but from time to time one can see the old aristocratic colors breaking through. | TOCQUEVILLE |

Early American political thinkers were deeply influenced by both classical and Enlightenment political and economic themes. Informed by the normative impulse for equality, the American political project, in its most radical formulations, was concerned with wiping away the sediments of the feudal past that still dominated what America had inherited from English government and society and its influence on American life. Central was the notion that equality meant more than mere formal or political and legal equality; what was required was, as Noah Webster remarked in 1787, "a general and tolerably equal distribution of landed property," and the need to give individuals control over their own lives in the form of economic autonomy.[1] The need to labor for another meant to be under the control of another; it was tantamount to servitude. There were no illusions about the problem that economic inequality had presented for centuries on end. Most important among them was the way in which inequality led to aristocratic institutions, the distortion of the public aims of republican government, and the destruction of human liberty. As the reality of economic inequality became more entrenched after the revolution, it became clear that the American republican experiment could also be endangered by the same forces that had plagued "Old World" European economic and social life.

At the core of the early republic was a concept of equality that seeped through the boundaries of politics and economics. Early American thinkers inherited both liberal and republican ideas, but both traditions were tied to the idea of property. Liberal thought emphasized the nature of work and the idea that the natural right to property was inherent in the capacity to labor. The very notion of property, in Locke's famous words, was anything with which one mixed one's labor. Republican ideas were also premised on property, but on the notion that an equal dispersion of property needed to be maintained by some political means to ensure that political power was also evenly dispersed. The republican impulse saw that the institutions of the state had to protect against the formation of blocs of power derived from property in order to prevent the reemergence of feudal relations of mastery and subservience. Republicanism, in this sense, was not simply an "ideology": it was a political theory which sought to prevent the growth of actual inequalities of power within society, and many radical republican thinkers saw inequalities of property as the source of inequalities of power. The concept of liberty that these thinkers employed was defined by both of these ideological traditions simultaneously: on the one hand, it was generally assumed that the labor theory of property would result in a tolerable distribution of property; at the same time, the social bonds of society would need to be cleansed of master-servant relations and the inequalities of social power that characterized the older forms of feudal social relations. Inequalities of property were seen as the result of corrupt political institutions that would grant economic, political, and social privilege based not on merit but on rank and status; each individual's ability to labor, to work and manipulate nature and acquire property meant that each person had an equal ability to obtain property and self-sufficiency.

Both of these impulses—the first, an economic ethic that preached a natural move toward equality, and the second, a political project that would remake social and political institutions for the purpose of eliminating hierarchical forms of domination—are crucial for understanding how the idea of economic inequality was perceived by early American thinkers.[2] The first doctrine—derived from Lockean roots—was radical in a political context where social inequality was fused to political inequalities and status distinctions. But the two found affinity with each other. Jeffersonian republicans argued that an agrarian economy would produce the ideal synthesis of liberalism and classical civic republicanism: the individual farmer who earned what he produced and participated in public life not out of self-interest but out of a civic republican impulse. But in either case, the complexity of the American discourse on economic inequality comes from the fact that over time, the liberal and republican ideas that defined it in the beginning would cleave from one another as the economic context changed. The liberal republic that was envisioned in the eighteenth century would slowly give way, as capitalism began to emerge, to liberal capitalism. The shift is not simply a historical reality; it also gives us insight into the ideational framework of the present because it is the ways that ideas and the material context of society come together that explain how economic inequality and economic life more generally are conceived in the American mind.

Both republican and liberal ideas railed against power and undue privilege. They both saw property as a source for power, and, roughly speaking, both sets of ideas saw that equality was the backbone of any just political order. But within each of them resided a tendency for conflict. A republic would be established that would, it was hoped, limit the ability of the few to take power over the many, but this was not anathema to markets and commerce. True, Jefferson and other classically minded republican thinkers saw commerce as destructive to any sentiment of civic virtue, but in the end, the idea of personal industry and individual self-reliance was consonant with republican ideas of the public good and the absence of domination. Economic inequality was debated, but it was generally seen that a natural economy characterized by industriousness and equality of opportunity would produce rough equality of condition. The feudal arrangements of the past would be kept at bay as long as property was not allowed to be accumulated in extremes.

Despite this, the reality of economic inequality in the pre-revolutionary years was stark. In urban areas such as New York, Boston, and Philadelphia, inequality was more prevalent than in rural areas. Predominantly an agricultural economy, inequalities of the more modern variety were seen as the result of the emergence of a society based on commerce and modern forms of manufacture. In time, this would lead to a tension with the liberal economic ethos and its labor theory of value and property. But during the earliest years of the nation, the problem of economic inequality was seen as a propensity of a commercial republic, a problem that would only worsen as commercial institutions deepened their influence. Some thinkers, notably Alexander Hamilton, would come to embrace inequality not only as a necessity but as a public good. Others were concerned about the fate of the republic once wealth began to concentrate, knowing the economic course that Europe had taken, and they were aware that a similar fate could plague America as well. The return to aristocracy was a paramount concern, and economic inequality was known to be its root. The concern with economic divisions was therefore inherently political.

It is true that, from a transatlantic point of view, America was seen as egalitarian and unmarked by the social divisions familiar to Europeans. Tocqueville's comment that "in a democratic society like that of the United States . . . fortunes are scanty," was not so much empirical reality as it was a relative truth contrasting Europe and America. Indeed, Tocqueville himself also saw the problem that an aristocracy of manufacturers would pose for the future of American democracy; the real question was whether or not the ethos of egalitarianism would be able to sustain itself. But more important for Tocqueville was the fact that there existed an "equality of conditions" that "gives some resources to all the members of the community" and "also prevents any of them from having resources of great extent."[3] The "egalitarian thesis" about early America argued for this kind of equality of condition—it was seen that America's scant population and vast endowments of land would be able to overcome the abysmal fate of Europe, whose land had been gobbled up by an aristocratic elite while masses of the poor were landless.

The republican nature of American democracy was premised on the ability to regulate the inequalities that a market-based economy would create, but mainly with respect to *landed* property. There was no way to prevent inequalities from emerging, but there were ways of preventing excess. Here many thinkers differed, some pessimistic, some the opposite; but all knew that once economic divisions became apparent and once they were allowed to deepen, the probability for tyranny, or the subordination of the many by the power of the few, would become more likely and the very fate of republican government would be at stake. Thinkers like John Adams, Thomas Jefferson, James Madison, and others therefore advocated for the government to regulate economic inequality through taxation and the elimination of debts, as well as the regulation through law of property distribution and inheritance. They saw that economic inequality was a threat to any kind of government based on popular sovereignty, and they saw—just as the thinkers had throughout the Western political tradition on the topic had also seen—that it could only lead to a disintegration of political freedom and to social fragmentation.

Optimism also existed about the economic system that would begin to emerge in the early decades of the nineteenth century. This was countered by radical critics of inequality who saw that the emergence of modern forms of industry and finance were leading toward a stratified economic hierarchy that corrupted the labor theory of property and was destroying the ideal of economic autonomy and the fundamental notion of equality upon which American society was premised. These radicals did not critique private property, but rather what they saw to be the new aristocracy: a new class that lived parasitically off of those who labored. For the radicals that dominated the Jacksonian period, the American egalitarian tradition would find its first coherent group of thinkers who would articulate an indigenous argument against inequality and its pernicious effects.

LIBERALISM, REPUBLICANISM, AND THE EMERGENCE OF THE AMERICAN ECONOMIC ETHIC

The notion that the American political tradition is in some way uniform, monolithic, and defined by a historical "exceptionalism" simply misses the larger political context.[4] The wider literature on early American political culture unearthed this long ago, while also beginning a huge debate between liberalism and civic republicanism. The radical concerns of the anti-aristocratic impulse, which has its roots in the English commonwealth tradition and was translated into American political consciousness, informed the critique of inequality. But the political concerns that attached to this theme need to be highlighted. As a political doctrine, Lockean liberalism—with its emphasis on the labor theory of property and the importance of a society based on contract rather than status—was fundamental to the American political project since it eliminated encrusted forms of social and political inequality by emphasizing the universal character of individual labor as the only true source of wealth and property. Much ink has been spilled on the debate about whether liberalism or republicanism were central in the making of the political ideology of early America, but the debate between the primacy of either is largely misguided.[5] Themes from both traditions were salient, and it is more correct to characterize early American political thought as a fusion of the two traditions rather than emphasizing the predominance of one over the other.[6]

Both republican and liberal streams of political thought saw property as a central concern, but each conceptualized it differently. Liberals saw property as the result of individual labor and industry, and republicanism was to be the framework within which a new society and polity would be formed, one characterized by the elimination of "dependencies and subordinations that still lurked everywhere in their lives."[7] This would take the form of an equality of property, though not a mandated absolute equality. The liberal assumption was that once people were free to live and work as they pleased, a rough equality of condition would result. The republican insight, as I showed in the previous chapter, was tied to the idea of an equal distribution of property. Thinkers such as Harrington, in his *Commonwealth of Oceana*, and Walter Moyle, in his *Essay on the Roman Government*, saw property and power as united. Liberals, too, were aware of this, and they sought—as did the English radicals before them—to eradicate forms of privilege inherent in feudal society. For liberals, once there was equality of opportunity—equal access for all to work, produce, trade, buy and sell—then the hierarchies of the past would melt away. The political messages of both streams of thought were the same in the sense that they sought to overturn an order where social power was held by only some and relations of domination still held sway.

Liberal republicanism held that equality would predominate as long as the labor theory of property was allowed to operate unhindered. Ideas about the economy and economic life were therefore built on the foundations of a moral economy of individual labor, and this was something distinctly Lockean in nature. Lockean liberalism also justified the acquisition of property, but this, too, was seen in a broader moral and political context based on the modern understanding of equality: the only true source of wealth and property was labor—this would serve as the basis for egalitarian slogans during the Jacksonian era—and labor was a universal human possession. The emphasis on individualism and property has been used as a stick to beat the political and egalitarian implications of Lockean-inspired ideas and the kind of liberalism that it established.[8] Lockean natural right has been seen by some critics as little more than a superstructural cover for an emerging bourgeois class or as an argument for atheistic hedonism. This does not capture how eighteenth-century Americans interpreted

Lockean natural right, however; they saw its egalitarian implications in the face of oppressive and feudal institutions and highlighted its "natural" mode of distributing property and wealth equally and with fairness. They also saw that in terms of equality, any distinction made between economic and political spheres was essentially meaningless. True, equality in terms of property and wealth would not be absolute, but it would be rough enough so that political power would not aggregate into the hands of the few, who would dominate the many. The key was therefore opposition to the emergence of any kind of hierarchical social formations, and both liberal and republican ideas were seen as capable of reaching this end. America therefore provided a thoroughly new context within which a new form of political and economic life could flourish, and the liberal economic ethic was a central part of this.

But we cannot be content with leaving the analysis here. It is not ideas alone that can explain political history, but rather the ways that ideas and material conditions interact. As capitalism matured, industrialism began to surge, and wage labor displaced guild and farm labor, the republican themes begin to erode; liberal ideas become flattened into an equality of opportunity and an ethic of competition. Stripped of their political nuances, these ideas, which had been unified in the eighteenth century, split. We see this first, I think, with the radicals of the Jacksonian period, but from that point on, the republican themes wane. As Isaac Kramnick has observed, "Bourgeois radicalism directed its emancipatory message to the aristocracy, its authoritarian one to the poor,"[9] and it is this dual nature of liberalism that is central to understanding the way that the historical idea of economic inequality progresses through American political thought and political history.

Viewed historically, the concern with republicanism needs to be seen in light of the impulse to wed this liberal ethic with the secular, early-American institutional concern for public ends. Although some writers have argued that early allusions to republicanism in America were not substantive but rather metaphorical in nature, this misses the larger concern that these thinkers had for the problem of social and political power.[10] The concern with a secular political regime that would balance the unequal powers inherent in society in order to provide for a broader sense of public welfare was derived from the English commonwealth tradition, which itself was, in fact, heavily influenced by the ideas of Greek and Roman political thought. American political thinkers had no intention of replicating the Greek polis; the central concerns were eliminating the hierarchical power relationships that were rooted in the institutions of Europe and creating a society of equals. A political state based on contract and secular institutions; an economy grounded in individual labor and effort; individual political conscience rooted in civic mindedness; and a public spirit and public institutions characterized by equality and the absence of domination and inequalities of social and political power were the broad political goals that pulsed throughout the political and social thought of radicals of the time. It is therefore not a distinction between liberalism and republicanism for which we should look, but the affinities and the fusion between the two that are actually so important.

This is crucial for understanding the approach to economic inequality not only during the first few decades after the founding of the republic but for the decades that preceded the Civil War, as well. It is even more important to see that the real essence of the American approach to the problem of economic inequality would develop out of the political understanding that this fusion of liberalism and republicanism fostered. Political history is not explicable simply through the transmission of "ideas" and political "languages"; it can be comprehended only as a result of a confrontation with the political and economic realities of power relations, which are resolvable only through the ways that the participants could make sense of them. Certain political ideas therefore can unmask the power relations of any given moment or legitimate them; but in either case, the interpretation of political ideas through time must take into account the arrangements of concrete power relations of the time in question because it is those that the ideas are reacting to or supporting. This is the importance of political tradition and political ideas: they help political actors make sense of the political constraints they face, and central to the various political constraints are *economic constraints*: the limitations to mobility, to the access of property, to the ways that lives are lived—all are shaped by the nature of economic life that surrounds them. The point is not that political interests are mechanically connected to economic interests; rather, it is that economic relations shape other social and political relations and that these give rise to competing interests. The various ways that individuals relate to one another, to themselves, and to how they view their interests are deeply shaped by the economic context within which they live and work, and this was true for people in the early American republic. In particular, many thinkers saw property as the source of social and political power, and its distribution was a crucial issue for the early republic through the antebellum period, as both liberal and republican ideas stressed property as a central element in achieving political liberty.

The antifeudal impulse that was a key feature of the new political theory emerging in the early republic emphasized the need for equality and freedom simply in both ideological and concrete terms: freedom could only emerge within a society of real equals since the absence of equality was assumed to indicate the existence of unequal relations of power and, hence, the existence of domination, constraint, or some other form of nonfreedom. And this is something particularly important for understanding the way that many early American critics of inequality viewed the relationship between economics and politics—unequal property produced an unequal polity and power and economic life were deeply braided with one another. It is not as a hidden bourgeois ideology of economic interests that we should interpret early American political thought, but as an optimism about the ability of the commercial system to buttress the political ideals of liberty these early critics thought accompanied it. Nor is it the case that republicanism was an ideology that can be interpreted outside of the economic concerns of the time.[11] Liberal republicanism was an ideology supported by the economic context of its time: small-scale economic production, agrarianism, and guilds of skilled craftsmen. Economic life was small scale, confined to local sites and still largely provincial. This meant that the Lockean liberal economic ethic was easily compatible with early American economic life and institutions, and it was decidedly against the forms of economic life of the past, where rank and privilege were supported by the unequal holding of property. Only when capitalism deepened its development, the scale of the market began moving toward the national level, and small-scale production and agriculture were being swamped by industrial behemoths would this situation change and the meaning of the liberal economic ethic change with it.

But economic inequality has to be seen in the light of the disastrous implications it would have for eighteenth-century Americans on the dual ideals of the economic autonomy of the individual and the project of wiping out forms of servitude and domination—irrespective of either their Lockean liberal or republican roots. These ideals were viewed as essentially a single economic and political project. What early American political thinkers saw as distinctive about American society was the result of a synthesis of economics and politics—liberty was grounded in certain political principles and required certain economic conditions. Indeed, the ethos of political liberty in America always had a material base. Grounded squarely in the tradition of natural law as it was used in the English liberal tradition (i.e., in Hobbes and Locke), the idea of individual liberty was deeply affected by its historical relationship to European feudalism.[12] The emphasis on the idea of private ownership of property was meant to protect from the arbitrary use of power unleashed by the aristocracy. Property was a means for self-sufficiency and autonomy; it highlighted the goal of most early Americans in thought and in practice, which was to attain a "modest economic independence based on honest individual labor over the extremes of capitalist wealth or desperate pauperism."[13] The American economic ethic as it developed in the eighteenth century was therefore concerned primarily with independence from forms of dependent labor and with the moral-political end of small property ownership, and it forged a more abstract ethic over time, which would regulate the way that institutions that created inequality would be judged: the idea that one ought to keep what one produces. As the economic context changed more than 150 years later, this ethic would take on very different meanings indeed. Rather than serving as a radical call against quasi-feudal institutions and for equality, it would be turned on its head to justify some of the greatest disparities of wealth and power in the nation's history.

Some thinkers, such as Jefferson, were suspicious of the moral dimensions of the market. His famous argument that "venality suffocates the germ of virtue, and prepares fit tools for the designs of ambition," was an example of the way that the lines between economics and politics still held sway. Jefferson was not against commerce by any means, but he, and others, too, saw that the excesses of the market could lead to corruption. Although not all republicans shared the same skepticism of the market, they mostly agreed that political life ought not be subservient to economic life. Markets may be mechanisms for the free exchange of individuals, but they were also based on narrow self-interest, as opposed to political life and its emphasis on the preservation of commonwealth. The complexities of a commercial society were crucial to many of the early American political thinkers, and the key was to preserve what they saw as a sense of social cohesion in the face of accumulation, individualism, and hedonism. For these early thinkers, venality, luxury, and the fruits of the commercial centers in Europe were for centuries the root of political corruption and of political and social inequality. Rapid market expansion, therefore, would be subversive to the moral virtue of the citizenry; republican ideas of democracy could only survive in a place where a balance between politics and the economy could be maintained.[14] Once the economy was allowed to slip from its moral moorings, the result, many thought, would be nothing less than the erosion of the American political project itself.

It is important to emphasize historical and economic context. For the Americans of the eighteenth century, the institution of the market and the emerging market economy as a whole were widely seen as being characterized by the absence of privilege and hierarchy. Thus, the original ideology of laissez-faire should be seen in its proper historical, sociological, and philosophical contexts: as a reliance on individual initiative as opposed to authoritarian direction and on the production of wealth for the larger prosperity of society and not for the maintenance of status and the hierarchical relations of the "old world."[15] It was a conception of the market that was yet to be touched by the complexities of large-scale capitalism. And it is for this reason that the history of the political idea of economic inequality requires us to pay attention to the material or economic context of the time. It is not that the material context causes a reflex change in the ideas about inequality and equality; it is that certain assumptions that are made in one period no longer hold in the next—new ways of thinking about the relationship between political ideas and economic institutions and realities are therefore constantly required.

THEORIZING EQUALITY IN THE EARLY REPUBLIC

Much of the standard literature on economic and political life in pre-revolutionary America emphasizes political radicalism stemming from political agitation against monarchy and pre-liberal social relationships, that is, those relations that were characterized by inequality of power and by mastery and servitude.[16] But it is also important to highlight the role that economic inequality—most prevalent in the major commercial cities—had on the idea of equality that was embraced by revolutionary thinkers. These thinkers saw that the relations of the feudal past were the result of inequalities of property; the central issue of the republican enterprise was seen as resting on some degree of equality of property.[17]

The empirical realities of economic inequality were evident well before the revolution. From about 1720 through 1780, economic development in urban centers—spurred on by the evolution of merchant classes and clustered urban markets—marked the beginning of serious disparities in wealth and income.[18] Those at the lower ranks were propertyless, while wealthy merchants were beginning to accumulate larger shares of property and wealth.[19] But at the macroeconomic level, it is important to note that the economic inequality was generally low in the colonial period and that serious wealth and income inequalities did not begin to occur until the decades preceding the Civil War.[20] Indeed, urban inequalities were not so significant since the economy was not based in urban areas but in rural areas and small towns. What early American political thinkers and political economists saw was that inequality was on the horizon, that as commercial society became more complex, the distribution of property would become more and more unequal. In addition, as market relationships grew more sophisticated, there were also movements against market pricing, especially of foodstuffs, culminating in more than thirty food riots between 1776 and 1779.[21] Coming to terms with this economic reality would be one of the core problems that a democratic republic would need to face, and the social theories of early American political thinkers would take up the issue in earnest.

In addition to the evidence from quantitative historical studies, the effects of economic inequalities and their severity are made clear in many of the newspapers and political pamphlets of the day.[22] In 1750, a Boston pamphleteer using the pseudonym Vincent Centinel published *Massachusetts in Agony; or, Important Hints to the Inhabitants of the Province: Calling Aloud for Justice to Be Done to the Oppressed*. He made his disgust known for the emerging merchant class that was enlarging its share of wealth as a result of the rapid marketization of the city when he wrote that "poverty and discontent appear in every Face (except the Countenances of the Rich)." The *New York Gazette* asked whether it was equitable "that 99, rather 999, should suffer for the Extravagance or Grandeur of one? Especially when it is considered that Men frequently owe their Wealth to the impoverishment of their neighbors."[23] The writer continues by saying "it is to the meaner Class of Mankind, the industrious Poor, that so many of us are indebted for those goodly Dwellings we inhabit, for that comfortable substance we enjoy, while others are languishing under the disagreeable Sensations of Penury and Want."[24] Such diatribes were in no short abundance in the middle to late eighteenth century, and they are a testament to the prominence that economic inequality had in the minds of pre-revolutionary

American colonists. This was certainly a concern that did not dwindle after the revolution was over.

The formation of a radical consciousness that militated against economic inequality and the realities that the maturing commercial centers were producing was therefore clearly not only political in nature. Economic conditions in urban areas, however, did not characterize the American economy as a whole. The reliance on economic liberalism—even within the confines of broader republican themes and attitudes—is most distinctive when it comes to seeing what was most important in American political economy. Since Lockean liberalism and much of the dominant English and Scottish political economy and social theory of the eighteenth century were based on the labor theory of value and its ability to ground political liberty, the economic ethic of Americans was largely liberal in nature. Jefferson, Madison, and Hamilton, may have believed in the inevitable truth of a laissez-faire approach to the economy. For various reasons, the people who lived through such institutional changes rightfully did not share in this optimism.

The American economy in the years after the revolution was seen by most observers of the time as resulting in a strong egalitarianism of economic and social condition. Before the revolution and the founding of the republic, there had been a tradition of hierarchy that had militated against any form of equality.[25] The discourse of "levelling" in the seventeenth and early eighteenth centuries was branded as utopian and seen as fanatical. Equality in economic terms, in terms of property, was a clear threat to a social order based on rank and privilege. Conservatives could always stress that leveling meant the fragmentation of social life, the elimination of the moral and structural center that gave security and peace to the small communities of the New England colonies.[26] The specter of leveling would continue to have deep resonance in American politics through to the present. But the irony was that the conservatives of the time were in fact not fearful of regulation or the control of markets and private property. They were fearful of market society and liberalism itself because these would lead to the erosion of encrusted forms of power and elite status. With the emergence of the market, older forms of economic privilege would be broken and the hierarchies of old would be threatened. But this older argument against leveling would continue to plague those who argued for any form of economic equality. In spite of this, early American political thinkers after the revolution were more realistic, and they were certain of at least one thing, among their many disagreements: economic inequality would be a decisive threat to the democratic republican experiment that they were seeking to inaugurate.

|70|

The predominant view of political economy of the time saw a kind of natural liberty and natural equality arising from an economy that did away with the older forms of mercantilist policies and their monopolistic consequences. What Smith termed "natural liberty" was to be unleashed by the opening up of economic freedom and private property. From this economic equality would arise since the elimination of older forms of land holding and the even playing field that markets created would allow the overcoming of the stubborn inequalities of the past, which were rooted in feudal social arrangements of land and orders. James Steuart's idea of a participatory economy argued that when all individuals and classes participated in the national economy it would allow for a social harmony unknown in a past marked by privilege and hierarchy.[27]

In purely political terms, early American thinkers were split between the kind of "naturalistic" discourse of the Scottish political economists and the political realities that they actually faced. Essential was the question of political power and stability: how could a commercial society and the inequalities that followed from it be prevented from destroying the democratic republican experiment? Thinkers like John Adams and James Madison saw this as the primary issue, and they sought to remedy the problem through political architecture. The key was to arrange institutions so that inequity of power could be minimized. Although they were convinced of the egalitarian nature of Americans as opposed to Europeans, they wanted economic progress and development. Knowing this would lead to class antagonisms, they wanted to avert political crisis before it actually began.

Madison's claims that "differing interests necessarily exist in different classes of citizens"[28] and that "the most common and durable source of factions has been the various and unequal distribution of property"[29] admitted not only that classes exist but that their diverse economic interests would lead to a splintering of the political community. What was at issue for Madison was the conflict between factional interest and what he vaguely terms the "public good." The crux of Madison's argument was preventing the emergence of a social order that was in any way based upon the privilege or the interests of a single class. Madison feared the same thing as many other early political thinkers in post-revolutionary America: the dissolution of democratic government and the reemergence of a social order based on inequalities of economic power. This kind of economic power was only possible once economic interest was entwined with political institutions. Political modernity was to be marked not by utopian illusions of leveling or absolute equality but by the absence of extreme inequalities of power—a state that could only be achieved by a government legally grounded in popular sovereignty with the appropriate checks on excesses of power. Madison rightly saw the source of these disparities: inequalities of property and differing economic interests. But his mistake was to think that these could be resolved within an impartial framework guided by the institutional constraints of the Constitution, one that would not obey the interests of faction but rather the principles of the public good.

John Adams was less optimistic about the prospects of economic equality in America. His central premise was, like the other writers of the *Federalist*, to protect republican government from the social divisions that were sure to arise with a developing economy. Without illusions, Adams approached the problem of inequality in straight political terms. It was clear that inequality would be a consistent dilemma facing a commercial society; the key was to embed the very structure of government with protections against these divisions. It was not an affection for the poor and the propertyless that drove Adams's argument—he was fearful of the ideology of leveling and denounced those that followed Shay's Rebellion as "lawless, tyrannical rabble"—it was the protection of society itself from the social and political convulsions that inequality would surely create that concerned him. His fear of the impact of economic inequality on society is expressed in his *Defense of Constitutions of Government of the United States*:

> Property is surely a right of mankind as really as liberty. Perhaps, at first, prejudice, habit, shame or fear, principle or religion, would restrain the poor from attacking the rich, and the idle from usurping on the industrious; but the time would not be long before courage and enterprise would come, and pretexts be invented by degrees, to countenance the majority in dividing all of the property among them, or at least, in sharing it equally with its present possessors. Debts would be abolished first; taxes laid heavy on the rich, and not at all on the others; and at last a downright division of every thing be demanded, and voted.[30]

The fear of the poor was matched by the fear of an emerging aristocracy. Adams recognized that an economic aristocracy could emerge from even the humble classes that made up the small-scale economy in early America, dominated as it was by merchants and small manufacturers. He saw that inequality would increase in the United States as long as a too rapid course was followed toward modern industry and the production of national wealth; the result would be social divisions, political strife, and, most important for Adams, the corruption of republican virtue.[31] The poor sought economic relief through redistribution, which was therefore opposed to the interests of the propertied and the wealthy, who, through their desire to consolidate their positions of privilege, would push toward aristocracy. This has an Aristotelian ring to it, and for good reason. Stability—or what Aristotle knew as the "secure constitution"—was premised on the absence of great disparities between rich and poor. There could be no justification for inequality since it would, by historical necessity, cleave society into parts and fragment the public.

In any case, republican virtue could not be maintained in the face of the expanding market, and, without the moral and political cohesion that such virtue provided, the only pragmatic course was to strengthen political institutions. Political authority invested in firm institutions—although legally grounded—would be the only way to counteract the effects of economic division and its fruits. Unlike Madison who thought the problems created by unequal distributions of property could be solved through electoral politics, Adams saw that there would be two great opposing interests, the wealthy and the propertyless, and that this division would only grow over time as economic development intensified. And Adams was keen on measuring this distribution of wealth, making the effort to look at statistics and estimate income and wealth distribution. His political ideas rested not on abstraction but on the actual empirical trends he was perceiving. Things did not bode well for the future.

Adams's political philosophy was simple enough. Since all men by their nature seek power, economic inequality needed to be kept in check, for it would result in political tyranny or domination by one class in one form or another. The bicameral system could therefore provide a check on these opposing interests and defend the republic. But the real problem was clear: economic inequality and the divisions it produced were permanent features of a commercial society, and the idea of reclaiming the moral ideal of a political community founded on republican virtue was nothing more than illusory. Ideally, property should be widespread to prevent the emergence of an aristocracy, but the complexity of the market system presented thinkers like Adams—and others who agreed broadly with the same idea—with the difficult reality of controlling the *effects* of inequality rather than eliminating the problem itself or the mechanisms that caused it.

The fear of a return to aristocracy in the early republic was widespread, and it was commonly thought that this would result from an increase in economic inequality. Inequality arising from economic divisions was a threat to the democratic experiment, and Adams feared that it would produce the very things that the American republic was defined against: tyranny, demagoguery, and aristocracy. Adams was hardly alone on this front. The Pennsylvanian George Logan, writing in 1792, commented on the corporate charter that was given to Alexander Hamilton's Society for Useful Manufactures by asking, "will it not, by fostering an inequality of fortune, provide the destruction of the equality of rights, and tend strongly to aristocracy?"[32] James Lyon, the editor of the *National Magazine*, wrote in 1799, "Any person who pays attention to the subject, will discover that the aristocratic faction, which is growing into influence in the United States, is built by various classes of citizens, as opposite in their interests, as their designs are to honesty, or light to darkness."[33]

Conceptually speaking, the critique of economic inequality was quite different in the early years of the American republic than it would become in later periods in history. The liberal republicanism of these early years saw the connection between politics and economics through the institution of property. It was clear that property itself engendered political and social power, and, as a result, republics needed to ensure that property did not become unequal. "In what then does *real* power consist?" asked Noah Webster in his defense of the Constitution in 1787. "The answer is short and plain—in *property*."[34] Webster's analysis of Roman history via Tacitus sought to prove that freedom could only be obtained if the people were able to hold "the power of governing in their own hands."[35] When the property of the plebeians had been acquired by the nobility of Rome, they were able to consolidate their power in the state. The lessons of Roman history were to be applied to eighteenth-century Europe:

> But in no government of consequence in Europe, is freedom established on its true and immovable foundation. The property is too much accumulated, and the accumulations too well guarded, to admit the *true principle of*

republics. But few centuries have elapsed since the body of the people were vassals. . . . Our jealousy of *trial by jury, the liberty of the press,* etc., is totally groundless. Such rights are inseparably connected with the *power* and *dignity* of the people, which rest on their *property.* They cannot be abridged. All other nations have wrested *property* and *freedom* from *barons* and *tyrants; we* begin our empire with full possession of property and all its attending rights.[36]

Webster's analysis sprang from a simple dictum: *"property* is the basis *of power."* This was a variation on his Scottish contemporary John Millar, who put forth the thesis "power follows property." Millar, a student of Adam Smith and cohort of the great Scottish political economists of his time, saw that political history ought to be interpreted as having a fundamentally economic basis. In his study *The Origin of the Distinction of Ranks* (1771), Millar showed that the basis of all political and social power and authority rests on the distribution of property. Forms of dependence and servitude emerged only when landed property was held for long periods of time in unequal hands. Then, feudal forms of social and political life would emerge because those without land would be forced to work for those who possessed it. Only the emergence of commerce, he observed, could reduce the older order of rank and distinction since no one would be able to hold on to property long enough to form such relations of power and control:

> This fluctuation of property, so observable in all commercial countries, and which no prohibitions are capable of preventing, must necessarily weaken the authority of those who are placed in the higher ranks of life. Persons who have lately attained to riches, have no opportunity of establishing that train of dependence which is maintained by those who have remained for ages at the head of a great estate. The hereditary influence of family is thus, in a great measure, destroyed; and the consideration derived from wealth is often limited to what the possessor can acquire during his own life.[37]

It was clear that property and power were linked in the minds of early American thinkers and that a commercial society was the best way to combat its inequality. But these were precapitalist ideas. Only several decades later, as industrial capitalism began to dawn on America's political horizon, would this theme of power and property once again emerge in force to combat what the radical critics of the time saw as the reemergence of feudal social relations.

Jefferson's views on economic inequality and its political impact also synthesize republican and liberal themes. Although Jefferson's conception of politics was deeply influenced by classical Greek conceptions of political life and human nature, it was also deeply influenced by the labor theory of property. He saw that the new American republic would be an opportunity to realize that humanism that was fostered by Greek philosophical thought as well as Christian ethics.[38] In Jefferson's political philosophy, economics was therefore subordinate to the sphere of politics. Even more, he saw that economics was a private affair of the household, fostering self-sufficiency and precluding dependence and unfreedom. He inherited this insight from his reading of Aristotle, held that economic activity was a private affair: one manages one's household to obtain self-sufficiency, which thinkers like Jefferson saw as central to the function of a free society since it stands in direct opposition to forms of dependency.

The core of many of Jefferson's economic ideas was derived from Aristotle. He saw the economy as both a private and an associational affair, and he saw that only through individual labor could true equality ever arise. Inequality was the product of privilege, and the amassing of fortune from the labor of others was a corruption of what he would have seen as a natural economic state. Although Jefferson's economic and political ideas are rightly seen as creating what Richard Hofstadter has called America's "agrarian myth," his wider ideas on politics and economics require—especially when talking about economic inequality in American political thought—a more nuanced look.[39] Indeed, Jefferson's thought is notoriously antisystematic, and isolating broadly consistent themes and positions is a difficult task. Jefferson's republicanism, however, is in tension with his economic liberalism, and this makes him an important contributor to the way that the discourse on economic inequality evolved in American political thought and history. Jefferson's essential view of economic inequality is that it is a fundamental obstacle to democracy and human development and happiness. This is a consistent theme throughout his varied writings, but the way that government is to handle this problem is a very different manner. In his *Notes on the State of Virginia* he is influenced by the liberal separation between state and society as well as economy and government. When considering the plight of the poor, it is through charity alone that they are to be helped; the state ought to play no role in alleviating such social ills. "So it is of the maintenance of the poor, which being merely a matter of charity, cannot be deemed expended in the administration of government."[40] Since it is "the manners and spirit of a people which preserve a republic in vigour,"[41] and this spirit is to be—in Jefferson's agrarian republic—devoted to working one's own soil, government aid to the poor will create a dependency that, in its own right, becomes a form of servitude ("dependence begets subservience").[42]

Jefferson wrote the *Notes* in 1781, and his ideas on the problem of economic inequality were naïve at best at this time. By following the intellectual logic of Lockean liberalism, his arguments against the state's alleviating the plight of the poor was essentially apolitical—it remained an abstraction. It was not until Jefferson's visit to France and his long sojourn there that he saw the real effects of economic inequity and its concrete moral and social implications. His experience in France showed him the threat that inequities in wealth and property can have on the population as a whole and its political climate, and he began to modify his views on the role of the state in responding to inequality. In a letter to James Madison in 1785, he writes:

> I am conscious that an equal division of property is impracticable. But the consequences of this enormous inequality producing so much misery to the bulk of mankind, legislators cannot invent too many devices for subdividing property, only taking care to let their subdivisions go hand in hand with the natural affections of the human mind. The descent of property of every kind therefore of all the children, or to all the brothers and sisters, or other relations in equal degree is a politic measure, and a practicable one. Another means of silently lessening the inequality of property is to exempt all from taxation below a certain point, and to tax the higher portions of property in geometrical proportion as they rise.[43]

But Jefferson did not abandon his belief in a minimal state that would leave men, as he says in his First Inaugural Address, "otherwise free to regulate their own pursuits of industry and improvement, and shall not take from the mouth of labor the bread that it has earned."[44] This is not a contradiction. Jefferson's ideas were in tune with the basic premises of economic thought of the age: namely the liberal economic ethic that saw that an economic system based on liberty was grounded in individual labor. The distribution of wealth and property would therefore be naturally distributed; the fruits of labor would be based on effort and work, not on privilege.

But Jefferson does argue in his letter to Madison that there is a need for the state to mollify economic inequality, and this apparent contradiction is intimately tied to Jefferson's understanding of political society as a whole. Although based primarily on the notion of political liberty, Jefferson's idea of freedom was not a narrow liberalism founded on the establishment of private property. It was also thoroughly shaped by the classical republican ideal of political virtue—the idea that self-interest needed to be subordinate to the public good or the interests of political society, of which the individual was inextricably a part. This virtue could only arise from the cohesion of society as a whole, not from a society divided against itself. Even more, property for Jefferson was not simply defined by possession, but by its moral overtones. Indeed, Jefferson's his letter to Madison reflects not only his evolving conception of the role of the state in mitigating economic inequality but his complex views of property and the moral status that he attached to it.

Jefferson makes a tripartite distinction when it comes to the subject of property.[45] He defines property by the activity with which it is worked, and each kind of property has a different moral implication for individual and society. *Feudal* property is defined by subservience and domination. It is based on a refusal of natural rights and leads to despotism and tyranny as well as the moral depletion of its subjects. *Commercial* property—because of its ability to allow its owners to accumulate wealth—also creates hierarchies and distinctions. It is only *agrarian* property relations that allow for true independence and the breaking down of social hierarchies. Only through agrarian property relations can individuals cultivate the virtues needed for self-governance and therefore the proper preparation for the pursuit of the common good. Property for Jefferson is not a Lockean natural right; it is not something natural to humans within some kind of prepolitical state of nature. Rather, Jefferson sees property as decisively factitious: it is a social creation and therefore one that can be warped to serve the needs of the few rather than the many.

Combating feudal property arrangements was Jefferson's first attempt at dealing with inequality politically in order to eliminate it. This was not something that was controversial among most social thinkers in America at the time, since there was a general consensus among influential political thinkers and political economists—both in the United States and abroad—

that older forms of property and social order were the main causes of inequality, politically and economically. This was the appeal, after all, of the ethos of liberal economic individualism: the ability to keep what you worked for, to hold as property that for which you have labored. But this economic idea was never meant as a substitute ethics, for Jeffersonians at least, for politics. The public good was still at the core of republican politics; economic inequalities—whatever their causes—were seen as a threat to the kind of agrarian utopia that Jeffersonian republicans sought to erect.

But even as early political thinkers like Adams and Jefferson, among many others, saw economic inequality as a threat to republican virtue and therefore to the constitution of political and social freedom, there was also another view of inequality that saw it as necessary and even as justifiable. Any analysis of political ideas and traditions needs to take into account this dialectical dynamic. In early American political thought, this defense derived from certain conceptions of human nature and the importance of inequality to social organization. In this sense, inequality was often seen as not only necessary but as beneficial, and attempts to eliminate it were not only utopian but also contrary to public welfare. Thinkers that defended economic inequality did so for a variety of reasons, but what unites them intellectually is their emphasis on inequality as the necessary and, in a sense, natural outcome of either human nature, the nature of free economic activity, or both.

Alexander Hamilton is the most forceful and articulate thinker on the subject of inequality and the idea of an aristocracy of wealth. Hamilton's ideas resonate with much contemporary thought when it comes to the relationship between wealth, industry, government, and national prosperity. Simply stated, he believed that economic inequality would not just be a consequence of economic growth; it would be an enduring social reality grounded in what Hamilton saw to be the nature of class society. The masses of people could not be trusted to make decisions with respect to the political and economic fate of the nation. They were driven by immediate interests, not long-term goals. They were largely ignorant; the wealthy tended to be intelligent. This did not mean that inequality needed to be as rampant as it had been in the medieval period. Instead of mass poverty and want, the bulk of the population was to maintain itself by the employment given to them by the ideas, money, investment, and effort of the wealthy elite.

This made sense in the conception of economic progress that drove Hamilton's model. He saw the encouragement of a commercial- and manufacturing-based society as the only model for economic progress and the development of national wealth and prosperity. Unlike Madison, Adams, and certainly Jefferson, he opposed the expansion and support for the agrarian sector and saw the only path to national economic progress through the development of modern industry. But at the same time, he saw that stratification between the wealthy and the mass of workers was to be a permanent feature of a developed economy. Class conflict would intensify as economic growth continued, but as long as a strong central government was in place, there would be little fear of political conflict. At the same time, inequality would persist in Hamilton's model since the mercantile and industrial classes would require all the financial help possible from the central government. To manage the swelling national debt that would emerge from such a policy, tax burdens were to be thrown onto workers, especially planters, whom he saw as representing the economic past rather than the future. Taxation on the wealthy was to be essentially nonexistent: taxing capital and profits went against the basic idea of liberty and, more pragmatically, it would hinder investment and stall the course of national economic growth.

Hamilton's views on inequality are important because they offer the first glimpse into a depoliticized conception of economic activity, growth, and policy. In this sense, especially, he could not be more different from Jefferson (and even Adams) in that he did not subordinate the function of economics to politics. In place of a labor theory of property linked to notions of liberty and anti-aristocratic privilege, Hamilton saw that economic inequality need not be associated with the old world's political institutions. What was to be new in the American experiment was the lack of state intervention in the economy outside of the subsidies for industry. Human progress was to be tied to the growth of national economic prosperity, a prosperity that itself was driven by a class of men that were wealthy and intelligent. But the enduring aspect of his argument was in the depoliticization of capitalism and his unabashed inegalitarianism, something that would only see its like in American writers such as William Graham Sumner seventy years later and, of course, in the late twentieth and early twenty-first-centuries. Inequality was not to be based on ascripitve foundations—the door was "to be open to all"—but on economic merit. Those who were able to accumulate and therefore expand the powers of industry were to be encouraged to do so for the common good.

But despite this argument, which embraced economic inequality, it is undeniable that for many thinkers in the early American republic, economic inequality posed a threat to the idea of a morally cohesive and politically ordered republic and also threatened the kind of freedom that they envisioned for that republic. Like the Greeks well over two thousand years earlier, they called into question the simultaneous existence of economic inequality and democracy. Economic divisions were the source of political divisions and, ultimately, the seed from which the tyranny and the end of republican government would grow. This was seen as one of the most important problems facing the social, economic, and political maturation of the nation. The solution was not to be found in economic policy but rather in political architecture. Inequality would have to be tolerated, but it could not be allowed to distort political arrangements, to allow certain factions to co-opt power, or to destroy the balance of interests that economic divisions created and that political arrangements would theoretically contain.

The general view was that rising economic growth would relieve the strains of inequality, but some were not so optimistic. By the first decade of the nineteenth century, it was becoming increasingly evident that the reality of economic inequality in America was actually threatening America's republican experiment. The political economist John Taylor wrote in 1814 on the emergence of new monopolies and their legal protection by the state: "The idle, who seek for wealth by chartering laws, are wiser than their equalizing brethren [laborers]. Law has never been able to produce an equality of property, where industry exists, but it can produce its monopoly. . . . [L]aws for this end are as unconstitutional as those for reestablishing king, lords, and commons. Legal wealth and hereditary power are twin principles."[46] A new generation of thinkers would emerge in the decades leading up to the Civil War. For some, economic divisions could be smoothed out; the interests of opposing classes harmonized. Classes—defined as different kinds of producers, agrarian or otherwise—would become more harmonious in an economic and political context defined by liberty and individualism, and the problem of economic inequality might be able to work itself out on its own. For others, the rising inequality was signaling a new economic order that was hardly benign and had to be transformed by organized action. Economic inequality became one of the most important issues in American political and social life, and from the early nineteenth century through to the present, it would be the one truly consistent set of divisions in American society.

THE DISCOURSES OF HARMONIZATION AND RADICALISM

For the thinkers of the early republic, economic inequality was an immediate reality, but its consequences remained little more than an abstraction. For the next generation and beyond, the reality would be considerably more concrete. Since the idea of a natural distribution of wealth based on individual effort and talent and regulated by the uncoerced nature of the market was the predominant paradigm for early American political economy, when it became obvious that the development of capitalism continued to have inegalitarian effects, approaches to the problem of economic inequality began to take on deeper political ramifications. The stakes were clearly higher since, in the minds of many thinkers in the first half of the nineteenth century, the debate about distributive justice was now being related to the fate of the democratic republican experiment itself.

American economic life was seen by some observers of the time as promoting a sort of economic equality that would prevent the emergence of hierarchical social relations reminiscent of feudalism. Tocqueville, in his second volume of *Democracy in America*, observed: "As the rules of social hierarchy are less strictly observed, as great ones fall and the humble rise, as poverty as well as wealth ceases to be hereditary, the distance separating master from workman daily diminishes both in fact and in men's minds."[47] Tocqueville reasoned that this was coming about since because was a market for labor and capital that promoted a "constant struggle about wages between those two classes," where power was "thus divided."[48] This would be a common theme in the decades running up to the Civil War: the idea that a free market for labor would lead to equality of condition was an optimistic view of the emerging economy.[49] But even Toqueville's optimism was clearly tempered by what he saw as the emerging threat to equality and democracy that was at the root of American economic life: "But in our time there is one great and unfortunate exception. I have shown in a previous chapter how aristocracy, chased out of political society, has taken refuge in some parts of the world of industry and established its sway there in another shape. . . . As one must be very rich to embark on the great industrial undertakings of which I speak, the number of those engaged in them is very small. Being very few, they can easily league together and fix the rate of wages that pleases them."[50] This would become an issue of hot debate for the remainder the antebellum period, not to mention still coloring the present debate on the relationship between classes through the twentieth century.

|82|

For the first time, especially for the group of radical critics of inequality, economic inequality and the new forms of organization that an emerging capitalism was putting forth were viewed as contradictory to the imperatives of political equality for which the American Revolution had been fought. Political and social thinkers saw rising inequality as more likely once modern industrial capitalism—something many of them knew was on the horizon—took footing. Only then would the corrosive effects of modern economic life threaten the republican fabric of moral, political, and economic cohesion that many of them saw as the hallmark of American society. Even more, it would threaten the equality of conditions that most Americans and foreign observers, such as Tocqueville, saw as America's truly exceptional quality. If the first generation of American political and social thinkers saw the enemy as an outdated feudal aristocracy crushing equality, the new generation of the first half of the nineteenth century would see it as the emerging industrial and corporate class. They did not see the liberal conception of labor and property as a problem, however. Their ideas still mixed republican themes and a liberal economic ethic. The two were still cohesive in their minds since as long as individuals were allowed to work, produce, and accumulate according to their own labor, there would be no threat to republicanism. Only after the state sanctioned corporations was it seen that both the liberal economic ethic and the republican framework were in jeopardy. For the masters of industry did not labor for themselves but had others work for them, and the result would be the distortion of republican government since the few would soon have the power to subvert the ends of popular government.

But even as economic inequality began to surge in the few decades before the Civil War, the idea that there was, hidden beneath these inequities, a harmonious relationship among the various economic classes remained resilient. For early-nineteenth-century political economists, economic differentiation did not necessarily mean an unevenness of power. This kind of equality was envisioned through the discourse of "harmonization." This notion had its roots in physiocratic ideas. Francois Quesnay's *Tableau economique* argues that there was an inherent interdependence among the three classes that make up any economy: a "proprietary" or landowning class, an agricultural or "productive" class, and a "sterile" class of manufacturers and merchants. Quesnay's argument was that a harmonization of interests among the three classes would emerge once the government saw that the productive class was the source of economic value since it was the only class capable of producing a surplus of goods.[51] The surplus produced would pay for the goods of the manufacturing and merchant class, and the landowners would simply receive their payment as rent. In this way, it would become obvious that the three classes were, in effect, interdependent and that their economic interests and activities were not in competition but in harmony with one another.

This basic notion of the "harmonization of interests" was not lost on influential American political economists and social thinkers in the early nineteenth century. The American economy was still largely agrarian in nature, and the predominant view was that an associational economy—as opposed to a competitive one—led toward relative economic equality, preserved the ethos of economic autonomy and independence, and also would lessen the kind of social and political strife that would derive from extreme inequality. An associational economy also underscored the liberal ethos as the backbone of American political economy and the American character more broadly—not simply in terms of property but in the idea of individual labor and economic autonomy. It delineated a middle position against the radicals who called for the redistribution of property and denounced the intractable reality of the onslaught of the new capitalism.

The more radical set of ideas that emerged did not come out of imported European notions (with the exception of Robert Owen's experiments), Rousseau, or the Levellers; they were derived from what was seen to be the initial ethical tenets of the American Revolution and the founding principles of American society and politics. The radical critique of economic inequality stressed the need for redistribution, the ending of special privileges, and an opposition to banks and new financial institutions that acted only as means for wealth accumulation. These institutions were regarded as tending toward a new aristocracy, one built on the backs of true and honest labor. The radical critics held that a moral economy based on the liberal ethic of individual labor and property was being shattered at the expense of self-interest and a narrow search for profit, which would result not only in inequality but in the destruction of the republican principles that American society embodied. Their critique was a defense of the economic autonomy of workers and an attack against all forms of wage servitude. The moral context of a free society was an economy that was based on labor that was itself oriented toward the ideal of self-sufficiency. Since this was seen as the sole purpose of labor and the market was simply a means of fair trade between honest producers, the appropriation of labor by others and the accumulation of profit from that appropriation was therefore the central object of the radical critique.

For both moderate and radical strands of thought, the liberal idea of labor and property informed the critique. But whereas the radical critique of the maldistribution of property, income, and wealth was explicitly an opposition to a kind of economic modernity that was gathering power, strength, and momentum, harmonization theory was an attempt to see the egalitarian kernel inside the shell of a newly emerging form of economic organization. The early nineteenth century saw the emergence of capitalist enterprise. New forms of investment and credit systems were erected; the need for larger pools of labor meant a departure from the small-scale and agrarian forms of production that were taken for granted by the earliest American political thinkers. Social thinkers in the first decades of the nineteenth century viewed the coming transformation with skepticism and, in some cases, with dread. Although most Americans were still living and working on farms and within small economic communities, it was a testament to their sociological perception that these thinkers saw the coming divisions of society. Their critiques were arrayed against lingering feudal elements in economy and society, and they would lay a foundation for the post–Civil War era's ideas about the new economic landscape.

The theory of the harmonization of interests was most lucidly formulated by the political economist Henry C. Carey, and it would mark one of the first attempts by American political economists to deal with the problem of inequality in an overly optimistic way. Egalitarian in its outlook, Carey's ideas were unwittingly an apologia for a new form of economics even as they were firmly grounded in the assumptions of agrarian and small-scale economic organization. His interpretation of the interaction between labor and capital accidentally supported the new, moderate economics because he wanted to show that the two groups' interests were, in fact, one and the same and that inequality would in fact lessen as economic growth increased. Derived from his critical confrontation with the ideas of Ricardo rather than the older theory of Quesnay, Carey sought to prove a harmony of interests—that economic divisions between "labor" and "capitalists" were apparent at the surface but were, in actual fact, nothing more than illusion. He knew that arguments were raging about inequality and the need for distributive justice. But for him the American economy did not promote divisions and opposing interests, and a growth economy ought to be looked upon with optimism rather than the forecasts of doom that others hung upon it because it would, in the end, promote equity and prosperity at once.

In both *The Harmony of Nature*, published in 1836, and in *Principles of Political Economy*, published in 1838, Carey would put forth an argument that, he believed, penetrated the essence of the economic system, revealing its interdependence and its ability to produce equality or harmonization. Like Hamilton, he wanted to see the economy as unrelated to politics. But he was different in that he favored a view of the economy as self-regulating and—as long as it was contained in small- and medium-sized enterprises and economic communities—benevolent to all its participants in terms of egalitarianism. In this sense, there was no need for political intervention into the economy—his system articulated a combination of laissez-faire, prosperity, growth, and economic equality. For Carey, "economic man" operated within a nexus of cooperative interchange that traded in skills, services, and goods. "Capital," in his usage of the term, was "any artifact or skill or knowledge that increases man's power to direct natural events."[52] Wages and profits were one and the same, and when a situation of free competition existed, they would be fairly distributed by effort and skill.

Crucial for Carey was the idea that wages would rise as a competitive capitalist system grew. Competition for labor by capitalists would raise wages, but the real equalizing tendency would come from the nature of economic growth itself. Technical progress would allow capital to become more productive, and the quality of labor would increase. In this way, the ratio between the amount of capital needed to produce goods and the amount paid to workers would fall, and wages would rise relative to profits. Workers would become more valuable to employers since their productivity was rising. Similarly, since Carey made no distinction between capital and wages but saw them as essentially one and the same, he argued that the total amount of capital would increase even as employers' profits decreased and the wages paid to workers grew. The result was a harmony of interests since workers and owners needed one another, and, in the long run, equality would result from the very dynamics of economic growth in a laissez-faire economy.

Despite the optimistic political economy posited by Carey, the literature of the time from 1820 to the Civil War was deeply marked by a radical discourse against inequality that was, interestingly enough, wholly home-

grown. Indeed, in contrast to the post–Civil War era, when American radicalism was deeply affected by European ideas such as Marxism, the radical critique of inequality during the antebellum period was derived from the moral-political imperatives behind the ideas of the revolutionary generation. This critique held that equal rights in the political sphere was an impossibility without an equality of property. But this was not as crude as it was made out to be by opponents. Grounding their argument in a radicalized conception of the liberal theory of labor and property, these critics argued that the arising new form of economic complexity—that is, the evolving capitalism that was gaining in strength—was antithetical to the basic, natural rights that America supposedly embodied. Chastising what theorists like Carey saw as a benevolent economic system, they saw it as annihilating economic autonomy, eroding what they referred to as "civil rights," and as ushering in a new aristocracy that would live parasitically off the labor of working people, the only real producers.

But even more, these radical critics of inequality saw that the force of property was once again emerging to destroy the liberal republican notion of political freedom. Indeed, what drove their critique was the realization that relations between employers and employees—characterized essentially by master-servant relations of power—were untouched by the revolution. Instead, these critics held that the new form of economic life that was emerging—industrial capitalism—articulated relations of domination and control reminiscent of the feudal past. The individual was no longer able to keep what he had labored for, on the one hand, and the relations between citizens were refeudalizing, on the other. They sensed what we know today to be the case: that the rise of market society itself was unable to destroy the preliberal labor relations that carried over from the feudal era. And it was these relations that they sought to overturn.[53]

The American economy would change rapidly and drastically from 1820 through 1860, and this would set the stage for the radical egalitarians and their attack on inequality and what they saw as the emergence of a new form of servitude and aristocracy. By 1860, income and wealth inequality were staggering. Brought on by the introduction of the factory system and the proliferation of wage labor—as well as the decreasing ability of the "family farm" to provide an adequate living standard—a pattern

of distribution emerged that would not only invoke the wrath of the radical egalitarians but also set the stage for the post–Civil War era and its own
battle with inequality.[54] By 1860, the top 5 percent of American families
held ownership of over half of the nation's total wealth, and the top 10
percent possessed over 70 percent. In Philadelphia alone, 1 percent of the
families owned over 50 percent of the city's total wealth; the lower 80 percent controlled a mere 3 percent.

These patterns of inequality, as well as the growing power of banks and
corporations, were setting the stage for the discourse of the radical egalitarians and their attack on the changing American economy. They were
radical precisely because they sought to use the political ideals of equality
to confront the economic order of their time, an order that was increasingly defined by wage labor and an inequality between labor and capital.
Their radicalism consisted in this opposition and their commitment to extending the economic egalitarian impulse of the American Revolution and
the project of constructing a republic founded on liberty and equity. They
upheld the ideal of liberal republicanism, but they were reacting to new
shifts in economic life and economic structure. They saw that the state
had to regulate economic life in order to protect republican principles—
whether in terms of redistributing property or preventing the excesses of
monopoly—but this was to be done in order to protect the ability of each
individual to labor and preserve his independence. The liberal economic
ethic and the ideas of republicanism were inseparable. They made the
connection between labor, power, and property. The basic idea was that
property flowed from labor; but when labor itself became the property
of others, then the very foundation of independence, the freedom from
servitude, was placed in peril.

All the radical critics of inequality during the period saw the political
nature of economic inequality, and the institution of wage labor, charters,
and other moves toward modern capitalism were the immediate targets of
their critique. In *The Rights of Man to Property!* (1829), Thomas Skidmore
made this evident in his opening preface:

> One thing must be obvious to the plainest understanding; that as long as
> property is unequal; or rather, as long as it is so enormously unequal, as we
> see it at present, that those who possess it, *will* live on the labor of others,
> and themselves perform none, or if any, a very disproportionate share, of
> that toil which attends them as a condition of their existence, and without

the performance of which, they have no *just* right to preserve or retain that existence, even for a single hour.[55]

|88| For radicals like Skidmore, the link between inequality and politics was clear: by allowing an unequal distribution of property to proliferate and worsen, let alone exist at all, the political ideals of individuality, liberty, and equality would all be subverted to the interests of capital, opulence, and idleness. The country's workers would forfeit any semblance of economic independence, and the social and political liberty that it bestowed, to economic dependence, which would mark the beginning of the decline of political freedom and justice. Economic and political equality were therefore inherently connected since they were one and the same thing: a man could not be free if his labor was appropriated by another. Skidmore summed it up in a moral slogan that was as simple in its formulation as it was profound in its implications: "all men should live on their labor, and not on the labor of others."[56] Skidmore's solution was redistribution by the state. Property was not to be handed down generation after generation but taken by the state after the owner's death. The state would hold this property in common only to divide and redistribute it for the next generation. This republican policy sought to encourage the liberal economic ethic: since there was no way for equality to flourish in the midst of unequal wealth and property, the state would need to enforce that equality so that each man would be able to work for himself. Radicals like Skidmore saw that the republican and liberal ideas about economic and political life needed to be applied in tandem.

The ideas of critics like Skidmore were hardly unique. Rather, they fit into the context of the larger worker movement that was beginning to thrive in Philadelphia and New York, which also railed against inequality and the kind of economic servitude that would emerge from it.[57] But these ideas also fit into the broader context of the egalitarian tradition. These radical thinkers confronted inequality and highlighted not only the negative effects that it had with respect to economic affairs and "fairness," but the larger impact it had on morality, happiness, servitude, and freedom.[58] They did not back away from characterizing inequality as patterning a new set of social relationships bent on re-creating aristocracy and barbarism. Theophilus Fisk, another of the radical critics, addressed a crowd of the "mechanics" of Boston arguing that "the history of the producers of wealth, of the industrious classes, is that of a continued warfare of *honesty* against *fraud*, *weakness* against *power*, *justice* against *oppression*."[59] Many of these thinkers, such as Langton Byllesby and John Pickering, were influenced by the ideas of Robert Owen and the New Harmony colony in Indiana, a radical experiment in equality and economic cooperation. Owen theorized that the growth of technology—or, as he referred to it, "mechanism"—was inherently accompanied by extreme economic inequalities. This was attributable to the fact that human selfishness was a product of unrestrained competition and greed. As a remedy, he advocated expanding public works and education to help workers in times of economic stagnation and depression and, most important, basing the economic organization of society on small, self-sufficient, and cooperative communities.

Even more, the radicals highlighted the power relations that were inherent in these emerging patterns of economic inequality. There is no mistaking the fact that they approached the subject from the point of view of political equality and that they did not see a separation between the abstract equality of political rights and the substantive equality that ought to be inherent in the economic sphere. There was a very real consciousness that America's political project of abolishing servitude and bondage— with the obvious exception of Southern slavery—was now under assault. There was no questioning the fact that a new set of power relationships— which were replicating the old feudalistic patterns of the aristocracy—was emerging with the onset of modern capitalism. Stephen Simpson, writing in 1831 in his book *The Working Man's Manual*, saw the stakes clearly. Unequal wealth was caused by the new legal institutions such as corporations and chartered monopolies (essentially one and the same for the radicals) and their ability to re-create the hierarchical power relations of the past with great ease. This, Simpson claimed, was due to the growing influence of "Law" rather than the rightful place of industry, of working men. "I use the term Law as a generic word, embracing all the details that affect the distribution of wealth, such as moneyed corporations, chartered monopolies, and that endless chain of levers which move industry to empty her gains into the lap of *capital*, and which effectively frustrate and defeat the grand object of rational self-government on the basis of individual freedom and personal merit."[60]

For Simpson, there was no mistaking the fact that this was leading to a re-creation of the servitude of working people to the wealthy and the essential destruction of equality and freedom. Drawing a parallel to the feudal systems of all nations of the past, Simpson was able to make his claim that America was witnessing a degeneration of its most cherished and important political and moral ideal, that of equality itself.

> Having shaken off, renounced, and branded those [feudal] systems of anti-quated barbarism and monkish superstition, by all the great leading docu-ments of our national existence, we are bound by the highest and most sacred ties of moral, religious, and political obligation to bring the condi-tion of the people, in respect to the wages of labor and the enjoyment of competence, to a level with their abstract political rights, which rights imply necessarily the possession of the property they may produce, on principles of equity congenial to the equal rights guaranteed by the organic law. To substitute Law for the distribution of labor is to introduce the chief feature of the feudal systems of Europe into the free, self-formed, and equitable republic of this country, and amounts to a virtual repeal of the very first principle of the Declaration of Independence and the Constitutions of the Union and the States.[61]

This emphasis on the connection between political rights and economic reality was no mere rhetorical device; it expressed the confusion and the anger that the emerging economic system was evoking in working people as the economic society was changing it basis from small economic com-munities to larger ones of wage and factory labor.[62] Inequality was a con-sequence because the divide between owners and workers had grown in intensity. For radicals like Simpson, there was no questioning the effects of inequality: it was leading to a condition of serfdom less than half a century after the revolution had shaken off those archaic institutions of servitude.

Politics could be used against economics. Indeed, it had to be used to reign in the excesses of the new economy and defend the political ideals upon which the "principles of the Declaration of Independence" had been founded. Simpson, like the other radical egalitarian critics of his time, saw that the political principles of equality and the emphasis on the common good were being eroded by the ability of economic interests to outweigh the political interests of the whole community. Working people therefore had a political obligation to use politics against the interests of a minority that sought nothing less than their oppression and the elimination of their political and social rights:

Like the abolishment of the laws of primogeniture and entails, we must commence with laws establishing the true principle of the distribution of wealth. To do this, the producers of wealth must cooperate through the usual means of commanding a majority of voters and of representatives, by parties, by combinations among the wronged never to vote for men who will favor the principles that oppress them.[63]

Radical critics of inequality therefore were not intent on a radicalization of politics; their intent was simply the utilization of already present political institutions against the interests of corporate wealth. Working people were not unlike a universal subject "placed by nature in a moral and physical attitude which conspire to carry perfection all the attributes that ennoble his mind and procure happiness to his being, presents to the world the imposing spectacle of Liberty and Reason combining to consummate Justice."[64]

Langton Byllesby's *Observations on the Sources and Effects of Unequal Wealth* was also the product of this emerging worker culture. Published in 1826, it was the first sustained analysis of economic inequality in America, and at its core was the political imperative of the equal right of all to the pursuit of happiness and the "Inaptitude of the primitive and existing institutions to admit that right, by their generation of unequal wealth, and warlike inclinations, through the assumption of fixed property in the soil, the introduction and perversion of the uses of money and the system of trafficking."[65] Wealth was the product of labor and this was, in Byllesby's view, a universal truism: man had the right to the products of his own labor, and this was the source of the pursuit of happiness and of true equality. With the rise of new economic systems of ownership and production—specifically the erosion of the older forms of craft production and the move toward industrial production—new forms of ownership began to arise. Inequality was the result of this transformation, and for Byllesby, what was at stake was nothing less than the possibility of true freedom as a result of this new system and its inegalitarian implications.

The ownership of property was not at issue, but that property was supposed to be the product of individual labor. Unequal distribution of wealth was therefore tied to the destruction of the pursuit of happiness because the economy was the means to that end. The rich capture labor that is not theirs, amass great wealth, and tie workers to their own economic interests, "thereby destroying the equality of means, and essentially the *equality of right*, to the 'pursuit of happiness' and enjoyment, however the sufferers may be deluded with the notion that they still retain that right."[66] In an argument similar to Rousseau's philosophical explanation of the origin of inequality, Byllesby held that it was perpetuated by the ignorance of the majority, who unwittingly accept their own systemic disenfranchisement. As a solution, he advocated the emergence of labor organizations that would be able to press for equal divisions of the fruits of labor. The link between political rights and economic conditions would prove important for the radical critics. They were able to see that the move toward economic modernity would effectively change the character of their political rights, that a move toward wage labor was consequently a substantial move away from the conception of economic autonomy that they held dear and that was seen as the material foundation of all political notions of liberty and self-determination. Unlike Carey or the economists of the late nineteenth and early twentieth centuries, they did not invest the economic system with seemingly natural powers, and they were able to see that economic inequality was the beginning of a long slide toward servitude.

Theodore Sedgwick pointed to the destructive capabilities of "corporate grants," which would give power to a minority of the community over the whole. Writing in 1835 as "a citizen of New York," Sedgwick cast his argument in terms of the direct relationship between government, corporate interests, and access to social power:

> It must necessarily follow, to every person whose mind is cast in that republican mold, the die of which is not yet, thank God, broken, that the principle of corporate grants is wholly adverse to the genius of our institutions; that it originates in that arrogant and interfering temper on the part of the Government which seeks to meddle with, direct, and control private exertions, and in that inefficient, petitioning, and suppliant temper necessarily engendered in a people taught not to rely on their own exertions but to beg aid of their rulers. Every corporate grant is directly in the teeth of the doctrine of equal rights, for it gives to one set of men the exercise of privileges which the main body can never enjoy.[67]

A distinction was made between "business corporations," which were essentially small in size and regulated by law, and banks, monopolies, and larger corporations; this distinction was based simply on the kind and amount of social power yielded. David Henshaw, writing in 1837, argued that "business corporations, excluding banks and all large corporations for trading in money, when judiciously granted and suitably regulated, seem to me generally beneficial and the natural offspring of our social condition. But if they are to be placed beyond legislative control and are thus to become monopolies and perpetuities, they assume an aspect the reverse of this and become alarming excrescenses upon the body politic."[68] The state regulated all kinds of activities, from certain limitations on free speech to certain kinds of "amusements," and, for Henshaw, there was no reason not to extend this to the sphere of corporations as well. Evoking the Constitution of the State of Massachusetts, Henshaw crafted an argument that held that corporate interests were against the common good because they sought to take advantages of others for their own benefit. It was therefore the responsibility of the state to reign in their excesses and to "correct" those who do not "conduce to the common good."[69]

What radicalism brought to the table—aside from its political perspective on equality and its populist rhetoric—was an analysis of the new economic organization of society and an analytical perspective that penetrated into the mechanisms of inequality itself. Whereas thinkers like Carey were concerned with analyzing the economic community and the interdependence of the different classes that were its constituent parts, the radicals—taking the labor theory of property as their central moral and social scientific lens—looked to the relation between employer and employee, between wealth and labor and the way that these relationships were constituted and the way that they perpetuated themselves. William Gouge, in *A Short History of Paper Money and Banking in the United States*, looks at the way that banking distorted the "natural" distribution of wealth by privileging owners over producers. The resulting inequality would affect more than the individual. "It is not easy to set bounds to the effects of a single act of injustice. If you deprive a man of his property, you may thereby deprive him of the means of properly educating his children and thus affect the moral and intellectual character of his descendants for several generations."[70] This, Gouge argued, was an effect of modern commerce, which was itself bound to a reproductive cycle that would continuously generate inequality in wealth between classes, cleaving society in two:

> Unequal political and commercial institutions invert the operation of the natural and just causes of wealth and poverty, take much of the capital of a country from those whose industry produced it and whose economy saved it, and give it to those who neither work nor save. The natural reward of

industry then goes to the idle, and the natural punishment of idleness falls on the industrious.[71]

| 94 |

The problem was seen to be more than the emergence of inequality itself. Many of these critics of inequality were reacting against the emergence of the banking system in the early nineteenth century. But it should be emphasized that this critique was not meant simply to bring down the banking interests; there was also the deeper, more important political issue of the emergence of monopoly, plutocracy, and aristocracy. John Vethake, writing in the *New York Evening Post* on October 21, 1835, described the reasoning behind the antimonopoly position. For Vethake, as for the other radical critics, the problem was a systemic one with civilizational consequences:

> Relatively considered, it is now precisely as if all things were in a state of nature; the *strong* tyrannize over the weak; live, as it were, in a continual victory, and glut themselves on incessant plunder. It is as humiliating now to be poor, as it is in the state of nature to be feeble of body; and although the ordinary difference between the rich and the poor, as between the athletic and the feeble, is clearly unavoidable and doubtless right, just, proper, and expedient, yet that such difference should be enhanced by legal enactments, that the rich or the strong should be enhanced by legal enactments, that the rich or the strong should be artificially legislated into still greater riches or still greater strength, is not only unnecessary, but decidedly improper and even *cruel*.[72]

The protection of incorporated interests was politically as well as economically unjust because, Vethake rightly claimed, there was "no such protection in existence for the mechanic or producing classes."[73]

Orestes Brownson's essay "The Laboring Classes" of 1840 pointed out that inequality was not simply the result of banks and privilege. The system itself worked in such a way so as to effectively rob those who labored of their own property. Merchants did this by artificially adding price to what was already produced. Remuneration was no longer based on effort, skill, and labor. It was increasingly becoming based on "mischievous social arrangements" created by the drive for profits and the manipulation of the market: "It may be laid down as a general rule, with but few exceptions, that men are rewarded in an inverse ratio to the amount of actual service they perform."[74] Readers of Marx's more sophisticated analysis of the labor process under capitalism will undoubtedly find a rough affinity with the theory of the working day.

Similarly, the opening lines of John Pickering's book *The Working Man's Political Economy* (1847) argue that "men do not accumulate property in proportion to their industry; but the reverse is the fact." Pickering saw that "capitalists" and the economic system that they were promoting was in contradiction with the basic tenets of American liberty: "the argument so often brought forward to sustain the positions of those who advocate the justice and propriety of granting special privileges, under a government based upon the principle of equal rights, *falls to the ground.*"[75] Going back to the labor theory of property was therefore a radical move: it stood in the face of wage servitude—something that Brownson and other radicals saw as particularly pernicious—and, more important, it would restore what was "natural" against what was "artificial." Reliance on the labor theory of property—perceived as a natural right—meant that the accumulation of great wealth was not the fruit of individual labor but of the appropriation of labor by capitalists. Herein was the crucial aspect of the new economic system that would crush the rights of man, equality, and liberty and usher in a new age of dependency and servitude as well as massive economic disparities of wealth and power.

In the decades preceding the Civil War, America was not falling back into the older political forms of aristocracy or tyranny, as the early revolutionary generation had feared. The economic inequality that manifested itself as the middle of the century approached meant, most immediately, the loss of the economic independence of workers. It is therefore little surprise that Whigs of the period and the rhetoric of the Jacksonian era were so critical of inequality.[76] Locofocos like William Leggett saw that the emergence of new ideas of property—such as those endorsed by "banking incorporations"—were overcoming the political ideals of equality. Opulence was being protected at the expense of the poor. Where did the wealthy gain the opulence one saw in New York, Philadelphia, or Boston? "They owe [it] to special privileges; to that system of legislation which grants peculiar facilities to the opulent, and forbids the use of them to the poor; to that pernicious code of laws which considered the rights of property as an object of greater moment than the rights of man."[77] The economy was becoming intertwined with political power, creating a legally sanctioned aristocracy, and the rights of man, which had previously been heralded by the revolution and its generation, were hanging on the edge of a precipice.

The radicals still wanted equality of condition, but they saw that it would be the natural outgrowth of an equality of effort and labor—effectively of an equality of opportunity. But the new economic relationships were smashing the foundations for any equality of opportunity, and the radicals therefore concentrated their critique on the system itself rather than a narrow emphasis on opportunity.[78] Their economic ideas were informed by a normative sense that wage servitude and economic dependence were fundamentally against the political principles of America's republican democracy. They would result in nothing less than the total disenfranchisement of working people and lead to a new form of inequality where wealth and opulence ruled over the laboring masses. Indeed, most Americans knew that anything akin to perfect equality was illusory and utopian, but they did recognize that relative equality of condition was the product of the rewards garnered from honest labor and a natural distribution of reward from individual effort and the freedom from economic and political dependency.

Since capitalism was evolving not in the agrarian sector but in the cities, it was the manual laborers and "mechanics" that were to feel its initial effects—but they were the minority of the overall American economy, which was still predominantly agrarian or bound to smaller economic communities. The problem was seen to be institutional in nature: capitalism had to be opposed because it corrupted the economic base of the time, which was, in itself, the realization of certain political principles such as equality and liberty. The small, self-sufficient, self-employed, independent, and unincorporated kind of enterprises that most people were engaged in was the realization of those political ideas. Any threat to that form of economic organization was also an attack on the realization of those American political principles. They did not seek state intervention in the economy—that, in their view, was not necessary. All that was needed was for charters and banks to be disbanded; for the law to properly award property and wealth to those that actually produced—that is, worked or labored—for it. Skidmore wanted a radical redistribution of property; Byllesby believed that "associations" of workers could organize to protect their interests from the effects or "evils" of unrestrained competition. For Carey and the radicals alike, free competition was not the cause of the problem, but the radicals knew that the manipulation of labor and property by a new economic class was the source of inequality and that the real mechanism of inequality was contained in the economic relationship between workers and owners.[79] Only the radicals were able to connect these concerns with the categories of political equality and freedom, and they did so through a curious blend of Lockean liberal ideas about the value of labor and the broader vision of which institutions ought to regulate the excesses of economic activity and the emergence of wealth. They were critics of asymmetrical social power, but they effected their criticism through a fluid combination of liberalism and republicanism. To be sure, they accepted the idea that individual labor was the source of wealth as well as equality, but they rejected Lockean ideas such as the ability to claim ownership through the payment of wages, a core aspect of Locke's prepolitical state of nature and a crucial addition to his labor theory of value. Instead, they argued that there was a conception of the common good that needed to be enforced: unequal wealth would be the path toward a new feudalism and the destruction of liberty.

Their movement failed, but not because their arguments were not heard. Their critiques of inequality resounded with skilled laborers and new workers in a rapidly changing economic system. The move to large-scale industrialism would render calls for the abolition of wage labor obsolete. The new economic imperatives gathering force as industrialism progressed were met with a demand for new forms of employment. The very culture and institutions of work were rapidly changing, and in the process, the radical call for equality would not diminish but would be overshadowed by the national crisis that burst onto the scene with the Civil War. In many ways, the legacy of the radical egalitarians was their insistence on an institutional critique of the production process as well as the links they constructed between wage labor, inequality, and the demise of worker autonomy and political and social equality. Even more, the radical critics of inequality showed that they were conscious that the principles of the American republic were intertwined with economic forces. Equality was not an ideological concern; it was a concrete political issue with fundamental economic dimensions.

It was becoming clear that discourse on economic inequality in America was reacting to the realities of economic modernity: the movement from small-scale agriculture and commerce to larger, more complex circuits of production and distribution and the formation of new economic entities such as the legal corporation. Movement away from the moral foundation of the American economy and toward the cash nexus meant a shift toward production, distribution, speculation, and investment, an emphasis on private interest and profit over the earlier aim of self-sufficiency. The maturation of the early American system of commerce was becoming a groundwork for industrial capitalism. The rise of inequality in the early nineteenth century was therefore not simply a matter for political economists; it resonated immediately with the political concerns of workers and those intellectuals who saw that the political rights of equality and liberty were under siege as capitalism developed. As the ends of economic activity were being reoriented, resorting to politics and political principles of equality was only rhetorical—the essential moment was the radicalization of the liberal theory of property and labor. By seeing the emerging system as being inherently against the interests of equality and liberty, Orestes Brownson was perhaps more prescient than he could have imagined when he wrote, "You must abolish the system or accept its consequences. No man can serve both God and Mammon. If you will serve the devil, you must look to the devil for your wages; we know no other way."[80]

3

The Transformation of American Capitalism

From Class Antagonism to Reconciliation

After the Civil War, the American economy began to change rapidly. Especially in the rubble of the South, markets became exploitive and predatory. Because of the attempted secession of the Confederate states, the older sectional constraints on Northern capital were no longer in place to contain the economic interests of the maturing industrial economy. The institutional shifts in American capitalism mirrored the great shifts in European society and its turn to economic and political modernity. However, Europe saw its own ensuing increase in inequality differently than the United States. Nineteenth-century European intellectuals did not see economic activity in such a benign light—for thinkers as diverse as Marx, Matthew Arnold, John Stuart Mill, and Eduard Bernstein, among many others, capitalism was premised on division, exploitation, and immiserization. Whether it was Durkheim's analysis of industrial society and its atomizing consequences in *Professional Ethics and Civic Morals*; Marx's understanding of the ways that modern life was marked by the processes of capital; or Arnold's critique of economic inequality as demeaning to civilization and humanism, the fundamental tenets were essentially the same: the barbaric effects of modern capitalism needed to be overcome and society transformed in order to preserve it against the forces of economy.

The sharp increase in economic inequality during the latter part of the nineteenth century was concurrent with rise of industrialism.[1] What Benjamin Disraeli referred to as "two nations" in England—the rich and the poor—was becoming an increasing social and political problem wherever industrial capitalism was expanding. Inspired by the legacy of Enlightenment moral and political principles, European radicals of the mid- to late nineteenth century were able to see the emergence of capitalism as simply the extension of previous forms of inequality. This resonated with the ideas of American radical critics of the Jacksonian era, but there was little cross-fertilization until the decades after the Civil War. In the American political discourse, economic inequality was intimately bound with political ideas. In antebellum American society, economic life was intimately bound with the understandings of equality and liberty. Through its Protestant work ethic and its secularized variant of a Lockean-inspired understanding of labor, property, liberty, and individualism, American ideas of economics were the necessary counterpart to political ideas of equality and freedom. And it is for this reason that the emergence of economic inequality—and its intensification—became such a political problematic, for without self-sufficient labor, dependency would result and inequality would cause excesses of power in the hands of a few.

But the concentration of economic power alone was not what motivated the radical critics of the first half of the nineteenth century, who took as their central problematic the emerging and intensifying economic disparities of their time. Their central target was the threat of economic dependence—and they thought this would emerge through the control of unequal property and wealth. The new economic order seemed to threaten everything that was unique about the American republic, specifically, its differences from European ways of life that were thought to be outmoded and hostile to the "natural" forms of human liberty embodied in American society. The concern with economic inequality was bound up with every aspect of modernity. There were constant worries throughout the nineteenth century that America would somehow not be immune to the degenerating social effects of industrialism evident in European economies. American travelers that visited industrial cities such as Manchester in England saw them as inherently opposed to America's republican civilization. The squalid and wretched conditions of the working class in these places was evidence of the brutal economic system that America had left behind. America's republican virtues were thankfully embraced as a barrier, at least for the time being, to such conditions.[2]

But despite this, the post–Civil War years witnessed the rise of concentrated economic power, the deepening of economic inequality, and a new, much wider pattern of social and political polarization. This period would see the clash of economic interests in the form of the "war of labor and capital," and it would also see the clash of ideologies on economic inequality. The rise of the large corporation and the massive transformation of American society had profound effects on the moral weight and political salience of economic divisions. The rise of laissez-faire not only as a doctrine but as an empirical reality in American society caused social convulsions and moral reprobation. Capital was able to operate without restriction, and there were no safeguards for the effects that industrialism was having on the lives and interests of working people. The economic change effected by capitalist development was therefore not only transforming the material relations of whole groups of people; it was also affecting the ways that members of society legitimized these new social and economic relationships. As capitalism was becoming increasingly entwined with legal doctrine and political institutions, it also was changing previously shared conceptions of what civilization and progress actually meant. The market transformation of society was beginning to take root, to proliferate, and to yield its fruit.

The connection between the changing discourse on inequality and the economic context of the time needs to be made explicit. Without question, the doctrine of social Darwinism was spreading just as the Gilded Age began to take off, indicating a tie between economic interests and social theories. Martin Sklar is correct when he argues that capitalist business activity "presupposes, and is permeated by, a complex mode of consciousness, that is by ideas and ideals about deliberate calculation of ends and means with respect to other persons; about the shape of society, its approved goals and moral standards; and about the law and jurisprudence, party politics, and the range and limits of government authority."[3] The arguments against economic inequality in this period therefore began to change, and not simply because a different set of interests were at stake—there was also a fundamental sociological transformation that produced a different sense of what economic equality was, how it related to the activity of the state, and how it related to political ideas more broadly.

In addition to the sociological shift that scholars such as Sklar emphasize, there was also an important change in class structure and the nature of the market as big business grew in size and in scope. Alfred Chandler argues that in addition to a concentration of capital and wealth, there was a simultaneous growth of a "new class" of professionals and managers. The older ideas about Adam Smith's "invisible hand" and the free operation of the impersonal market were being replaced with decisions made by a more highly complex bureaucratic corporate elite. The old economy was changing, and changing rapidly. It was becoming not only larger in terms of economic concentration—which began with new transportation technologies such as the railroad, more densely concentrated urban markets, and scale economies that were able to produce more and therefore simultaneously stimulate consumption—but in terms of its bureaucratic structure as well.[4] This would not only rapidly change the way the market would work, but eventually also undermine the older presumptions about the market as the impersonal distributor of wealth by means of "free labor."

The labor radicalism of the antebellum period railed against the onslaught of industrial capitalism—specifically the emergence of wage labor and the erosion of smaller, more cohesive economic communities—because it would lead toward conditions of servitude in economic and political life. Economic inequality was not simply an injustice; it meant—at a much deeper, more political level—the material destruction of the very political ideals upon which the American republic was founded. The intimate relationship among economy, morality, and polity in an earlier era began to unravel as capitalism developed and modernization proceeded. Equality of condition and equality of opportunity in this period were still one and the same for the radical thinkers since once everyone was able to enter freely into economic life, a rough equality of condition would result. Inequality of economic conditions was the result of the distortion of equality of opportunity and the concentration of economic power, the emergence of the modern corporation, and the dismantling of smaller economic communities, which were, for the most part, self-sufficient unto themselves.

Economic modernity—modern capitalism itself—was therefore seen as the genesis of a new kind of social stratification that would threaten individual liberty by creating conditions of dependence and control. But the new economic system that made industrialism possible changed the economic preconditions of this argument. The very nature of industrialism was mass employment, which meant the overshadowing of the older, smaller economic communities that Matthew Carey, Orestes Brownson, and others saw as the foundation of American economic life. Moralists such as Henry George and Edward Bellamy called for conquering economic inequality by overcoming the social atomism that modern industrial capitalism had proliferated. But others, such as E. L. Godkin, were not optimistic about the calls for reform or radical change, writing that "when a man agrees to sell his labor, he agrees by implication to surrender his moral and social independence"; workers were "legally free while socially bound."[5]

At issue was a change of social cosmology. The economic changes that ushered in the era of industrial capitalism were intimately tied to ideas of progress and innovation that were a function of the rise in technological production. This, in turn, had a profound effect on the goals and interests of the different classes. Inequality was becoming more central to many of the debates that plagued academics, policymakers. and popular writers. But the notion of "equality of condition" would become increasingly utopian in sociopolitical terms, and "equality of opportunity" would be emphasized by those criticizing the inegalitarian effects of industrial capitalism. This shift was not simply a change of emphasis, however; it reflected an acceptance of economic modernity, which was also constituted by the spread and general acceptance of the institution of wage labor. The radical critics of the early nineteenth century reacted against wage labor because it reduced the worker to a mere "hireling," or one who would serve for wages. As capitalism grew, so did proletarianization, and this acceptance of the wage system would have a deep effect on conceptualizations of economic inequality.

The radical views expressed by Thomas Skidmore's call for an equal redistribution of property and Orestes Brownson's call for the elimination of the system of wage labor would change with a new generation into arguments against the monopolistic character of the economy. The older notions of republicanism of the revolutionary generation were eroding, and the liberal idea of labor and the individual was beginning to eclipse republican themes. This tendency in American political culture—one brought about largely by the changing nature and structure of American capitalism—would inevitably serve as the guidelines by which capital and labor would deal with the problem of social divisions spawned by the great age of high industrialism. The liberal economic ethic that had evolved in American political economy and moral thought was being pitted against new and more complex historical conditions: the institution of capital, monopoly, and the nationalization of the economy.

The liberal economic ethos worked so well with the emerging democratic ideas of the nation because the assumption was that once labor was freely able to express itself and individuals accumulated property from their labor, skill, and talent, a rough condition of equality would emerge. Equality of opportunity and condition were therefore conceptually linked, but the new institution of capital—which Marx correctly termed a *process*, not simply property—would organize society in a decidedly different way, making these older conceptions of liberty and labor, economy and morality, obsolete. It was the task of critics of inequality to come to terms with this. Some did so better than others. In the end they would also have to confront a new argument legitimizing inequality, which derived from Spencerian ideas of social Darwinism but also was consonant with older arguments against equality in American social and political thought. In the end, inequality would only be successfully confronted once policymakers saw that capitalism was here to stay but also that labor as a force in and of itself was as well. With the settling of the industrial order, it was clear that democratic principles were being sacrificed to the workings of capital. In time, the radicalism of labor, on the one hand, and the newer arguments wedding the worsening condition of class inequality with social progress, democracy, and liberty, on the other, would be tamed, subdued, and brought into line. American social and political thought would therefore reflect the fractious nature of class society of the time, but it would move from a general condition of antagonism to one of reconciliation and consensus. These new policymakers and intellectuals—all of whom worked during either the Progressive or New Deal Era—would forge a liberal-capitalist consensus that would hold for decades, finding its apex in the New Deal and the social welfare programs of the 1960s.

RACE, CLASS, AND THE PROBLEM OF INEQUALITY

The aftermath of the Civil War presented the American discourse on inequality with a new set of problems. The debates over the project of Reconstruction revolved around the extent that equality ought to conceived and then extended to the freed slaves of the South. Dominant was the ideology of "free labor," which was crucial to the ideological core of the Republican Party even before the war.[6] Free labor was nothing more than the recognition that the liberal economic ethic was a crucial component to American values of liberty. The debates around Reconstruction centered on the extent to which a propertyless class would be able to achieve any degree of equality and social integration. Radical Republicanism—a civic ideology that encompassed thinkers and politicians such as Thaddeus Stevens, Horace Greely, Charles Sumner, and E. L. Godkin, among others—was primarily focused on the issue of civic and political equality for freed black salves rather than on economic issues. It was standard to distinguish between the natural and political rights that had been denied blacks, on the one hand, and the social and economic rights that were defined simply as the right to labor like any other man and own the fruits of that labor, on the other.[7] These radicals' interest in economic equality was defined by their faith in the liberal economic ethic: namely, that reward would come from the effort and labor of individuals and that equality could be nothing more than the equality of opportunity.

Blacks therefore had to be guaranteed their political rights in order to be integrated into American society, and it was presumed that this was the limit of what government would and could do in order to promote equality between blacks and whites. But economic equality was not something that Radical Republicans advocated in their vision of Reconstruction. Reconstruction, as it was broadly conceived at the time by the most radical in Washington, therefore had little to do with economic change but was wedded to the liberal economic ethic and its liberating impulse. The Radical Republicans saw that through guaranteeing equality of opportunity in politics and the economy, their duty toward racial equality would be complete. Aside from fringe calls for the redistribution of Southern property—Thaddeus Stevens advocated the seizure of plantation lands in order to turn them into homesteads—redistribution and economic equality were nonissues.[8]

Black writers and thinkers, however, did look into the issue of economics and the essential link between economic power and equality. The idea of economic empowerment became a crucial staple of black political thought during the early years of Reconstruction, in that without economic power—by which was meant the economic development of black communities with some degree of parity with their white neighbors—blacks would continue to exist at the whim of white economic institutions. There were no illusions that civil and political equality could be of any substantive value without economic parity with whites. Alexander Crummell—rector of St. Luke's Episcopal Church in Washington—was one of the first black thinkers to advocate the construction of black economic communities in order to construct a new force in American society. Without economic power, blacks could look forward to a continued dependence on whites and a re-creation of the conditions that they had suffered under as slaves. This would become a major theme in black political and social thought throughout the late nineteenth and early twentieth centuries. Booker T. Washington emphasized the development of skilled labor and thrift as a means for the accumulation of capital and the development of black communities. Crummell and Washington—despite their differences—both saw equality as requiring an economic dimension. Political and civil rights were one thing, but the reality of the situation was that without some degree of economic parity with white society, political and civil rights would be, at best, a mere pleasantry.

Washington, as Crummell before him, acknowledged that the economic empowerment of black communities was an essential first step in achieving and securing political and social rights and power. Although DuBois would chastise Washington for his "submission and silence as to civil and political rights,"[9] the reality was that the latter never accepted any form of restriction on black political or civil rights and that his advocacy for economic empowerment, thrift, and industrial education was primarily an argument that linked economic power with political and social power and equality.[10] Crummell and Washington saw that the need for economic development—through the growth of capital in the hands of blacks—would be the only way to achieve social integration and guarantee that there would be no dependence upon the white community. For Washington, the emphasis on economic empowerment and development meant that relations with the white South had to be maintained; it meant that there had to be some degree of accommodation and cooperation with white Southern leadership.

But as the project of Reconstruction went into crisis and terminal decline, many black intellectuals who had supported Washington's program for black empowerment—which was linked with a conciliation with the white South—became critical of it. DuBois, who had been a supporter of the Washington's Tuskegee position, began in the early years of the twentieth century to advocate protest and a break with the policy of accommodation and conciliation with the white South. In place of the ideas of economic empowerment, DuBois began to articulate a political-cultural critique of the Tuskegee position and pushed for a focus on civil and political rights and the development of a black cultural-intellectual elite. The move away from the issues of economic empowerment would not return until the 1920s, when DuBois began to look toward socialism as a possible alternative for black liberation. Indeed, DuBois's concern with politics and civil rights was—in the face of increased Southern violence and the quashing of equal opportunity for blacks in white society that became ever more real with the emergence of Jim Crow—understandable. But it can perhaps be argued that the move away from economic issues may have been a fatal error. Indeed, concern for the consequences of the economic disparities that severely affected the political and social life of black communities would reemerge in the black radicalism of the 1960s.[11]

What black intellectuals and activists—as well as their white allies in Washington and elsewhere—sought was, therefore, an equality of opportunity rather than equality of conditions. But this should be seen within the ideological context of the time. Blacks, from Reconstruction until the beginnings of the twentieth century, were—not unlike the radical critics of inequality during the antebellum period—concerned with the struggle for equality of opportunity. Although it would later be seen that propertied interests had destroyed many progressive aspects of Reconstruction in the South, taking away even the possibility of equal economic opportunity for blacks—what DuBois would call in the 1930s the "counter-revolution of property"[12]—during the Reconstruction era, an explicit discussion of economic inequality took a tertiary role to issues of equality of opportunity guaranteed through equal political and civil rights. But the post–Civil War period would also see the recurrence of the theme of economic inequality in America's critical political and social discourse. It was quickly becoming evident that the laissez-faire industrial economy that expanded rapidly after the war was leading America to economic, political, and moral crisis.

THE MORAL ATTACK ON INEQUALITY AND CAPITALISM

The central premise of the labor radicals' argument against the effects of economic modernity during the decades preceding the Civil War was that the emerging realities of capitalism were a direct threat to the kind of economic individualism and autonomy that characterized small-scale economic production and exchange. For those early radicals, Langton Byllesby and Thomas Skidmore, among the many others, economic inequality threatened to destroy democracy itself. The ideas of republican virtue that had idealistically characterized the thought of Adams and Jefferson and many others of the revolutionary generation were being squandered, and it was only by fighting against the effects of economic divisions that any semblance of democracy and liberty might be preserved.

In addition, the radicals saw the liberal economic ethic as being not only compatible with republican political virtues but necessary for their realization. Many of the next generation of reformers, radicals, and social and economic critics of the economic polarization of the nation would stick to an idea of liberal individualism but place it within the context of an already transformed culture of economic life and phase of institutional development. The earlier radical critics emphasized that equality of opportunity and equality of condition were essentially the same because opportunity meant the ability to produce your own goods (such as in agriculture) or sell your own labor time as an independent laborer and not a wage-earner. Wage slavery was tantamount to economic inequality and the disruption of the kind of cohesive society where wealth and income were distributed by talent, skill, and effort.

Not unlike the previous generation of labor radicals, many critics of inequality in the industrial age saw firm economic foundations for the generation and perpetuation of economic divisions. For some, progress itself was the cause of inevitable immiserization. Henry George saw that as both technology and productivity increased, the value of land would also increase. As rent rose, it necessarily pushed down wages because industrialists needed to pay for higher rents out of what they paid to labor: "with increase in productive power, rent tends to even greater increase, thus producing a constant tendency to the forcing down of wages."[13] Inequality was therefore tied to the economic foundation of modernity. It was not simply a matter of preventing the amassing of wealth through corrupt means. The new economy, the new industrial civilization that was being forged, would seal the fate of millions. Poverty and progress were inextricably linked.

George's critique of inequality was in the spirit of the antebellum labor radicals. Indeed, for George political rights were meaningless without economic rights, and economic rights still meant that each individual would have rightful access to an equal share of land—property and power were still linked in his thinking. By leveling a single tax on rents, George argued that, over time, monopoly could be broken down and there would be a return to an economy based on individual effort and skill. This would produce not an absolute equality but, rather, a rough equality that still rewarded differences in effort and skill. At the core of George's argument remained the ideal of individual economic autonomy. In this sense, George looked back to the past; unable to see the newest phase of capitalism—its national, industrial manifestation. He was unable to see that the old physiocratic notions of land as the source of all wealth was economically wrongheaded. But his moralism was a critique of monopoly and the exclusion of economic autonomy and individualism. Equal political rights are meaningless without economic equality—that is, equality of land—since land is the only source of individual wealth. After quoting Jefferson's line from the Declaration of Independence that "all men are created equal," George insists:

> These rights are denied when the equal right to land—on which and by which men alone can live—is denied. Equality of political rights will not compensate for the denial of the equal right to the bounty of nature. Political liberty, when the equal right to land is denied, becomes, as population increases and invention goes on, merely the liberty to compete for employment at starvation wages. This is the truth that we have ignored.[14]

This "central truth," as George referred to it, was the need to restore an economy and society based on "natural opportunities," and this meant that the basis of equality was still one grounded in assumptions from America's economic past.[15] The problem with the various theories of equality that were put forth by so many reformers of the period was not that they failed to recognize the barbarism of the new economy; rather, far too few of them possessed a broader understanding of the economic reality of the time. Many writers, such as George himself, were unable to think outside of the economic context and ideas that had defined the early American republic.

The moral revulsion against capitalism's deepening effects did not lessen as the nineteenth century progressed. Socialist ideas became increasingly prominent—which George was decidedly against—and they injected the idea that individualism and inequality were somehow connected. The problem with what Marx termed "universal egoism" was not only that it would lead to deeper social divisions at levels other than class, but also that this social atomization would inevitably reproduce the same problems that arose under modern capitalism. George wanted to preserve individualism and promote "association," by which he meant an association of equals—equal in the sense that all had an equal opportunity to work on land from which they could derive the fruit of their labor, something that the state would need to enforce through taxation. This was one of the final gasps of the older liberal republican conception of economic life. George believed that all people had an "equal right to the elements of nature," and since nature, or land, was the only source of wealth, its redistribution was essential to alleviating the ills of inequality. Discouraging the massive accumulation of property was at the heart of George's policy alternative and his "single tax" movement. The problem was not with the capitalists, it was with the way that monopoly squeezed out all opportunities for honest individual labor and thereby shattered any hope for equality.

But the socialists did not see it this way, especially the German socialists who were writing in defense of socialist ideas in America. For them, the problem was with monopoly, but monopoly was inextricably tied to capitalism and to egoism. Three years before George published *Progress and Poverty*, Friedrich Sorge wrote his "Socialism and the Worker," his only published piece in English. There he chided, "if you are a capitalist yourself, reflect how much nobler it is to help promote the welfare of the many than to serve only your own interest, ugly and hideous Egoism."[16] Sorge was tracing the moral critique of inequality down to the very ethical fabric of a market-based society. Johann Most attempted a more anthropological analysis. What he identified as the "beast of property" was any "man in connection with wealth," who, still unsatiated after accumulating beyond his needs, desired little more than the expansion of his greed. These "beasts of property" were at the core of capitalism, and capitalism was the source of monopoly, the one great threat to human liberty: "In America the place of the monarchs is filled by the monopolists. Should monopolism in the alleged free United States of America develop at the rate it has in the last quarter of a century, only daylight and air will remain free of monopolization."[17] In Marxian style, Most made clear that inequality was not a transitory condition of economic development; it was, rather, the essence of capitalist exploitation and a permanent feature of the evolving economic system. The immiseration of working people could therefore only be expected to get worse—inequality was not the problem in and of itself; it was the symptom of a greater illness: capitalism, exploitation, atomization, egoism, barbarism.

But early socialists like Most and Sorge premised their critiques on alternatives that were highly utopian, to say the least. They relied on a complete transformation of the economic life of nineteenth-century America: a massive, egalitarian redistribution of property and the common ownership of property. Whereas George held that the solution to the injustice of modern economic inequality was a matter of returning to the economic life of the past—of independent producers associating under conditions of equality—Sorge saw the emergence of associations and an emphasis on the common interests of society over "Egoism" as the key to overcoming capitalism. Most argued for the same end by promoting a war of workers against capitalists and the establishment of a "network of federations" of autonomous and independent communes. Lacking concrete institutional referents, the socialists had little to use in their appeal to those outside of the German-immigrant working community. George's economic ideas looked back to the ideology of economic liberalism and economic autonomy and independence and therefore had some possibility of resonating with American working people. George did not reject capitalism and did not have a problem with free trade; his aim was to restore equality of opportunity, which itself ultimately sprang from free labor and a single tax that would serve as a permanent barrier to the monopolization of land.

But this, in many ways, was the problem with the critique from the beginning. It is true that the German socialists saw capitalism as a more complete social, cultural, and economic system, but they were unable to pose alternatives outside of a crude collectivism. The socialists rejected capitalism without having a realistic institutional alternative, and their rejection was still, in essence, a *moral* critique of capitalism. Unlike Marx's more scientific examination of capitalism and his argument that it would essentially break down under its own internal economic strains and contradictions (such as the law of the falling rate of profit), American socialists were more interested in possibilities for immediate action and in extrapolating from some of Marx's insights for utopian ends. For his part, George was unable to see—through his highly flawed political economy—that inequality was not caused simply by the monopolization of land but rather by the very dynamics of capital and its need to constantly agglomerate more of itself at the expense of labor. George was unaware of the inequalities that arose from the production process under capitalism and the way this affected the system of labor, and he remained under the trance of an outdated and outmoded Physiocratic doctrine even though his critique was essentially grounded in a moral antipathy to inequality and social divisions.

The socialists differed from reformers such as George, Edward Bellamy, and Henry Demarest Lloyd, in the sense that they espoused an absolute equality of property, which the reformers thought was neither desirable nor possible. For George and Lloyd, the central idea was still to have some form of rough differentiation between individuals based on "natural inequalities." Property would still correspond to natural inequalities of ability, but this would not lead to great differences. After all, the point of critique for these reformers was the problem of monopoly, not capitalism or competition. True, they all shared a moral aversion to the decline of economic autonomy, of equality writ large, seeing the agglomeration of capital as the primary force destroying equality and freedom. But ultimately their calls for equality were based on the idea that the emerging divisions of society were out of tune with American political and moral ideals. This was an important period in American social and political thought because all three reformers were, in one sense, attempting to come to terms with economic modernity using what they felt were fundamental American ideas about economy and society.

Industrial capitalism was transforming America into a gluttonous society. Political economy was becoming the source of wealth, but it was also and more importantly the result of the abuse of liberty. "Liberty produces wealth, and wealth destroys liberty," wrote Henry Demarest Lloyd in *Wealth Against Commonwealth*. The inequalities that plagued America and that were at the core of what was being called the "social problem" by the 1880s were not a result of capitalism itself but rather its excesses: "Our bignesses—cities, factories, monopolies, fortunes—are the obesities of an age gluttonous beyond its powers of digestion."[18] For Lloyd, the "corporate Caesars" were nothing more than the ruinors of civilization. Inequality in wealth was, at its core, the inevitable result of what Lloyd referred to as the anarchy of self-interest. Wealth was destroying the republican virtue upon which the idea of commonwealth had always rested. Lloyd's critique of monopoly and inequality did not lead him to advocate the destruction of capitalism but rather to call for overcoming self-interestedness that opposed the general welfare and, more pragmatically, for the transfer of private monopolies over to state ownership. Lloyd's ideas were republican in nature: he insisted that citizenship be based on what amounted essentially to Aristotelian moral and political categories, that is, that the individual realize that he is part of the social whole and that self-interest should be in harmony with the interests of the political community.

> The true *laissez-faire* is; [sic] let the individual do what the individual can do best, and let the community do what the community can do best. The *laissez-faire* of social self-interest, if true, cannot conflict with the individual self-interest, if true, but it must outrank it always. What we have called "free competition" has not been free, only freer than what went before. The free is still to come. The pressure we feel is notice to prepare for it. Civilization—the process of making men citizens in their relation to each other, by exacting of each that he give to all that which he receives from all—has reached only those forms of common effort which, because most general and most vital, first demanded its harmonizing touch.[19]

Only through the reconstruction of a social ethic based on a harmonization of self-interest with the public interest could the principles of commonwealth overcome the forces of wealth. But Lloyd, too, was unable to prescribe concrete, institutional alternatives. He railed against monopoly and the unequal distributions of power, wealth, and resources that monopolistic capitalism created, but he was essentially unable to translate these critiques into concrete institutional alternatives—moral revulsion was considerably simpler than political practice. Aside from his idea for state ownership of all large industrial combinations, he was unable to peer into the complexities of economics and institution building. His moral vision lacked the material basis for any kind of viable political translation.

Outside of the more pragmatic politics of the emerging labor movement, the politics of inequality was still largely fueled by moral rhetoric, but it did not lack intellectual substance. Each of the thinkers saw economic equality—or some rough approximation of it—as being the material manifestation of political democracy and political equality. Nonetheless, their lack of social scientific expertise worked against them. Henry George's economic theories were easily countered, and during a debate at Oxford with the great English economist Alfred Marshall—the founder of modern equilibrium economics—he was decidedly defeated and his ideas discredited in a public setting. George's significance was in his moral revulsion against inequality; he, like Lloyd, wanted to show that monopoly capitalism and democracy were essentially incompatible and that it was a phenomenon that went heavily against the grain of American democratic principles. Since economic life had always been tied to American political ideals and values of liberty and equality, the disappearance of economic equality meant the imbalance of justice and liberty. The idea of the individual was not a problem for Lloyd, George, or Bellamy, unlike the German socialists. They sought reform—albeit radical reform—rather than radical upheaval and utopian schemes. Radical reform, however, consisted for them, at its base, of the moral regeneration of society, a return to the political ethics that were grounded in what they saw as the foundational principles of American republican civilization. The individual was not a problem, but individual self-interest had to be checked by social interests. Inequality was the result of self-interest unhinged from the moral moorings of political society, and all of society was being affected. It was a descent into anarchy.

The success of Edward Bellamy's novel *Looking Backward* was a testament to this moral appeal against the economic complexities of division and depression that plagued the late nineteenth century. On the surface, Bellamy's novel is one that exploits the well-used literary device of utopia—as opposed to the actual call for utopian social arrangements—to cast a critical glance on American industrial society from the vantage point of the year 2000.[20] Its central character, Julian West, wakes up in Boston in the year 2000 after having been in a trance for over a century. But at another level, it is a tale of moral growth and discovery. By the end of the twentieth century, America has overcome the problems of class conflict, social atomization, and poverty, and West's transition to life in that time is a tale of moral reinvention as he absorbs and learns to situate himself in a futuristic society characterized by abundance, equality, and peace. Social change of this magnitude could only be effected by what Bellamy termed—in an essay of the same name—the "religion of solidarity," which in Bellamy's novel and other writings becomes "nationalism." Inequality was the expression of a deeper cancer pulsing within American culture and society. Economics was not the problem; it was the motives of individuals in a society that was becoming increasingly fragmented, atomized, and unequal. Moral degradation—defined politically as the move away from social integration and toward social atomization, the fetish of individualism, and selfishness—was the cause of material inequality and the decline of America's republican experiment. Inequality was the ultimate social ill because of its manifold consequences, from human suffering to political imbalances of power. The economic ethic of liberal individualism would therefore need to be called into question.[21]

Even as George looked back to a kind of agrarian socialism based on individual labor and Lloyd's critique of monopolies and industrialism and his call for a return of commonwealth smacked of anti-modernism, Bellamy, not unlike Marx, held that the emerging industrial order would usher in a new era of human happiness and prosperity. The new American Jerusalem would be built on the foundations of machinery and technology, and equality and solidarity would be the very stuff of its moral collective consciousness. The key was the elimination of narrow self-interest and the cultivation of unselfishness. Bellamy saw the individual as comprising a "personal" and an "impersonal" self. The former was driven by narrow self-interest, greed, and the dictates of possessive individualism. When suffused by this ethic, society would drift toward inequality, and fragmentation and would produce individuals who had regressed to their most base, animalistic appetites. Bellamy's ideas had a distinctively Hegelian cast, arguing that a class of social engineers, the bureaucracy, would be responsible for mass economic planning and the maintenance of society economically and technologically.[22]

The impersonal self would tend toward solidarity, toward social brotherhood. Its ascendancy would mean the elimination of selfishness and a moral consciousness to serve the social whole, of which each individual was an integral part. Inequality was not a result of the institutions of the day, of capital or land-rent prices. It was, rather, the result of the drastic erosion of solidarity, wholeness, and social responsibility, of the turn to self-interest and the neglect of social cohesion and attention to collective welfare. Bellamy has Doctor Leete—Julian West's guide through the year 2000—say: "Now that industry, of whatever sort, is no longer self-service, but service of the nation, patriotism, passion for humanity, impel the worker as in your day they did the soldier."[23] The transcendence of narrow egoism and possessive individualism would therefore effect a redirection of political, social and economic life. It would enable society, as a whole, to see that what was in the best interest for all was also in the best interest of each. Economic life would shift from the drive toward personal accumulation and move toward the common good. Doctor Leete explains how this social ethic was able to redirect the economic life of industrial America:

Early in the last [twentieth] century the evolution was completed by the final consolidation of the entire capital of the nation. The industry and commerce of the country, ceasing to be conducted by a set of irresponsible corporations and syndicates of private persons at their caprice and for their profit, were entrusted to a single syndicate representing the people, to be conducted in the common interest for the common profit. The nation, that is to say, organized as the one great business corporation in which all other corporations were absorbed; it became the one capitalist in the place of all other capitalists, the sole employer, the final monopoly in which all previous and lesser monopolies were swallowed up, a monopoly in the profits and economies of which all citizens shared.[24]

The nationalization of production and distribution therefore harnessed the full potential of modern industry, and the concern for the collective whole would create a "Republic of the Golden Rule." But none of it would happen naturally; the yearning for equality would begin to promote the needed moral transformation, which would result in the system's collapse. As Edith Leete, Julian's lover and the Doctor's daughter, says, recounting late-nineteenth-century history from the vantage point of the twenty-first in Bellamy's less successful literary sequel, *Equality* (1897), "the American people began to be deeply and widely stirred with aspirations for an equal order such as we enjoy . . . very soon the political movement arose which, after various mutations, resulted early in the twentieth century in overthrowing the old system and setting up the present one."[25] Social struggle was an integral part of the move toward social equality, progress and the birth of a new American civilization.

The abstractness of Bellamy's prescriptions for social change were problematic when it came to translating them into practice. On the whole, the moral critique of inequality was probably correct: the maturation of capitalism and the intensification of modernity were causing massive social fragmentation. But the various moral critics were unable to link their ideas with organized political movements. They shared the political ideal of an integrated political and social community that would be unspoiled by the excesses of industrial capitalism. Each in his own way sought to overcome the social fragmentation that economic modernity and economic inequality fostered and they, like their socialist counterparts, believed that inequality was the means by which they could draw attention to the problems of capitalism and modernity as a whole. Their utopian schemes were extensions of their political interpretation of American republicanism, something that was being eroded by the advance of capitalism and the corrosive effects of laissez-faire individualism. With the move from small economic communities to industrial behemoths and dense urban centers, the sociological shift from *Gemeinschaft* to *Gesellschaft*, and the slide of the American economic ethic from individual labor and production to possessive individualism, these moral critics of inequality were the last gasp of the older liberal republican ideology of political integration in the face of a divided America and the modernizing transformation of American capitalism.

The Omaha declaration of 1896 had considerably more pragmatic policy proposals than the regeneration of moral life and its reformation. Although thoroughly populist in nature, it saw its political origins in the older republican notions of common middle-class farmers and small producers—not unlike those that the earlier generation of radicals sought to protect from the implications of a developing capitalism. In their addition to the Omaha Platform originally laid out in 1892, the National Farmers Alliance sought as their primary goal "to restore and preserve these rights under a republican form of government, private monopoly of public necessities for speculative purposes, whether of the means of production, distribution, or exchange, should be prohibited."[26] The theme of republican government was therefore wedded to the liberal economic ethic in the sense that individual labor was to be given primacy at the expense of combines and corporations. This populist strain was not surprising; the economic interests of the agrarian sector had always been opposed to those of capital.

The reformers and socialists all shared the critique of inequality and the yearning to repair the eroding social bonds that were, for some, the cause and, for others, the effect of industrial capitalism. These reformers were outside of the mainstream. More common was the kind of laissez-faire liberalism of people like E. L. Godkin, the essential premise of which was that individualism was the base of American society and that what they termed an "equality of rights" was the only kind of equality that was acceptable. Extending equality to conditions was tantamount to the destruction of individualism through the promotion of collectivism. Laissez-faire liberalism was critical of tariffs and any other special privileges that the government bestowed on corporations, but it was equally critical of the idea of economic equality because this would, in Godkin's words, "prove fatal to art, to science, to literature, and to law." The fear of equality as flattening out human distinctions, quashing creativity, and annihilating individualism would go on the offensive during this period. The maturation of a counter-discourse legitimating economic inequality was about to take place.

LEGITIMIZING INEQUALITY

The moral critique of capitalism and inequality was accompanied by a raging war between capital and labor, as Mathew Carey would refer to it in the early 1870s. Rutherford B. Hayes deployed the army to crush the Baltimore and Ohio Railroad strikes, an interstate manifestation of the growing "labor question," and the Haymarket Riot in Chicago became world news. Both were interpreted by the moral critics of the age as symbols of American decline. The corporate transformation of American capitalism had its apologists as well as its critics. It is probably more correct to say that they were apologists for a certain definition of liberty, or at least of a configuration of liberty and economic inequality. The legitimation of inequality would become, from this point forward, a distinct tradition in American political thought, with deep ramifications for the present. The apologists of inequality accomplished this by linking the economic realities that were unfolding around them with their interpretation of the liberal economic ethic. It was not a return to aristocracy and medievalism that they sought; rather, it was the understanding that inequality was not anathema to human liberty—as the previous generation of radicals had insisted—but rather its ultimate realization. The connection of liberty and economic inequality was therefore tied to the political sphere because it would now become necessary for the state, by and large, to refrain from interference with all economic activity.

More than in the antebellum period, the late nineteenth century saw the emergence of a tradition in social theory and political thought that would buttress arguments for economic inequality through the present. Although it is certainly correct to characterize broadly this school as marked by social Darwinist beliefs and ideas, it is more important to see these ideas in the context of American political thought and their implications for the further development of American political thought.[27] Not unlike Alexander Hamilton and John C. Calhoun, these thinkers—ranging from William Graham Sumner to Andrew Carnegie—represent the matu-

ration of an explicitly antidemocratic tradition in American social and political thought. That the rise of these ideas and their purveyors was tied to
the nuances of the new economic realities of capitalism should come as
little surprise.

The political dynamic of the new social theories that grappled with
the progress of industrial civilization fit into the broader transatlantic revulsion at bourgeois notions of democracy and equality. But in America
these ideas took on a very specific economic and social flavor. Criticism of
equality was, in many ways, inherent in the doctrine of classical liberalism
from its inception, based as it was on a political order that protected individualism and a moral one that was skeptical of collectivisms of all kinds,
including that of the state. In Europe, equality would be the rallying cry
for the burgeoning socialist movements, but for every Marx there was a
Nietzsche.

America, too, had its struggle with the question of equality and its relationship to democracy and human progress. But Americans, of course,
had a cruder, more brutal tradition upon which the discourse of social
inequality could be grounded. Decades of debate about slavery had convinced enough thinkers that any kind of absolute equality was anathema
to nature itself.[28] Hamilton's idea about the necessity of economic inequality—that it was the essential counterpart to economic development—was
not something that many political economists looked upon with admi-
ration. But Hamilton's ideas were still in tune with a predominant understanding of liberal thought in the eighteenth century: that the difference between "natural" and "political" equality needed to be delineated.
Equality before the law was—when it came to white, property-holding
men—taken as a given. But the idea of translating that into the physical
and material world—that is, the world of individual effort, skill, talent,
and property—was largely condemned as leveling and, in the end, utopian
and destructive.

Indeed, although Calhoun's ideas were primarily aimed at the debate
over slavery and the protection of that institution in the South, they also
touched upon a much broader notion of the danger of economic equality,
or the equality of condition. More than a defender of slavery, Calhoun was
also a deep critic of American democracy and the idea of equality itself.
He was keenly aware of the changing nature of the American economy
and knew that the future of the nation would no doubt see the exhaustion
of slavery as an economic order. It was therefore inequality as such with

which Calhoun was concerned. Conceding that the essence of popular government was an "equality of citizens, in the eyes of the law," to move beyond this into the equality of condition would undoubtedly "destroy both liberty and progress." Inequality in condition—that is, in material terms and economic welfare—was rooted in a kind of natural equality between individuals. Going against this natural inequality would therefore interfere with the realization of liberty:

> Now, as individuals differ greatly from each other, in intelligence, sagacity, energy, perseverance, skill, habits of industry and economy, physical power, position and opportunity—the necessary effect of leaving all free to exert themselves to better their conditions, must be a corresponding inequality. ... The only means by which this result can be prevented are, either to impose such restrictions on the exertions of those who may possess [ability] in a high degree, as will place them on a level with those who do not; or to deprive them of the fruits of their exertions. But to impose such restrictions on them would be destructive of liberty—while to deprive them of the fruits of their exertions, would be to destroy the desire of bettering their condition . . . and effectually arrest the march of progress.[29]

Calhoun knew that inequality would persist even after the present system of agriculture and slavery had been abandoned by the marching advance of the economic system. The coming industrial order that he saw from the vantage point of the late 1830s would pit capitalists and "operatives," or laborers, against one another. This was not to be seen as unnatural; it was the result of progress. And this conflict was the firm basis of civilization, Calhoun argued; the new industrial order would ensure a "contest between the capitalist and the operatives; for into these two classes it must, ultimately, divide society."[30] Calhoun's ideas may not have been hegemonic at the time, but they evince an interesting and oddly persistent intellectual linkage between economic or material inequality—grounded in natural distinctions of individual skills and talents—and political liberty. This view would become an ingrained perspective justifying inequalities in American social and political thought up through the present. Ideas in the post–Civil War era about inequality were not so much the intentional development of the older ideas like those of Hamilton and Calhoun; they were, instead, the theoretical articulation of the antiegalitarian impulse that had always been present in American thought.

With the rise of industry and the massive social stratification that accompanied it, a new generation of thinkers would deepen this inegalitarian tradition. The great industrialists of the day would see their efforts as entitlements. Inequality could be justified in the name of progress, development, and modernization. Jay Gould's famous phrase, "We have made the country rich, we have developed the country," was hardly mere rhetoric. It captured the way that those who wanted to defend and justify the newly stratified society would think. As moral critics such as Bellamy and Lloyd knew all too well, industrial capitalism was an assault not only on the doctrine of equality but on civilization itself. For the apologists of this new social order, the debate on inequality would be a matter not only of protecting their interests in intellectual terms but also—for those who did not have specific capitalist interests—a matter of reconciling economic modernity with notions of progress and prosperity. Capitalism may have begun to exhibit its true face, but it was in the same classic categories of individual effort and economic individualism that these apologists would cast their arguments. Hence, the idea of economic liberalism could be seen to cut both ways—it was now becoming a matter of interpretation rather than a contest between civilization and barbarism.

The ethical and social theories of William Graham Sumner would attain a high degree of intellectual influence in the late nineteenth and early twentieth centuries, and they would come to legitimize economic divisions through a thoroughly developed sociological and moral system. Sumner's writings were not intended as an explicit apologia for the new industrialized aristocracy, but they were the most coherent and most influential theoretical and moral notions about social divisions and inequality up until that time. Whereas political economists like Henry Carey had seen optimism in the development of the American economy through its inevitable ability to create inequality between various classes and hence a "harmony of interests," Sumner reversed this notion. He saw economy, polity, and society as grounded in the forces of nature, which Darwin had theorized and which prominent thinkers like Herbert Spencer had transferred over to society, but also as the product of social mores and customs that had set in over time. It was clear that Sumner's conservatism would prove a powerful defense of inequality and social division, and its resonance would not be lost on contemporary conservative thinkers in America. He would succeed in privileging liberty over equality and show that American society—its economy, legal system, and polity—was, without the meddling interference of the "social doctors" (his term for civil servants), the ideal political and legal system to realize human liberty.

Sumner's aim was to strip moral and "sentimental" impulses from social analysis and to show that the status quo of American society—and here he specifically meant to focus on the class inequalities of his day—best for the realization of human liberty. Reversing George's dictum that progress and poverty were opposite sides of the coin of economic development, Sumner also wanted to claim that the interference with the activity of capital was the cause of social misery and poverty, not the reverse. Society as a whole progressed and increased its standard of living as capital was freed to unfold and operate according to its own logic and the logic of its owners. It was only when the economy was allowed to work freely that liberty could be realized since liberty was conceived as a set of laws and institutions that "create great organs of civil life which can eliminate, as far as possible, arbitrary and personal elements from the adjustment of interests and the definition of rights."[31] For Sumner, liberty was to be emphasized over democracy; the former was a greater value than the latter because it accorded with the rational distribution of the fruits of labor, talent, and skill. To assume equality among individuals was sheer nonsense. Just as Jeremy Bentham had mocked the idea of natural law theory in the eighteenth century by calling it "metaphysics on stilts," Sumner was equally critical of natural law doctrines, preferring a positivist interpretation of political and legal categories.

At the heart of Sumner's economic and social theory was the notion that interests are grounded in innate human needs such as hunger, love, vanity, and fear.[32] This provided him with a naturalistic basis for economic motives, which were matched by innate differences in skill, talent, drive, and intelligence. But also there was the economic idea that the nature of society and politics is governed by the relationship between population and available land. With a low population and abundance of available land, society and government would be less competitive and less savage. The opposite ratio would necessitate intense competition; "earth hunger arises, races of men move across the face of the world, militarism and imperialism flourish, conflict rages—and in government, aristocracy dominates."[33] Inequality was therefore the direct outgrowth of this "natural" Malthusian-Ricardian economic framework: only the most fit would survive the social competition for existence. The fortunate by-product of this was that competition would result in social progress because it would allow the creative and talented to mobilize their skills and abilities, which, in the end, benefit everyone.

Sumner's ideas were therefore not simply a justification of capitalism, nor was he trying to align the new industrial order with what were seen as American political principles. Instead, Sumner wanted to show that the moral pleasantries of equality were a sentimentalism of the past. The scientific understanding of man's nature and of modern society made it clear not only that economic inequality was necessary but that interfering with it was essentially an intrusion into liberty itself. The justification for inequality was therefore one that had remarkable affinities with the ideas of Calhoun and other critics of the doctrine of equality on the basis that equality and liberty were not—as Tocqueville had believed—compatible. Modern industrial capitalism therefore required economic inequality; there could be no separation of the two. Hence, a rejection of the reality of economic inequality was not only a lapse into prescientific sentimentalism; it was also a rejection of modernity as well.

> Some have said that Mr. Stewart made his fortune out of those who worked for him or with him. But would those persons have been able to come together, organize themselves, and earn without him? Not at all. They would have been comparatively helpless. He and they together formed a great system of factories, stores, transportation, under his guidance and judgment. It was for the benefit of all; but he contributed to it what no one else was able to contribute—the one guiding mind which made the whole thing possible.[34]

Sumner's ideas about competition and social progress set the stage for the theories of economic inequality. Although they were to fall out of fashion during the Progressive Era, Sumner still was able to place the inequalities generated by capitalism in a quasi-scientific framework. His ideas rested on the simple dictum that "persons who possess the necessary qualifications obtain great rewards";[35] the legitimation of social stratification was a simple extension of the liberal economic ethic, depoliticized and transplanted into the context of industrial capitalism.

Even though, ultimately, the discourse that legitimized economic inequality was not powerful enough to hold back the massive strains that the system was causing, it provided an important conservative justification for the excesses of capitalism by wedding an antiegalitarian theory with the doctrine of personal liberty and political freedom. Before libertarians would attack the state for its redistributive mechanisms, Sumner was able to ground a thoroughly modern critique of economic egalitarianism, one that preserved political equality by splitting off the economic and political spheres from each other. No longer was it possible to see the relationship between economy and society as it had been interpreted in the postrevolutionary era. Indeed, the crucial transformation of the liberal doctrine during this period reflected the emerging differentiation among economy, polity, and society. Economic liberalism had always been the backbone of theories of social justice and equality because, in the presence of a precapitalist market society devoid of political influence, nepotism, and privilege, it was the only way to critique the kind of encrusted power relationships that were characteristic of preliberal society. But now that the economic context had transformed, the liberal economic ethic was being fused to a new set of social and economic goals, and economic inequality could be justified using the same liberal categories of individual labor, skill, and the right to property.

Sumner's ideas—as influential as they were—were only an aspect of the way that laissez-faire doctrines was adopted. Sumner's ideas were explicitly antiegalitarian, but laissez-faire became a serious issue in late-nineteenth-century America as well as England. Herbert Spencer's work *The Man Versus the State*, published in 1884, laid out the firm argument that state intervention was opposed to liberal individualism; state interference was inherently opposed to the idea of liberty. The state stood for coercion, and any extension of the state's role beyond enforcing contracts—what Spencer referred to as "anarchy plus the constable"—amounted to the erosion of liberty in economic affairs and, in the American interpretation of things, the elimination of freedom itself. This apologia for capital and laissez-faire therefore exploited a narrow interpretation of American political categories and transformed Hobbes and Locke from liberal thinkers at the roots of American democratic institutions to radical libertarians. It was an ideology that would rise again, with even greater power, a century later.

In this way, thinkers such as Sumner, and even Calhoun before him, did more than privilege the interest of one particular class over another; this is far too simplistic. What they were able to achieve was the purging of ethical and moral categories from social theory and analysis. They were able to reinterpret liberty and the entire American brand of liberalism itself as a radical individualism that was—when framed in the context of a capitalist economic framework—conducive to progress. It was not an ideology that embraced the past or a conservative ideology that sought to prevent progress and modernity. Sumner and others who followed his ideas were different from George, Lloyd, and even Bellamy in the sense that they saw moral categories as obstructing social progress. Although Carnegie would see the tragedy of the dark side of capitalism, for Sumner there was a natural order that was evidenced not by some static ordering of classes but, rather, in the free dynamic fluidity of society, which meant that the state needed to refrain from concretizing ethical impulses into state intervention. Unlike older conservatives who saw that equality was a threat to a social order of privilege, Sumner and Calhoun saw that the "natural" workings of the economy and of social progress functioned best when moral entanglements were effectively removed. Politics was therefore reduced to its most base Hobbesian elements: freedom was a freedom of contract and safety from a return to the state of nature.

Legitimating inequality ideologically went hand in hand with the structural realities of late-nineteenth-century economic life. The ability for working people to organize and make effective demands for higher wages and other improvements in their working life was also contested by what Sanford Jacoby has referred to as the "exceptionally high degree of employer hostility" that was present in the American economy from the late nineteenth century through the turn of the twentieth.[36] An ideological understanding of American life was being forged, and it would outlive the structural imperatives of the time. In the late twentieth century, the inegalitarian tradition in American political thought would reemerge, but it would have a very different reality to struggle against: namely, that forged by the ideology and policies of the Progressive and New Deal Eras.

BRINGING IN THE STATE: THE FORMATION OF THE LIBERAL-CAPITALIST CONSENSUS

Whereas both the moral critique of inequality and capitalism, on the one hand, and their pseudo-scientific defense, on the other, were unable to deal with the practical problems of a divided society, the intellectuals and policymakers of the Progressive Era were able to crystallize different ideas and moral impulses into social policy. For Progressives, the late nineteenth century was rightly seen as having left a legacy of economic divisions and an economy that was, for all intents and purposes, out of control. By the time that Edward Bellamy had written *Looking Backward*, the economist Richard Ely—the teacher of both Woodrow Wilson and John Commons—could write, addressing the "workingmen," that "[w]hile the majority of you reject socialism, I am certain that most of you agree with me that along certain lines the function of the state should be increased. Government cannot do everything, but it can do much."[37] In essence, this sentence encapsulates the direction that the discourse on inequality took during the Progressive Era, and it is one that was instrumental in forming a liberal-capitalist consensus that lasted essentially until the late 1970s. The turn was against radicalism but also toward the limiting of economic disparities through state mediation. The disasters of the nineteenth-century economy could no longer be denied, and, although there would be broad disagreement among them about specific policy prescriptions, thinkers of the Progressive Era would respond in order to deepen American democracy and preserve industrial capitalism.

The Progressive and New Deal Eras have been the subject of much analysis and interpretation, but one theme is dominant: the excesses of industrial capitalism and the laissez-faire doctrines of the late nineteenth century were viewed by the emerging academic and intellectual elite—not to mention the broader public—with deep suspicion. Critical of the ideas of people like Spencer and of judicial doctrines that upheld laissez-faire, they began to turn to the state to provide more public goods and to question the economistic and libertarian notion of "liberty" that was being privileged. These new thinkers saw what was at stake. On the one hand, the march of social, economic, and technological progress was bound to lead to some degree of social stratification; this was the price of modernization. Business elites were not to be seen simply as monopolists; they were also at the same time unquestionably the engines of economic growth and keys to the progression of a modern civilization. But the new theorists were also fully cognizant of the consequences of industrialism and unrestrained capitalist growth, most importantly economic inequality. And it was this latter realization that makes so many Progressive thinkers crucial in understanding the way that the discourse on economic inequality would change during the beginning of the twentieth century.

Pressure had been building for some time in America over the abuses of capitalism and the ineffectualness of political life to stop its excesses and corruption. In the late nineteenth century the literary and journalistic writings of the Muckrakers had broadened public attention to the worst aspects of American industrialism. Ida Tarbell's writings on Standard Oil, Lincoln Steffens's probing of the abuses and corruption of local politics, and the novels of Upton Sinclair and Frank Norris, among others, were all central in creating a new awareness of the abuses of capitalism. Norris's novel *The Octopus* focused on the politics and the social effects of railroad monopolization, while *McTeague* tells the story of greed and individualism that he—not unlike the moral critics of the late nineteenth century—believed were wreaking havoc on American moral and social life. Upton Sinclair's novels, such as *The Jungle*, *Oil!*, and *King Coal*, were instrumental in not only exposing industrial abuses and scandals but also in nourishing a broader trend that was emerging in American society: a critical discourse on laissez-faire economic life and its political, social, and moral ramifications. Their critical discourse was also being mirrored in intellectual circles, although there it would not tend toward outright radicalism.

The transformation of American society during the first decades of the twentieth century would therefore need to reconcile capitalism with some sense of democracy; it would need to integrate the state into economic and social life in order to mollify inequalities. Progressive intellectuals were by no means egalitarians, but they did see that the excesses of laissez-faire capitalism needed to be counteracted by the institution of the state. As early as 1886, the economist Richard Ely was explicit about this program:

> While all the monstrous inequalities of our times can by no means by upheld by good men, while many of those inequalities, the fruit of evil, can beget only evil, remember that nothing more disastrous to you could happen than to live in a society in which all should be equals. It is a grand thing for us that there are men with higher natures than ours, and with every advantage for the development of their faculties, that they may lead in the world's progress, and serve us as examples of what we should strive to become.[38]

Progressive thought saw economic inequality as a primary assault on America's democratic traditions and on any possibility for a democratic future. But more important, Progressive thinkers were able to see that modernity placed new demands on intellectuals and specialists and that the complex ordering of a modern, industrial society would need to be explicitly taken up. Ely was not alone in his view that the state simply had to be brought in and that inequality was an emerging moral as well as political problem. Charles Spahr's *Essay on the Present Distribution of Wealth* (1896) was the first major empirical study to show the massive inequities of wealth at the end of the nineteenth century, and it would be cited even a decade later as an empirical source describing a deeply and antagonistically divided America.

Issues about distributive justice would give way to the Progressive vision of the expanded state and to a more complex idea of the relation between the economy and the state.[39] But the apology for laissez-faire would still be able to assert itself. Christopher Tiedeman argued that the right to property protected individuals from any form of interference by the state or other organizational bodies who sought regulation or any kind of redistribution. His *Limitations of Police Power* was a defense of a kind of individualistic liberalism that Progressive thinkers would come to deride. The liberal idea of property rights would not disappear, but its influence would be considerably overshadowed by a newer idea of American democracy and an insistence that the economy had to be steered toward more democratic ends. The Progressive assault on individualistic capitalism would ultimately culminate, during the New Deal, in a political environment sensitive to the interests of organized labor, but it would also forge a consensus between capitalists and workers and the state that would last well into the twentieth century.[40] Progressives would hold the laissez-faire impulse at bay while formulating a newer conception of political and even economic rights.

Progressive thinkers began to have a dominant influence on the intellectual discourse in America beginning in the late nineteenth century, and their views would radically transform the way that economic inequality was viewed and the ways in which it would be confronted. In addition to Ely, Henry Carter Adams would attack the notion of laissez-faire in his essay "The Relation of the State to Industrial Action," and Charles Cooley would put forth a distinction between caste systems and the more dynamic and fluid class systems characteristic of the United States, arguing that the latter provided more impetus for innovation and personal self-expression and was less likely to lead to permanent forms of social inequality. All of these thinkers embraced a faith in market capitalism, but they saw that it was an imperfect system, one in need of regulation and reform. These thinkers collectively would begin a reorientation of American intellectual affairs, and the changed discourse they provided had a decisive impact on the way that economic inequality would be interpreted, viewed, and dealt with in policy.[41] But it would also lead to a legitimation of a certain kind of social order that would prevail throughout the twentieth century. In short, Progressive intellectuals wanted to avoid radicalism and, for that matter, egalitarianism, and this was the product of their particularly moral and even religious intellectual and ethical roots.[42] They were aware of the dangers as well as the immorality of the way that laissez-faire or individualistic capitalism wreaked havoc on the populace, and all of them saw—to a greater or lesser extent, depending on who it was—that a new understanding of democracy was needed that they would seek to provide. They would build an intellectual framework that would reconcile the fractious relationship between capital and labor into a new consensus and set the stage for a new conception of economy, polity, and society.

Although published well after the intellectual influence of the Progressives within the academy was firmly established, Herbert Croly's highly influential book *The Promise of American Life*, published in 1909, was the pivotal text for a set of ideas that emphasized the need for reform—reform which would reestablish and renew a sense of national purpose and democratic realization. First and foremost this meant attacking the problem of economic inequality. For Croly, the problem with inequality was simply stated, and it looked back to thinkers like Adams and Jefferson and their privileging of the political over the economic: "The existing concentration of wealth and financial power in the hands of a few irresponsible men is the inevitable outcome of the chaotic individualism of our political and economic organization, while it is inimical to democracy, because it tends to erect political abuses and social inequalities into a system."[43] For Croly, economic inequality in America was being systemically reproduced. He noted how the divisions of economic power were widening and that closing the gap between rich and poor was also becoming increasingly less likely as long as those that had amassed great wealth sought nothing less than the protection of their own interests at the expense of the public. Conservatives, he argued, put forth a narrow interpretation of rights that existed solely to protect contract and did not conceive of democracy as anything outside of economic utility. Political life was being subordinated to economic life, and since the logic of the market was seeping into the fabric of American life, the only way to combat inequality as well as the "chaotic individualism" of the time was through a reinvention of political life itself.

Croly's ideas about economic inequality were characteristic of a more advanced conception of democracy that insisted on what Croly referred to as "mutual ties and responsibilities." Inequality split the interests of individuals into different segments that, in turn, shattered the cohesive, underlying unity that democracy requires. He did not intend a radical overturning of capitalism but the elimination of gross inequalities by taxation and the returning of what he referred to as an "excessive measure of reward" to the community so as to "secure for the whole community those elements in value which are made by the community."[44] Croly's understanding of the connection between inequality and the erosion of democracy was important, for it pointed toward a more active role of the state (for regulation) and away from older ideas of democracy—what he referred to as "traditional democracy"—which were based on narrow interpretations of rights, individualism, and social welfare. Croly fused the political and economic spheres by connecting the problem of equal rights with that of the maldistribution of wealth under a system of private property: in no way was it possible, under such a system, for there to be both equal rights and equal opportunities for *exercising* those rights. If left unfettered, the result would be the gradual withering away of national purpose and of democracy itself.

The Progressive response to economic inequality spurred a new conception of political rights, one that brought issues of the economy and the inegalitarianism it created together with new conceptions of political democracy and public welfare. It envisioned, as Walter Weyl's phrase indicated, a "new democracy" that would no longer cling to its older Jeffersonian and Jacksonian manifestations, that is, laissez-faire individualism. The new democracy was emerging out of what Weyl called the "new social spirit," one that was separating America from its crude past and propelling it into a more democratic future. Weyl was one of the new proponents of a "socialized democracy," which saw the older individualistic form of society as crude because it halted progress and, more importantly, eroded the social foundations for the deepening and extension of democracy. The maldistribution of wealth was simply the highest form of social ill that this conception of society produced. Weyl was able to perceive that the "individualistic" democracy that had characterized American society from its inception was producing a fragmented, atomized, and anomic society where plutocracy was beginning to erode prospects for any kind of democratic future. What the new social spirit called for was a *"socialized democracy*, which conceives of society as a whole and not as a more or less adventitious assemblage of myriads of individuals."[45]

The foundations of liberal individualism needed to give way for a democracy built around assumptions of the public good to emerge. The new democracy was, in this sense, an interpretation of civic republicanism from the point of view of modernity: state institutions would pick up where the older forms of civic virtue had left off. Progressives like Weyl and Croly, as well as thinkers like Dewey, saw the need to embrace a more democratic modernity in order to overcome the shattering social consequences of the Gilded Age. Plutocracy was, in Weyl's estimation, merely temporary because it was being effectively counteracted by the emergence of "socialized democracy." Individualism was therefore no longer what it had been in the late eighteenth century, in its classical liberal guise—it was now little more than an apologia for propertied interests that acted at the expense of the public good.

> In the socialized democracy towards which we are moving, all these conceptions will fall to the ground. It will be sought to make taxes conform more or less to the ability of each to pay; but the engine of taxation, like all other social engines, will be used to accomplish great social ends, among which will be the more equal distribution of wealth and income. The state will tax to improve education, health, recreation, communication, "to provide for the common defense, and promote the general welfare," and from these taxes no social group will be immune because it fails to benefit in proportion to cost. . . . The political liberties of the people will be supplemented by other provisions which will safeguard their industrial liberties.[46]

Thinkers like Weyl and Croly would therefore effect a fundamental intellectual reorientation away from the older ideas about inequality and individualism and toward an attempt to halt the nation's slide toward economic society and away from political society. Weyl, Croly, and Dewey knew that such a slide had a grave impact on political life, morality and ethical life. They knew that, in Weyl's words, "to-day the chief restrictions upon liberty are economic, not legal, and the chief prerogatives desired are economic, not political,"[47] and that the effect of this was nothing more than the erosion of democracy and the sacrifice of human progress.

Unlike George, Bellamy, and Lloyd, the later thinkers were able to translate the critique of an atomized, fragmented society rife with economic inequality and social antagonism into a working alternative that contained institutional concerns and involved a moral redirection of the relationships among economy, polity, and society. Their critique was not merely moralistic; they were able to glimpse the crucial insight that the character of political and economic life was rooted in the particular ethical ideas that members of society held and that ideas could be concretized into political institutions. George, Bellamy, and Lloyd—each in his own way—looked to the past to ground their critiques of the present and their pathways to the future. George's economics embraced a liberal economic individualism and a variant of an outdated physiocracy; Lloyd's criticism cast industrial modernity as the source of a socially corrosive individualism; and Bellamy's notion of a "religion of solidarity" fed off of ideas that were foreign to a modern society marked by class divisions, growing ethnic diversity, and the notion of modern individualism. But this was not what characterized the ideas of Weyl, Croly, and their contemporaries. For them, the emergence of modernity required a reorientation of democracy by expanding what it meant as well as the role of the state in achieving common, public ends. Primary among their concerns were the economy and the amelioration of economic inequality. They were able to link the category of political rights with the problem of economic conditions. As a general movement, Progressivism sought national progress through a moral reinvention of the nation, and this was accompanied by a redefinition of the role of the state and a reconfiguration of polity, economy, and society.

It was this reconceptualization of democracy that would essentially transform the bases American society from economics and social laissez faire, marked by anomic individualism and inequality, to social responsibility and state intervention. The enemies of the Progressives were the familiar coterie—the adherents of the classical economists, especially Adam Smith, and other libertarian thinkers—but in the end this was hardly of any real consequence. What would emerge as a liberal-capitalist consensus was not the product of this struggle of ideas but the admission of Progressive intellectuals—from Ely and Cooley on through Clark, Croly, and Weyl—that capitalism, more specifically industrial capitalism, was one of the key elements of social progress, of human freedom and happiness. Unlike the socialist thinkers of the time, their opposition was not to the system itself but to the effects of the system's abuses and excesses.

This tendency in Progressive thought would have a deep effect on the conception of economic inequality for most of the twentieth century. There was no rejection of capitalism or even large-scale corporatism. Croly insisted that "the huge corporations have contributed to American economic efficiency. They constitute an important step in the direction of the better organization of industry and commerce."[48] But there was a reformist mentality that gave way to deeper ideas of political and social change. Fighting inequality and social fragmentation did not necessitate, for the reformers, the elimination of capitalism. Socialists like John Spargo, by contrast, would still insist that class divisions and social fragmentation could not be properly addressed without jettisoning capitalism itself.[49] But the American radical project would be thwarted by the emergence of the expanded state and its crusade for economic and social security. Progressive intellectuals saw that a reworking of state-economy relations would enable both economic and technological growth and a more just distribution of economic product. Capitalism in and of itself was not the central problem—the entire system of laissez-faire was, and to combat this, the state needed to be redefined, reworked, and brought in.

The erosion of the older labor radicalism, which had centered on the elimination of wage labor, was also a central aspect of the new consensus between labor and capital. The older ideology, which saw wages as an entrée into wage slavery and servitude, was giving way to the newer idea that working people—through labor unionism and activism—could increase their share of wages, thereby evening out the unequal power between labor and capital. The massive expansion of the American economy made the proletarianization of the American working class all but complete, and although this process began in the late nineteenth century, its political effects would begin to appear only in the early twentieth.[50] Indeed, the shift in labor ideology from anti-wage to the acceptance of the wage system was, as Lawrence Glickman has argued, "perhaps the most significant ideological development of the late nineteenth-century since it entailed a redefinition of the meaning of freedom, independence, and citizenship."[51] This shift meant an acceptance of capitalism as an institution and way of economic life, something that the radical egalitarian critics of the antebellum period would never have accepted. Now working people who suffered from economic inequality would be forced to confine their arguments to the push for higher wages rather than a transformation of the economic system as a whole. In so doing, they would embrace reform over more radical solutions to economic inequality and the friction-ridden relationship between capital and labor.

This ideological transformation would redefine the very ways that workers saw themselves: no longer were they "producers," as they had been in the early nineteenth century, but now consumers, primarily of wages.[52] The workers could achieve equality not by eliminating capitalism but by pushing for higher and higher wages through labor organization. Ira Steward, one of the main theorists of this shift in labor ideology in America, was direct about this point when he argued that "the way out of the wage system is through higher wages, resultant only from shorter hours." The emphasis on equality was therefore shifted to a new set of ideas; the improvement of wages was only part of the argument for equality. Working people would be able to improve their overall quality of life by insisting on higher wages and shorter hours. This would soon become the vision of the American labor movement, as Samuel Gompers would point out in 1919 when he argued, "I believe that as time goes on the wage-earners will continue to become larger sharers per dollar of the wealth produced."[53] Gompers wanted to see rights of working people tied to their ability to live according to civilized standards of living—to do this, workers would constantly need to push for higher wages to accommodate their needs. This new emphasis on a "living wage" would come to dominate the rhetoric not only of the labor movement itself but of the broader political debates of the early to middle twentieth century.

As an extension of Progressive thought about the economy, inequality, and the role of the state, New Deal thought became the institutional paradigm for American politics and political and social theory through the 1960s. The philosophy of society that began to emerge with the Progressive thinkers codified a new relationship between state and society even as it served to deradicalize the conflict between labor and capital.[54] The scarring effects of economic inequality brought to American political theorists the consciousness of a need for a new conception of the state, one defined against the laissez-faire minimalism of the past century and oriented toward new moral-political goals. The stubborn existence of economic inequality had convinced many American political thinkers that the narrow liberal individualism that was born in the eighteenth century and that had coexisted with the growth of a grotesque social order during the nineteenth had to be reformed, even transcended. Against the older ethos of liberal economic individualism, the move toward conceptualizing the public good came to be cast in social terms rather than individualistic ones. It emphasized the need to abandon the encrusted view of powerful elites that individualism was akin to liberty and that private property and resource ownership were the only paths to efficiency, fairness, and social progress. Thus Thurman Arnold argued in *The Symbols of Government*, "Those who rule our great industrial feudalism still believe inalterably the old axioms that man works efficiently only for personal profit; that humanitarian ideals are unworkable as their principle aim of government of business organization: that control of national resources, elimination of waste, and a planned distribution of goods would destroy both freedom and efficiency."[55]

The older moral critique of capitalism and inequality that was so vibrant in the late nineteenth century was largely seen as utopian, but not incorrect in its perceptions. Then as now, the key concern behind the critique of economic inequality was not a simple concern with distributive justice but a deeper fear that inequality was eroding social cohesion and threatening the ends of democratic social life. What thinkers such as Arnold sought to overturn was the mythos of the corporation and rugged individualism that occupied the American mind. He called these widespread ideas about economic life the "folklore of American capitalism," and in a book of that title (1937), he argued that this mythic idea of capitalism had led to the destruction of democratic life and ushered in an age of "corporate feudalism." The interests of capital were inherently opposed to the interests of labor—and where the state did not intervene, the result would be wholesale impoverishment:

> This folklore which denied that labor had a moral claim on an industrial organization produced most interesting results. The textile industry in New England had a supply of docile labor which it exploited for years. Then it took the so-called "capital" thus accumulated and invested it in the South where labor was still cheaper. This enriched a few trust companies in Boston but left whole communities impoverished. Nevertheless, under the creed of rugged individualism, primitive-minded conservatives of New England fought to the bitter end to preserve this manner of doing things. The relationship of governmental organization to industrial wreckage of this sort was entirely confused. Necessity compelled government action; theory denied it.[56]

A new kind of democratic theory was beginning to arise that identified the public as the central locus of democratic accountability, and this would serve as a theoretical and regulative ideal, judging and, in many cases, guiding the institutional reforms of the New Deal Era. But more important, thinkers such as Arnold saw that the institutions of the state had to step in to regulate economic life and curb the excesses of inequality and corporate power. John Dewey's book *The Public and Its Problems* was one of the more prominent texts that would provide new normative insights for the understanding of the interaction between state, society, and economy.[57] Dewey argued that the "public" was defined as "all those who are affected by the indirect consequences of transactions to such an extent that it is deemed necessary to have those consequences systematically cared for."[58] For Dewey, modern life posed new problems for the older understandings of community and state. Before the modern era, it was commonly seen that deliberate transactions between two or more people were essentially isolated acts circumscribed in and of themselves. But the modern understanding of a "public" meant that the new economic institutions of the time, modern technology, and so on had unintended effects on others; as such, the public interest could not always be served by the activity of self-interested individuals.

Dewey was able to conceive this in Hegelian terms. Economic modernity had created a situation where civil society—which in Hegel's formulation was defined by atomistic individualism—had overcome moral obligations of individuals toward the public good. Economic inequality was effecting a breakdown of social bonds, but it was also corrupting the ability of individuals to lead creative and free lives. The individualistic atomism that accompanied the economic nature of civil society (Hegel's *bürgerliche Gesellschaft*) could only be overcome through the machinations of the state, through institutions that objectified the public good through rational law guided by what best for society as a whole. The problem with American liberalism was not its original existence but its inability to change with the historical context. The early forms of liberalism that had railed against political oligarchies, feudalistic social arrangements, and church authority had also created the ideal of economic autonomy as a means to those ends. But in the modern context, this form of liberal individualism had a corrosive effect on society—economic inequalities were the empirical referent for this breakdown of social bonds and also for the breaking down of America's democratic political and cultural order. What Dewey termed "social liberalism" was, as he saw it, the most developed phase of liberal philosophy, one that relegated individual autonomy to the realm of thought and free inquiry and expression and placed concerns of the public good and broader social interests into the hands of the state.[59] What was needed, in Dewey's formulation, was a reconstruction of liberal theory to accommodate the complexities of the modern age, but in reality he was tapping into the republican ethos of earlier thought. The "old liberalism"—by which Dewey meant classical liberalism—rested on outdated conceptions of the individual and community, let alone the state. All this had to be reworked in order to create a new republic.

The turn away from individualistic liberalism and toward the institutional construction of the welfare state was therefore a reaction against the economic effects of modern capitalism, but also toward a different vision of the American republic.[60] Inequality was foremost among these newly framed concerns because the question of distribution and redistribution—and the role of the state in this activity—was of primary importance before and during the New Deal Era. True, the Great Depression was the primary motivator for the emergence of the welfare state, and the Roosevelt administration was forced to take the interests of labor into account because of the labor movement's growing influence. But the intellectual environment in which the welfare state was born requires emphasis; without the intellectual and moral reorientation of both the bureaucratic elite and public intellectuals, these new state institutions would have scarcely been possible. A new sympathy toward labor unions, the poor, and the expanded role of the state required a transformation of the moral-political sphere. American political and social theory effected an intellectual and moral-political reorientation away from the crude, atomistic individualism that marked the previous century and a half and toward a new conception of state-society relations. The effects of economic inequality in the late nineteenth and early twentieth centuries therefore had a profound effect on American political thought, leading to ideas that called for the state not only to enter into the activity of redistribution, but to take over where the market was unable to provide. This would remain the active ethic of the welfare state well into the 1960s, when the Great Society programs of the Johnson administration were extensions of this shift in relations between state, society, and economy.

The equality in income and wealth distribution that was achieved during the 1940s and 1950s was not only the result of the sharply progressive tax policies of Roosevelt's administration. It was more importantly the result of the expanded power given to labor. The Wagner Act, the Walsh-Healy Act and the Fair Labor Standards Act were integral to raising the wages of workers and to combating the systemic inequalities that had been increasing since the middle of the nineteenth century between capital and labor while the Tax Act of 1935 worked to reverse the trickle-down economics of the first three decades of the century. Economic inequality was now on the agenda of American politics and policy, and it was politics more than ideology that limited the expansion of this institutional crusade. Roosevelt's policies had thoroughly alienated capitalist interests in favor of labor.[61] Labor's radicalism was decisively curbed in the immediate postwar years as conservative forces surged against the growing power and influence of labor. Groups like the National Association of Manufacturers (NAM) and other probusiness organizations mobilized. But the conflict between labor and capital would take on a different flavor than in the late nineteenth century, one contained by the liberal-capitalist consensus created by Roosevelt's policies. By being given participation in the economic and political process, labor was able to have a hand in raising wages, and the federal government's progressive income tax provided further redistribution relief. Inequality was by no means eliminated, but it was so attenuated among such a broad section of the population that labor's reconciliation with capitalism was approaching completion.

But at a deeper level, an intellectual crisis emerged in New Deal liberalism. Although Dewey had called for a "social liberalism" that would accentuate the need to oppose individualistic capitalism, which had created the economic divisions of the recent past, it was not clear that this project would be successful. Indeed, although the institutions of the New Deal would be created and a shift in American politics had been effected, Dewey's "social liberalism" and the emphasis on the state as the solver of public problems that was current in the late 1930s began to give way. The issue of individual liberty once again became a key topic for liberals as the war progressed and Soviet collectivism was seen for what it was.[62] The older liberalism that Dewey had pointed to, its antistatism, its skepticism of collectivism, and the fear that it would quash personal choice and opportunity in the economy would all contribute to counteracting the more radical promises and potentials of the New Deal. The turn toward individualistic liberalism would have deep consequences for economic inequality and the future ability to respond to it.

Of course, the New Deal reforms were contested. Some critics asserted that the New Deal had not gone far enough, others that they had gone too far. Norman Thomas called Roosevelt's reforms nothing more than "pale pink pills" and castigated Roosevelt's New Deal for not going far enough to free labor.[63] Thomas was not confronting the realities of Roosevelt's policies—especially that they were giving preferential treatment to labor and allowing its increased power to result in a more reasonable equality of income and wealth. For the most part, liberals and many socialists were won over by this new orientation toward labor. Dewey himself was of mixed view. He saw that the reforms had yet to establish equality as the central political and moral category around which a new socioeconomic order should be arranged: "The means have to be implemented by a social-economic system that establishes and uses the means for the production of free human beings associating with one another on terms of equality."[64]

But despite the criticisms, it was clear what the New Deal had accomplished when it came to addressing the problem of economic inequality. For the first time in American political history and thought, it became imperative for the state to enter into economic affairs for the purpose of redistribution. The classical liberal conception of the state had always protected private property rights at all costs; now the state backed labor unions against the larger interests of capital for the purpose of economic justice. And in the end, it was not simply a transformation of institutions that made this possible: it was also—and more importantly in many ways—a reorientation of the intellectual and moral-political dimensions of state-society relations that consisted in an overturning of the older, more entrenched understanding of liberalism and democracy. Moving away from the ideas of economic autonomy and individualism that were championed throughout the long evolution of American political culture, thinkers of the Progressive and New Deal Eras reworked the older idea of a liberal democracy, premised on possessive individualism, into a socialized democracy that recaptured the older republican themes of the public good and social equality.

Of course, the problem with this—as Dewey and Thomas, among others, had seen—was that the reforms did not go far enough in remaking a new socioeconomic order. Inequality was ameliorated and for the remainder of the twentieth century; radical forces that were once active in the labor movement would no longer control the movement's ideas and programs. What the labor movement was able to accomplish—through their fights in the courts—was the liberalization of labor relations. Collective bargaining became the solution to the age-old problem of master-servant relations in the workplace, but it could not eliminate the problem of inequality.[65] The liberal-capitalist consensus was therefore an agreement by labor and capital to accept the terms of the New Deal and preserve—although on contractual terms—the system of production that industrial capitalism had put in place. Ideologically, it would preserve a liberal notion of property and a liberal work ethic; institutionally, the reality of labor's collectivism allowed workers to share in the growth and expansion of America's postwar industrial growth. But in time, this phase of capitalism would also pass, and with it the mechanisms for maintaining the modicum of economic equality obtained from the 1940s through the 1960s. But even more, it set the stage for a reified expression of the republican impulse. Whereas in earlier periods, the more radical expressions of republicanism sought to protect against the amassing of unequal property and wealth, now the interests of labor were narrower, moving from the domain of society itself to that of the shop floor. The discourse on economic inequality would therefore operate within very different institutional and cultural constraints.

In the end, the reconciliation between capitalism and corporate liberalism was able to usher in an expanded conception of democracy. The welfare state was an admission that the autonomy of the market would continue to plunge society into chaos, division, and turmoil. In its earliest manifestations, liberalism articulated an ethic of social cooperation against anarchic individualism; in its later, New Deal manifestation, it would turn this into a call for economic and social security, expanding the responsibilities of the state and its powers.[66] The desire for equality was tempered by the relative equality brought about by the New Deal and the welfare state. Through the next several decades, until the reemergence of a newly reformed political culture of conservatism in the late 1970s and beyond, the product of reconciliation worked as John Bates Clark, writing in 1905, predicted when he asserted that "the new condition will not put an end to socialistic agitation, but it will reconcile so many classes to the present order that the agitation will have no radical effects."[67]

4

Embracing Inequality

The Reorientation of American Democracy

The American Economic Association's Richard T. Ely Lecture of 1999 was titled "In Defense of Inequality." Its author, Finis Welch, was simple and direct in approaching his subject: "I believe inequality is an economic 'good' that has received too much bad press."[1] But Welch's assertion was not meant to generate controversy. Indeed, it became painfully obvious by the end of the twentieth century that the ascendancy of the market in American society has been accepted at the expense of broader political aims and goals. Whereas the Progressive and New Deal Eras sought to privilege politics over the workings and effects of the economy in order to realize more substantial political conceptions of democracy and human liberty, the contemporary consensus has decidedly shifted toward a hostility to state intervention and, I would argue, away from the very goals of economic equality itself. Not only are market processes regarded as the fundamentals of modern economic and social life, but market outcomes are tolerated as final. Contemporary views on inequality have been shaped by the curious mixture of liberalism and capitalism that has been at the heart of American political culture. Indeed, the liberal-capitalist consensus that was forged during the 1930s and 1940s was not something imposed from without; it was simply the reconciling of liberal ideas of "fairness" and "opportunity," which were inherent in American political conceptions of individual liberty, with the economic conditions of the time. Confronting economic inequality in any radical way therefore requires insight into the mechanisms of inequality, into the various ways in which inequality is generated. But it also requires that a conception of political rights that goes beyond a liberal framework be adopted. It is the entrenchment of liberalism—and its elective affinity with modern capitalism—that has produced the broad acceptance of economic inequality as a just aspect of modern American social organization.

A crucial aspect of the importance of political ideas lies in their ability to legitimize institutions and ways of social and economic life. An important dimension of the underlying ideology of American political culture has been its economic liberalism: the emphasis on the importance of hedonic individualism and property. Although there were variations on this theme, the overwhelming force of the liberal economic ethic in American life has resulted in a skepticism of the state and an emphasis on equality of opportunity. The radical link that was made during the few decades before the Civil War between equality of opportunity and equality of condition was slowly drowned out as the evolution and spread of capitalism made the possibilities of such a link less realizable. The formation of new markets for labor as industrial capitalism developed transformed the discourse of economic inequality in America by breaking apart the smaller economic communities of the early nineteenth century, and with them the associational ideals of equality that were advocated by the radicals of the time. The aftermath of the Civil War saw the ascendancy of industrial capitalism, rapid economic development, the nationalization of the economy, mass urbanization, and massive economic disparity. The ascendancy of wage labor formed a new economic context wherein the ideas of economic equality would shift from equality of condition to equality of opportunity and from a political ideology that was specifically anticapitalist to one that sought reform and a reconciliation between capital and labor. This change was made necessary by the new economic context of wage labor and the erosion of the smaller, self-sufficient economic communities that had predominated in the late eighteenth and early nineteenth centuries. The enemies of the radical critics of the 1820s through the 1850s—such as wage labor and the evolving legal rights that corporations or "combines" were winning—gave way to newer economic foes such as monopolization and an economic aristocracy that possessed the capacity to choke off economic opportunity. Even at their most radical, Americans rarely moved away from their liberal economic ethic and the emphasis on individual labor as the sole criterion for the accumulation of property.

The economic and social crises of the late nineteenth and early twentieth centuries, such as the economic depressions that spread massive unemployment and social strife, made reform a major issue and prompted a reorientation of intellectual and political life. Franklin Roosevelt's claim in his second inaugural address that "we refuse to leave the problems of our common welfare to be solved by the winds of chance and the hurricanes of disaster" was evidence of the extent to which a new conception of the market and its relation to society and the state was in bloom. Antipathy toward the "free," or unregulated, market was generated by the massive economic inequalities of industrial capitalism and the social crises that resulted from them. But despite the gains of the labor movement in pushing labor into more parity with capital, the vision of the New Deal went into crisis in the late 1970s, and its deeper vision for remaking American economy and society was derailed. Although state assistance in recovering from the Depression was welcomed by an overwhelming majority of Americans, there was a clear limit to the extent to which they would tolerate the concentration of state power.[2] The crisis of a "socialized democracy" was therefore the result of the skepticism of the state that a liberal American society had always harbored, and the implications this would have for economic inequality would not take long to manifest themselves.

By 1980, the conservative forces in American society and politics had acquired new legitimacy and power. Their ideas were formed by a new intellectual and ideological orientation that blended populist ideas of economic liberty, as well as the identity of American economic life, with liberal capitalism opposed to the collectivism and state-centered economies of communist countries and the social democratic countries in Europe. What Bruce Schulman has referred to as the "southernization" of American politics and society began in the 1970s with the crumbling of the old Northeastern industrial belt and the rise of the "sunbelt" economies of the South and Southwest.[3] Kevin Phillips's argument that this new economic Sunbelt would serve as the foundation for a political and cultural split in American politics and society proved to be correct, and with this divide came a deeper attack on the state and a renewed emphasis on economic liberalism and deregulation.[4] A return to the individual in political and economic discourse was therefore a crucial turning away from the kind of social integration that the Progressive and New Deal thinkers had been developing, away from public institutions and toward a renewed skepticism of the state and its institutions and programs. The "new democracy" that thinkers in the first few decades of the twentieth century, such as Herbert Croly, Walter Weyl, and John Dewey, had seen emerging, with its emphasis on a socialized democracy, a shift away from the autonomy of the market and laissez-faire individualism in economy and society, and the investing of the state with a new, common purpose, was withering.

The empirical nature of economic inequality would also become something qualitatively different in nature. Whereas capitalist development in American history was an explicitly exploitive process that made class identification easy and class differences highly acute, the new inequality does not wear such obvious trappings. The postindustrial, service-oriented economy has bred anew the older forms of economic exploitation that were characteristic of the nineteenth century. The crucial question is no longer whether inequality exists, but why, even as it continues to grow in scope and magnitude, it has become more tolerated and, to a certain degree, accepted. Even though American political thought has always had its apologists for economic inequality and class hierarchy—whether through naïveté or through sheer ideology—there was always an egalitarian discourse that saw America's republican traditions at risk as long as inequalities in wealth were in existence. The fact that this egalitarian tradition has receded to the background in contemporary American politics is therefore an important concern that requires investigation.

The most salient aspect of the change in political and social thought in the last several decades in America has been the slow ascendancy economic society over political society. The liberal economic ethic that at one time was a force against stubborn feudal institutions and precapitalist economic relations has been reduced to a kind of "chaotic individualism," to borrow Croly's phrase from the early twentieth century. The decline of civic engagement, the erosion of political life, and the shattering of a once vibrant public sphere has been the result of a possessive individualism that has also come to legitimize economic inequality as the result of what are seen to be the "natural" processes of the market. The various thinkers and their ideas in this chapter were largely responsible for this intellectual reorientation; of course, it has intellectual roots that go back to the beginning of the twentieth century and the renewed attempt, in the midst of the Progressive Era and during the New Deal, to give a renewed legitimacy to laissez-faire and to the kind of capitalism that the reformists of the time sought to overcome.

The long and embattled discourse on economic inequality in American thought shows that there was a constant unease about replacing political ideas of democracy and equality with market-based ones of individualism and hierarchy. But the erosion of political society and a vibrant and democratic public sphere allowed for a shift in this orientation. John Kenneth Galbraith saw the shift coming as early as 1967 when he argued, "If we continue to believe that the goals of the industrial system . . . are coordinate with life, then all of our lives will be in the service of these goals. . . . Our wants will be managed in accordance with the needs of the industrial system; the policies of the state will be subject to similar influence; education will be adapted to industrial need; the disciplines required by the industrial system will be the conventional morality of the community."[5] The revival of laissez-faire and what the older theorists and critics of the Progressive Era termed "individualistic capitalism," as well as the shift to economic society, has meant the acceptance of the market and its consequences. It has resulted in the embracing of a culture of consumption and a dependency on new social relations that have deemphasized class as a category of social identity and solidarity. It has undergirded a newer, deeper conception of individualism that has reified market relations in contemporary society even to the extent that it opposes the most immediate material and political interests of an overwhelming majority of the actors involved.

The retrenchment of economic equality and the renaissance of anomic market liberalism was therefore not merely the result of an ascendant capitalism in the post–World War II context; it was also aided by an intellectual shift that put emphasis on a conception of the market that was fused to ideas of liberal individualism and political freedom. Over time, this new market ideology has come to legitimize economic inequality as a necessary byproduct of capitalism. Just as Thomas Paine lamented the need for government among a society of free individuals in "Common Sense," the idea of economic inequality as a necessary function of modern economics has become akin to gospel. But this has also been reinforced by a distinct cultural dynamic, one that has—through the reification of the market—allowed for the emergence of what Lizabeth Cohen has called the *"consumer/citizen/taxpayer/voter*[s]," who view "government policies like other market transactions, judging them by how well served they feel personally."[6] In the midst of rising affluence in the postwar years, the ascendancy of the market was coupled with a renewed skepticism of the state. Depoliticization, increased consumption, and inequality have gone hand in hand, and, since 1980, all have increased in intensity. What Paul Krugman has referred to as "permissive capitalism," or the expansion and inflation of the compensation of business elites, has led to a substantial shift in inequality.[7] The cultural component is important to understand since it is the key factor in seeing how economic inequality has become legitimized and why elites and their theories of a renewed laissez-faire have been so successful in their project of reworking American democracy.

Both the economic and the cultural shifts are important when understanding the rise and mass acceptance of economic inequality. These shifts were not simply a matter of a change in economic structure; they were also attributable to the political and cultural change that occurred during the final decades of the twentieth century.[8] The retreat from political life and the erosion of the public sphere that has marked the past quarter century in America is a symptom of this change. In American history, as I have shown in preceding pages, economic inequality has always been critiqued, fought against, and denounced from the sphere of politics, but this was a politics of equality premised on equality not as an end in itself but as a quality of freedom, the annihilation of hierarchy, privilege, and servitude. This political vision held that the economy was a set of power relations and was therefore political. The emphasis on economic equality was therefore the outgrowth of the insight that any economy and society marked by social atomism, individualism, and inequality would constitute a movement away from the ideals of political and individual freedom that had always been seen as the heart of America's republican project. The rise of a consumer society and the erosion of political participation and the public sphere more broadly therefore constitute a cultural component that has found an elective affinity with certain structural elements of the modern American economy. The move of capital away from its traditional mass-industrial base in the North and Northeast to the South and Southwest meant a move toward states with weaker or even nonexistent unionization. Thus eagerness for economic development developed, even at the expense of workers' rights.

The egalitarian tradition in American political thought had always critiqued the effects as well as the workings of the emerging capitalist system. Thinkers in this tradition saw that property was unequally distributed, but they also peered into the mechanisms of how this was systemically reproduced. From Byllseby to Pickering and Brownson to George, Lloyd, and Croly, there was always some understanding of the ways that capitalism worked. They may not have been correct in all of their analyses, but the need to see how inequality was produced was always an essential dimension of their egalitarian project. They did not put emphasis on "economic democracy" because the term itself would have been viewed as absurd: democracy was a way of organizing social life as well as a way of organizing political institutions, and the economy was simply seen as the material domain of that process. Economic equality—albeit a rough approximation of it—would be simple to maintain once each individual was liberated to keep the fruits of his labor. This liberal economic ethic did come into conflict with economic modernity, but amid the rubble of the interventionist state in the late twentieth century, the acceptance of capitalism as a way of organizing society has replaced the older egalitarian ideas upon which American political thought and culture had rested for almost two centuries.

THE MERGER OF LIBERTY AND MARKETS

Throughout its development, the inegalitarian tradition in American political thought was constrained by a crucial flaw in the way it communicated its political ideas. It was one thing to argue that economic development would always require class divisions and inequalities, as Hamilton had; or to argue that human nature itself required that inequalities would present themselves as Calhoun had; or that such "natural inequalities" were, in effect, beneficial to human progress and should, on those grounds alone, be embraced rather than critiqued by an out-dated moralism as in Sumner. What the modern conception of inegalitarianism emphasized was the liberty that markets unleashed, the way that individuals would be freed from the fetters of any trace of authoritarian control. For these thinkers, laissez-faire was indeed a theory of economic individualism. Even though some of the staunchest proponents of free market economics—such as Friedrich Hayek—did maintain that the state ought to step in where the market obviously fails (such as for health insurance and a minimal safety net for the poor), the central premise of modern laissez-faire economics was the emphasis on a split between economy, society, and state. Margaret Thatcher's remark that "there is no such thing as society; there are only individual men and women and there are families," was an extreme formulation of this view. Gone was the discourse that had dominated American political thought on the topic of economic inequality since the economy began to develop along capitalist lines. In its place would rise a new form of liberalism, the foundations of which were not the political imperatives of old but the economistic reductionism of a capitalism reborn.

The defense of inequality that has emerged in the late twentieth century was unique in another way: it was able to root itself within the political culture of America. Although thinkers like Sumner and Carnegie articulated a thorough doctrine defending economic inequality not only for the interests of an elite class but for the entirety of society as well, they were never able obtain any kind of popular support. When Matthew Arnold named the "religion of inequality" in the late nineteenth century, he referred to a climate of intellectual opinion. What American political culture has now accepted is the populist variant of this ideology, which has been able to embrace the most disparate classes in American politics by finding affinities with traditional American cultural and political understandings of individualism, liberty, and economic life. The turn toward libertarian conservative ideas was begun during the 1960s. The major intellectual forces behind this movement—Hayek and Milton Friedman, among others—were still an intellectual minority, and their ideas had yet to filter into the formulation of policy or into ideas of public life.

The origins of the contemporary assault on the ideas and political traditions that emphasized economic egalitarianism in America are complex, but they are grounded in the critical turn in economic thought that sought to invent new arguments for economic laissez-faire. In Europe, during the late nineteenth and early twentieth centuries, an anti-Marxist discourse began to emerge around thinkers like Hayek and Ludwig von Mises; this reasoning emphasized the liberalizing character of free markets and the fundamental irrationalism of and a moral revulsion toward state intervention in the economy. The tropes of classical mechanics once again came to influence economic theory: the ideas of neoclassical economics are still replete with the ideas of "friction" caused by state institutions and vertical as opposed to horizontal institutions. But at the heart of the ideas behind the new laissez-faire was a political and ethical theory that put primacy on the market as the only means to satisfy want and reward labor, and this would become core of the new intellectual reorientation that would redefine the discourse on economic inequality.

Upon closer examination, the intellectual and philosophical roots of the return to laissez-faire and the legitimation of economic inequality possess a fair amount of intellectual sophistication, delving into the epistemological as well as ethical concerns of individual knowledge and conduct. Well before the ideas of thinkers like Friedman and Hayek were to have influence, the ideas of economists like John Bates Clark and Frank Knight were laying a groundwork for what would become a libertarian economic and ethical framework that would overturn the legacy of the political ideas of a "socialized democracy." For Clark, the key insight was that each factor of production—be it capital or labor—would, under the conditions of an unregulated and freely operating market, receive the proper and just returns to its input. Beneath what looked like a chaotic marketplace lurked a hidden logic that, when allowed to work unfettered of regulation and monopolistic distortions, would work "naturally" to produce efficiency and the just distribution of the fruits of difference kinds of "labor." The ideas of the neoclassical economists would therefore seek to invest the market with an autonomous status with its own laws of operation and development.

In the early 1920s, in *Risk, Uncertainty, and Profit*, Knight put forth a comprehensive theory of laissez-faire with the business entrepreneur at its center. Knight held that individuals in society are unable to have absolute knowledge and information about the world and, therefore, about economic processes. Knight's epistemological assumptions about subjective knowledge were central to his ethical justification for laissez-faire, and they allowed the doctrine as a whole to regain ascendancy in American economics and, in time, in political and social thought as well. Knight saw that the crucial flaw in the arguments for political intervention in the economy revolved around the concern with *uncertainty*. Progressive and, in time, New Deal thinkers were arguing for the socialized management of the economy in order to limit what they saw as the excesses and inefficiencies of the market. But for Knight, their policies were plagued by what he viewed as their unscientific and, therefore, potentially damaging nature, namely their idea of the relation between society and individual.

The very nature of human subjective experience was chaotic and in flux. Reaching back to the Hobbesian (materialist) and Lockean (empiricist) roots of epistemology, Knight began his analysis from the root of experience and knowledge itself. Human knowledge was grounded in the individual, in subjectivity, and in the interaction between individual consciousness and nature. But since individuals could only ever know their own experience, it was always only partial and could never obtain objective knowledge about universals—whether about nature itself or about society. Uncertainty was the essential condition of knowledge, but it was most acute in modern industrialized societies. Possessed of a complex division of labor and a massive, nationalized market, producers were constantly faced with uncertainty with respect to what and how much to actually produce.[9] For Knight, the solution to this problem of uncertainty was the entrepreneur, the individual who faces risk and does so because of the possibility of reward but in the process is able to close the information gap by responding to market pressures and their consequences. It is the entrepreneur who can hold economic organization together, ensure efficiency in the use of resources, and, in the end, promote social progress. Despite the fact that Knight himself was skeptical of the market's ability to lessen inequalities and the fact that his ethical beliefs were against economic inequality, the basic building blocks for a renewal of the attack on economic egalitarianism was already in the making.

In Knight's work, the central premise of a new economic outlook was being born. Since the social world—which for Knight was defined as a collection of individuals and not an entity in itself—could be coordinated by the market, it was an inherently more efficient system that socialism or any form of state capitalism. But the ethical basis for Knight's system was not Sumnerian in any way. What he sought to do was overcome the epistemological and sociological problem of the interaction between individuals in a state of advanced industrialism. Advanced capitalism was a fact not to be justified but rather a phenomenon to be explained. For Knight, competitive societies did not rest on firm ethical foundations; in fact, he was skeptical of the ability of laissez-faire economics to distribute wealth justly (from an ethical point of view, he was a critic of economic inequality), but his philosophical ideas about the nature of society, mind, and "uncertainty" led him to privilege economic laissez-faire over socialism and other state- and social-interventionist models of the economy.

Knight's ideas were reflected in Europe with the rise in Vienna of the Austrian School of marginal utility. Thinkers like Carl Menger, August Böhm-Bawerk, Mises, and Hayek would be the most important names to emerge from this school, and their theoretical emphasis on a neo-

Kantian conception of the individual—with consequences not all that different from what Knight had pointed out, such as uncertainty, risk, and reward—were instrumental in constructing a new theoretical approach not only to the economy but to philosophy and politics as well. With their emphasis on the "subjective theory of value" and the centrality of marginal utility, these thinkers would come to have a deep influence on economic discourse in the English-speaking world after fleeing Europe and taking up residence in England and America. Their dual emphasis on the market and on the primacy of the individual would shape the American discourse on economic inequality, pushing the hegemony of Keynesian economics and state intervention to the periphery and creating, with thinkers like Milton Friedman and numerous others, a new libertarian social theory that would mark the intellectual climate of the late twentieth and early twenty-first centuries.

The American tradition of laissez-faire had been deeply discredited by the historical excesses and failures of capitalism from the late nineteenth century through the Great Depression. The reality of economic laissez-faire had given way to a moral and political discourse about the nature of American democracy during the Progressive Era, in large part because of the problem of economic inequality and the inability of intellectuals and ideologues of the time to bring together the realities of inequality and the social atomization that resulted from it with the ideas of democratic equality that were inherent in American political culture. The turn away from economic individualism was therefore a response to the growing problem that class society posed to American political thought. But the resurrection of laissez-faire found support as a response to the rise a fascism in Europe and the solidification of the Soviet Union in the decades after the war. The Austrian School was instrumental in this regard; its approach to economic theory was extended by social and political ideas that rested on a radical understanding of liberal individualism.[10]

But it was the emphasis on a new synthesis, that of liberalism and unrestrained capitalism, that would make the ideas of thinkers like Mises and Hayek so tempting to Americans and come to change the trajectory of American political thought on the subject of economic inequality in the late twentieth century. It was Mises who, writing as early as 1927 in his book *Liberalismus*, made one of the first arguments for collapsing liberalism and capitalism into a unified system:

> A society in which liberal principles are put into effect is usually called a capitalist society, and the condition of that society, capitalism. . . . [O]ne is altogether justified in calling our age the age of capitalism, because all that has created the wealth of our time can be traced back to capitalist institutions. It is thanks to those liberal ideas that still remain alive in our society, to what yet survives in it of the capitalist system, that the great mass of contemporaries can enjoy a standard of living far above that which just a few generations ago was possible only to the rich and especially privileged.[11]

This would become the standard argument in America decades later. Capitalism and liberalism were one because, as Mises, Hayek, and others in their circle perceived, both worked on the principle of free individualism, which was, by definition, opposed to the rank and privilege of preliberal societies. But for Mises, capitalism was not a component of liberalism; it was the concrete application of liberal ideas and principles—where liberalism was truly put into practice, there you would find private property, a minimal state, and unrestrained markets. This would be the beginnings of the later neoliberal ideology in the United States. In this sense, classical liberalism's approach to the problem of equality was simple enough to understand: individuals were only equal insofar as they had the right to pursue the exercise of their own free labor—it was nothing more than a condemnation of involuntary servitude.

Classical liberalism—as opposed to what Mises saw as the distortion of liberal doctrines of equality that existed at the time, what he ironically termed "neoliberalism"—was therefore at one with capitalism since capitalism was simply the economic system that resulted from free labor, markets, and private property. The illusion of equality outside of the legalistic conception of the individual and his right to property and free labor was not only an absurdity in terms of empirical fact, it was also economically regressive. Mises's argument in defense of economic inequality would become the standard credo, one that continues to dominate what we today refer to as "neoliberalism" in quite a different context. For Mises, inequality was a social good specifically because it created a dynamic, productive, and creative society:

> Only because inequality of wealth is possible in our social order, only because it stimulates everyone to produce as much as he can and at the lowest cost, does mankind today have at its disposal the total annual wealth now

available for consumption. Were this incentive to be destroyed, productivity would be so greatly reduced that the portion that an equal distribution would allot to each individual would be far less than what even the poorest receives today.[12]

Capitalism—the application of true liberalism as the embodiment of individual liberty, choice, and action—was the very engine of human prosperity and the real guarantor of human freedom. The concept of capitalism that began to emerge with the renewal of economic liberalism was that the market, capital, and wage labor, the entirety of the system, should be interpreted as a manifold, dynamic system of freedom and progress. The problems that capitalism had actually caused—whether political society violently divided by class strife or violent business cycles that caused unemployment and recession—were not of concern because such things were the result of the ignorance of what liberalism and capitalism actually were. Even the aristocratic wealth seen during the Gilded Age was also to be praised. "The luxury of today is the necessity of tomorrow," and although it might seem ethically intuitive to despise the rich idler who does nothing for his wealth, "he sets an example of luxury that awakens in the multitude a consciousness of new needs and gives industry the incentive to fulfill them."[13] Inequality was now being reinterpreted as a social good by redefining the classic examples of economic injustice as in the best interests of the public and of social progress.

It must be admitted that Mises's book was radical for its time. The justification of economic inequality was not capable of generating a serious audience, but it used ideas and arguments that would prove remarkably resilient, as indicated by the fact that they would continue to be advocated and have influence decades later in the ideas of Hayek and Friedman, among other, more contemporary conservative thinkers.[14] Indeed, while the course of economic thought as well as social policy was moving toward Keynesianism for moderates and for radicals, socialism was still the politics of hundreds of thousands of workers. This was the reason for Mises's overstating his case. But when *Liberalismus* was finally translated into English in 1962, Mises and his ideas were already gaining considerable ground intellectually, and, in time, they would be part of a comprehensive new conservative economic doctrine that would come to influence both social policy and political culture. Even more influential than Mises would be his younger colleague from Vienna, Hayek, who would make a firmer and more complex case for liberal capitalism and its logical and ethical primacy over all other forms of economic and social organization. In so doing, he would also shore up the case for economic inequality under capitalism as a social virtue and an attribute of social justice and of social progress.

For Hayek, just as for Knight before him, the argument for laissez-faire and the need to reintroduce a cleaner, more precise conception of liberalism was undergirded by the uncertainty of human knowledge and its fundamental inability to obtain anything more than partial truth. Hayek and Mises took socialism as their common enemy, and they sought to prop up arguments for libertarian capitalism that would be grounded in the nature of human psychology and provide the most advanced system for an efficient, free form of social organization. Socialism rested on the false assumption that economic planning by a bureaucratic elite could have access to the totality of economic knowledge. Socialism was therefore plagued from an epistemological point of view, and this political and economic critique of socialism emphasized the case for radical liberal economic individualism. The Austrian School had been characterized by, among other things, its emphasis on the subjective theory of value, which argued that economic values were not assigned objectively—as in the labor theory of value—but by subjective preferences and the value that individuals placed on a particular good. It was an extension of methodological individualism, and, as Menger himself said, "value does not exist outside of the consciousness of men."[15]

This was at the heart of Hayek's economic theory and his social philosophy as well. Just as Mises had argued in *Liberalismus*, Hayek saw that "true" liberalism needed to be recovered, and this meant, first and foremost, a recovery of the idea of the individual, or what Hayek would refer to as "true" individualism. By politicizing the economic sphere, the "social liberals" and social democrats—let alone socialists and communists—of the 1930s and 1940s had made exaggerated assumptions about the power of human reason and its ability to guide social institutions.[16] Hayek's claims therefore would take Knight's ideas about uncertainty and use them to justify a more comprehensive laissez-faire doctrine. In his reading of Western thought, Hayek wanted to show that thinkers such as Adam Smith, Bernard Mandeville, and David Hume constituted an intellectual tradition that emphasized an essential truth of liberal individualism, namely, that there exists "a constitutional limitation of man's knowledge and interests, the fact that he cannot know more than a tiny part of the whole of society and that therefore all that can enter into his motives are the immediate effects which his actions will have in the sphere he knows."[17] This would serve as the philosophical, ethical, and psychological basis for the market. Since "society," in this view, is little more than the assemblage of individuals, the random actions of this collection of individuals would create a spontaneous order, one that functions "without a designing and directing mind" and that rests on the sociological insight that "the spontaneous collaboration of free men often creates things which are greater than their individual minds can ever fully comprehend."[18]

This philosophical assault on the economic and social policies of the age would not gain ground for some time, but it would prove to be a rigid critique of egalitarianism. In the style of classical liberalism, Hayek sought to limit the scope of the state and to unleash the powers of the market. Drawing the line between economy and the state more deliberately than previous thinkers, Hayek did not simply resort to an ethical argument for laissez-faire or a set of class interests or, as in Sumner, an outdated conception of social progress (e.g., social Darwinism). Instead, his argument was grounded in the foundations of logical positivism and a liberalism that spoke to all as political equals. At the time this served as a counterargument to calls for socialism and communism based on the intellectual grounds of methodological individualism and classical liberalism. But it would also serve as the bedrock of a new assault on the evolving ideas of the welfare state and the new philosophy of social liberalism that had been emerging in the early twentieth century, something that Hayek referred to as "unlimited democracy." For Hayek, the distinction between equality before the law and other forms of equality—specifically economic or material equality—was the key to understanding how to move beyond, and more specifically against, the ascendancy and dominance of the welfare state. His arguments would not only become a new defense of inequality, they would also serve as a highly persuasive way of preserving a form of liberal political equality while simultaneously guarding against claims for social justice.

Hayek's ideas about the market and its relation to state and society therefore shored up his notions about inequality and the ethics of distribution. Inequality was disparaged not simply because of the epistemological arguments that Hayek and Knight had put forth; there was an ethical argument that set the foundation for their ideas as well: namely, that human freedom was equated with the absence of coercion. This would resonate with the libertarian strain in American economic thought, and it would allow Hayek's work to become highly influential. His book *The Constitution of Liberty* would obtain manifesto-like status, and it would become the intellectual touchstone for modern conservatism. His discussion of liberty and economic equality would also set the stage for contemporary understandings of the phenomenon—both popular and, in many cases, academic and professional as well. The argument was not particularly original: since there was no way to argue for the "factual" equality between different individuals, any other form of equality outside of equality before the law was not only immoral and nonsensical but also dangerous to the concept of liberty.

> From the fact that people are very different it follows that, if we treat them equally, the result must be inequality in their actual position, and that the only way to place them in an equal position would be to treat them differently. Equality before the law and material equality are therefore not only different but are in conflict with another; and we can achieve either one or the other, but not both at the same time. The equality before the law which freedom requires leads to material inequality. Our argument will be that, though where the state must use coercion for other reasons, it should treat all people alike, the desire of making more people alike in their condition cannot be accepted in a free society as a justification for further and discriminatory coercion.[19]

The opposition between economic equality and liberty was necessary for Hayek because he thought that inequalities were generated by differences in ability and talent. It was a conception of inequality that ignored institutions and was both antisociological and ahistorical. Achieving economic equality—of even the most weak variety—would always entail coercion since it would always be necessary to take from those who have achieved and accumulated wealth and property and give it to others. Economic equality was the result of envy, not a genuine political or ethical imperative for social justice. The desire for economic equality was the result of "factual" inequalities between individuals, and it was the fact that all people were different and hence unequal. As a result, in countries with a liberal political framework guaranteeing equality before the law, economic inequality would be seen wherever true liberty existed. And the emphasis on liberty was not an end in itself. Rather, the emphasis for Hayek—unlike thinkers of a similar vein such as Friedman—was on the implications it would have in liberating knowledge and the aggregate social benefit that would accrue to all members of society, serving as a mechanism for social progress.[20]

Hayek examined what he saw to be the basis for the drive for economic justice. It was essential for him to point out that there was no objective mechanism that created inequality, only natural differences among skills, talents, and rewards. Thus, the drive for equality was cast as a function of envy. Inequality was natural, and a truly free, liberal society would therefore need not only to tolerate inequalities in wealth and income but also to accept them as socially beneficial and an expression of a free society. But still, Hayek knew that drives for equality would persist, and part of his project was to explain this phenomenon. The problem, he argued, was in the perception of how merit was rewarded. There existed a moral objection "not to the bare fact of inequality but to the fact that the differences in reward do not correspond to any recognizable differences in the merits of those who receive them."[21] But this was merely an error in perception. Reward and merit should not be seen in terms of what people have objectively done; they were the result of how another's talents and skills were valued by others. The impulse for social justice, for equality in material and economic terms, was therefore the result of not comprehending the real way that market society worked. It required that people understand that the market was not only a guiding force, but also unpredictable. In a free society there would be no injustice in the outcomes of market forces since all desired and valued skills and talents would be properly remunerated; and proper remuneration was a subjective, not an objective, phenomenon.

Hayek's discussion of inequality and the mechanisms that produce it was therefore able to shift significantly the debate on economic and political affairs. With his emphasis on the subjective notion of value, Hayek was able to see economic inequality as the product of "factual" inequalities, or real differences, between individuals. Differences in income and wealth are the result of subjective preferences, not institutions. The concept of "justice" itself can only apply to actions, never to systems or institutions. But by exempting institutions and processes from his analysis, Hayek's ideas become blind to the actual mechanisms of inequality that had been identified by, and were the primary focus of, the critiques of inequality that had developed in American political thought. Looking back to the first radical critics of inequality—figures such as Langton Byllesby, Thomas Skidmore, Orestes Brownson, and others—the initial insight that drove the most robust critiques of economic inequality in American thought was that inequality was generated not simply by market relationships but specifically by the new economic system itself and the way it shaped, indeed, distorted previous market relationships. The problem was—as Marx would later identify it—institutional in nature; inequality was generated by the production process itself and not simply by differences in skill and ability.

By taking institutions out of his analysis of how inequality is generated, Hayek sidesteps the problem of how capitalism generates economic inequality. Indeed, it is important to point out that Hayek's discussion of inequality does not mention capital at all or even wages. Instead, he investigates inequality ahistorically. By specifically avoiding the Marxian critique of the production process and the mechanisms of inequality that it generates, Hayek confined himself to "natural" differences among individuals and their subjective preferences, which themselves turned into values and prices. In further contrast to earlier critics of inequality, Hayek was able to extricate the economy from politics, sealing off each sphere from the other. The argument for economic equality had always derived from the political principles of equality that had been articulated after the American Revolution. It had a firm basis in an anti-aristocratic and anti-hierarchical conception of society that was being threatened by new forms of economic life and class differentiation. The character of such claims did not diminish as time went on, but with the renewal of the laissez-faire project, the economy would not only be seen as separate from politics, it would also be theorized as the very source of liberty itself. Whereas, in the past, political ideas of equality and justice were seen as penetrating all dimensions of social life, the economy began to be seen as the source of liberty. Hayek was not alone in making this transition, but his ideas were central and influential in effecting a major intellectual shift in the ways that inequality would be viewed and how the economic sphere would be privileged as the source of human freedom.

Although Hayek's influence would, in time, be without dispute, Milton Friedman's libertarian reinterpretation of liberalism, politics, and economics would have a much more pervasive effect and much deeper influence. With his renewed defense of capitalism and his staunch advocacy of laissez-faire, Friedman would transform the discourse on economic inequality, pushing politics and economics further apart. Friedman was successful in integrating the laissez-faire ideas that had been developing in American and Austrian economic thought and merging them with what he set out as traditional American understandings of equality, fairness, and justice. In so doing, he would be one of the next great defenders of economic inequality, helping to pave the way for the intellectual and popular acceptance of economic hierarchy in modern American thought and culture. At the heart of Friedman's analysis is the idea that the redistribution of incomes and wealth or property constitutes political coercion. What informs his analysis is the same basic argument that had been used by advocates of laissez-faire throughout American political and social thought: that liberating markets will serve rather than undermine the public interest and individual freedom. For Friedman, this view was informed by the notion that markets inherently disaggregate social power. Free markets in the context of competitive capitalism did not, as the critics of capitalism had always asserted, lead to an uneven distribution of social power. Rather, free markets dispersed power, and, as a result, the connection between capitalism and freedom was clear. Free markets, capitalism, dispersed social power and they were therefore the foundation for the free individual and a free society.

By placing emphasis on the connection between liberty and markets while at the same time chastising the state for its intervention in economic affairs, Friedman was able to revive the radical dimensions of a new form of liberalism inspired by libertarianism. Just as Thomas Paine had focused on the division between society and government and the necessity of that separation for the purposes of individual liberty as a call for political liberty and political revolution, Friedman's ideas worked out a theory of society that would not only tolerate economic inequalities but would also further marginalize the critique of capitalism as a system responsible for generating inequalities. In place of concerns for democracy and the public interest, Friedman's ideas grounded themselves in a utilitarian conception of the individual, reviving the kind of atomistic understanding of society that was at the heart of liberal philosophy from Hobbes to Locke. And just as Knight, Hayek, and Mises had emphasized the notion of uncertainty and the subjective theory of value, Friedman would bring this perspective to a new level of intensity. Attempts by the state to redistribute income and fight inequality rested on the false assumption that the state could even know what ethical categories such as "fairness" actually were; state policies would therefore always work against their own intentions and, in the process, continue to erode liberty.

"Fairness," like "needs," is in the eye of the beholder. If all are to have "fair shares," someone or some group of people must decide what shares are fair—and they must be able to impose their decisions on others, taking from those who have more than their "fair" share and giving to those who have less. Are those who make and impose such decisions equal to those for whom they decide? Are we not in George Orwell's *Animal Farm* where "all animals are equal, but some animals are more equal than others"?[22]

Friedman's ideas were not new; they were synthesized out of the laissez-faire liberalism that had been emerging throughout the early twentieth century. By linking government to coercion, the assault on what Walter Weyl had referred to as America's "socialized democracy" was being put into place. Friedman reinterpreted social life and saw—as thinkers such as Locke and Paine had to a certain extent as well—the market and private property as the foundation for individual liberty. Markets are noncoercive and cooperative at the same time. They reward individual labor and allow for the expansion of free choice. Free markets can and do produce inequalities, but the reasons for inequality are not to be found in what Friedman castigated as the "Marxist syllogism" where value and capital were seen as embodied labor. Inequalities were generated by the fact that different individuals have different preferences and make different choices in the face of risk, Friedman's extension of Knight's category of uncertainty.

Underpinning Friedman's analysis was the idea that distribution takes place "according to product." Since the "central principle of a market economy is co-operation through voluntary exchange," the market did not distribute goods and services; it allocated them based on how much each individual produced, how productive each individual was. It was not a question of "fairness" or justice since these were invariably political concepts that were applied to the market; the normative ideal was not equality of resources but the efficiency of allocation. "Payment in accordance with product is therefore necessary in order that resources be used most effectively."[23] Payment in accordance with product was, for Friedman, "ethically fair" because it was reward or remuneration for activity, for production, mental or physical. In classical liberal style, Friedman saw that only through the voluntary exchange of the products of individual labor can there be any semblance of political freedom. Capitalism unhinged from the interventionist state would therefore become the key philosophical and policy goal of this new brand of conservatism, one that would provide a broad justification for inequality as well as its effects.[24]

The justification for inequality was also based on the notion that inequality under capitalism was of a fundamentally different nature than that of non- or precapitalist societies. Just as Cooley had argued in the early years of the twentieth century that classes in American society constituted a fluid, dynamic social order, Friedman argued that the kind of inequality produced by free-enterprise capitalism was not based on status or social rigidity. Social mobility was part of the essence of capitalism, and this mobility was part of the overall argument for the linking of capitalism and freedom. Freedom was the result of the wide distribution of economic opportunity that market capitalism fostered. Inequality in noncapitalist, nonmarket societies "tends to be permanent, whereas capitalism undermines status and introduces social mobility."[25] Equality of opportunity was essential in this regard. Just as late-nineteenth-century thinkers saw the importance of equality of opportunity—something they saw threatened by monopolization and the massive inequalities bred by industrialism—Friedman's argument was well situated in the liberal tradition. Since his conception of freedom was so narrowly stated as the freedom to pursue one's ends in market transactions, he could easily make his case that "government measures that promote personal equality or equality of opportunity enhance liberty; government measures to achieve 'fair shares for all' reduce liberty."[26] They reduce liberty because they act as frictive barriers on the free play of individuals to pursue their own ends, while at the same time coercing others to distribute the reward of their product.

Inequality was also the price of efficiency. One of the key elements of the libertarian defense of markets was that although inequality was a product of actual differences among people with different skills and abilities who competed freely in a marketplace, the generation of inequality ought not to be the central concern. Just as Sumner had chastised the moralism of focusing on social inequality, casting it out into the abyss of historical irrelevance in a modern scientific and rational age, the new defense of inequality put forth by the libertarian vision rested on the idea that economic efficiency, in the long run, would relieve inequalities. Interpreting the long history of American economic development, to them, was enough to prove their theories correct empirically. Long-run economic growth via capitalism had produced an affluent society. This emphasis on market efficiency would become a key component of the contemporary inegalitarian tradition. By placing inequality in a subordinate position to other economic concerns such as efficiency and vesting markets with an autonomous logic not unlike a vast automaton, inequality ceased to be a direct result of the system of production and was relegated back to the more archaic discourse of "natural inequality."

Friedman's defense of social and economic inequality under capitalism was a vigorous assault on the social democratic tradition that was emerging in America in the early part of the twentieth century. By emphasizing the idea of "distribution according to product" Friedman was able to reconnect the liberal notion of economic individualism that was predominant in the early republic with a libertarian economic framework, and it is here that the attack on the "social liberalism" of the Progressive and New Deal Eras was most clear. Indeed, one of the core insights of figures such as Herbert Croly, Walter Weyl, Thurman Arnold, and John Dewey, among so many others of the period, was that capitalism was an inherently imperfect economic system that was not in accord with the new philosophical understanding of political freedom emerging at the time nor with the tenets of what they interpreted modern democracy. The "social liberalism" that Dewey had advocated thirty years before Friedman's most influential writings were published emphasized that the democratic ideal did not consist of naïve, egoistic forms of liberalism but insisted on the need to see political democracy as encompassing a form of economic democracy as well. Dewey and thinkers like him saw that capitalism created inequalities not only in wealth and material well-being but in power relations as well. They saw that economic constraint was a key factor in limiting the advancement of democracy and in realizing a more just social order that was in accordance to what Croly had referred to as the "promise of American life."

But the libertarian ideas of Friedman, Hayek, and their various colleagues and disciples would radically reverse this reinterpretation of liberalism and reintroduce a more basic understanding of a liberal society structured by market relationships and atomistic individualism. Economic constraint was now seen as a fiction since workers and employers simply entered into contracts that were mutually voluntarily. They would introduce, to borrow a phrase from Arnold, a renewed "folklore of capitalism" that would legitimize inequality and put pressure on the state to recede from economic affairs, reinvigorating and redefining liberalism not as "social liberalism" but as the need to reduce the concentration of power.

> A liberal is fundamentally fearful of concentrated power. His objective is to preserve the maximum degree of freedom for each individual separately that is compatible with one man's freedom not interfering with another man's freedom. He believes that this objective requires that this power be dispersed. He is suspicious of assigning to government any functions that can be performed through the market, both because this substitutes coercion for voluntary co-operation in the area in question and because, by giving government an increased role, it threatens freedom in other areas.[27]

This emphasis on individual liberty and the skepticism toward the state would soon become an entrenched ideology, one that would dominate large segments of American political culture and transform the understanding of the politics of inequality.

The ideas of Friedman, Hayek, and their numerous followers were the product of a prolonged reaction to the emergence of the welfare state and the radical turn in American institutions that it set in motion. Understanding the state as anathema to human liberty, they saw in the oppressive Soviet state and in the modern welfare state as well the very antithesis of democracy, liberty, and progress. The extension of state into the economic realm was, in this sense, one of the key transgressions that classical liberalism specifically denounced. The extension of political claims into the economic sphere would therefore become the very issue at debate as the twentieth century progressed. The older ideas that inequality arose out of the system of wage labor, which made equality of condition impossible, and that equality of opportunity became impossible as monopoly capitalism evolved with industrialism gave way to an altogether different explanation for inequality. Both Hayek and Friedman saw interpersonal differences in skills, talents, and, at times, mere luck as the mechanism of inequality. They saw natural—or as Hayek termed it, "factual"—differences among individuals as the groundwork for inequality in economic rewards and outcomes. But they succeeded in taking the emphasis off of the institution of capital, the unequal exchange between worker and capitalist, and returning the argument to one about the efficacy of markets and not the economic constraints that capitalism as a system had always created.

These ideas become even more important in the light of older American ideas about inequality. When viewed in the context of the long history of the egalitarian tradition in American political and social thought, it is clear that the move away from an immanent critique of capitalism as a system of production—rather than as a system of distribution—was the central pivot on which the recent shift toward justifying inequality turned. It was one thing to reject the Marxian-inspired critiques of capitalism, but it was quite another to move understandings of inequality away from the production process itself, as the egalitarian critics of capitalism had done as early as the 1820s. The critique of inequality of the Jacksonian period had always emphasized the fact that the relation between wage earner and owner produced inequality. Independent of, and in most case quite prior to, Marx's work, these critiques did not locate the market as the producer of disparities of economic power. Rather, they diagnosed the evolving division between ownership and the working class. The modernization of economic life—the birth of modern capitalism—was their object of inquiry and critique. Inequalities in material terms would simply reproduce themselves, causing a process of cumulative causation from which individuals would be unable to escape, a road to serfdom of a very different kind.

Although the critiques of capitalism and inequality had always been vibrant in American thought, the arguments in defense of capitalism, laissez-faire, and inequality itself had rested on the notion that progress had to come at the expense of equality, and it was this emphasis on a sterile notion of progress that held the various arguments—from Hamilton through Sumner—together. The libertarian attack on the incipient social democratic tradition and institutions that had emerged with the New Deal and the expansion of the welfare state cast its argument in a very different guise. Now it was freedom itself that embracing inequality offered. Class divisions were simply a mythology because inequality had to be viewed on an interpersonal basis and not as a function of asymmetrical power divisions. Inequality in economic terms was no longer seen to have political implications. The market had to be depoliticized, and this had become the task of the intellectual defenders of capitalism and freedom. The older anti-aristocratic discourse that had been vibrant throughout the nineteenth century—and that had slowly taken the form of a radical movement against class inequality by the early twentieth century—had dissolved into a radical vision to liberate the market from the shackles of state intervention and, in so doing, liberate individuals as well.

Redefining the idea of economic inequality and the mechanisms of its growth was also dependent on reconceptualizing the relationship between freedom and economic life that thinkers of the Progressive and New Deal Eras had advocated. The central insight of the advocates for state intervention in the economy was that corporate capitalism produced excesses of inequality—of economic condition, opportunity, and political power. They saw that only the state could steer economic activity toward the national interest and away from the plutocratic tendencies of the late decades of the nineteenth century. Implicit in this was the notion that the freedom of individuals, which they saw to be the political and ethical project of American politics, rested not simply on what we know as "negative liberty"—as classical liberalism had essentially held—but on positive liberty as well. This idea followed from the realization that political equality and individual freedom rested not simply on the removal of what Hayek referred to as the "coercion of some by others,"—that is, on the arbitrary external restraints placed on the individual and his actions and decisions—but on the context in which that individual was placed.[28] Friedman also emphasized that a transformation of the liberal discourse—from its classical to its social form—had taken effect since "the catchwords became welfare and equality rather than freedom. The nineteenth-century liberal regarded an extension of freedom as the most effective way to promote welfare and equality; the twentieth-century liberal regards welfare and equality as either prerequisites of or alternatives to freedom."[29]

Of course, the social liberalism of the early twentieth century had emphasized welfare, security, and equality not as moral ends in and of themselves but as means to a more complex, more nuanced conception of human freedom and agency. The experience of laissez-faire capitalism had shattered the confidence in the naïve assumptions of classical liberalism. The realities of capitalism and the ravaging effects of industrialism in the nineteenth century had shown that the doctrines of laissez-faire did not benefit prevailing notions of the public good and instead caused class antagonism and social fragmentation. The workers' movement of the late nineteenth and early twentieth centuries had sought to deal not only with issues of wages and economic interest but also with despotic working conditions.[30] Bringing the state in to regulate economic affairs was therefore more than a concern with wages and economic distribution; it was also a matter of the way everyday life had become structured by capitalism and industrialism. By replacing the assumptions of classical liberalism—a political doctrine that had largely matured before the evolution of modern capitalism—Hayek and Friedman put forth a notion of liberty or freedom that had effectively shed the 1930s idea that a certain degree of material equality was needed for democracy.

This new face of the inegalitarian tradition in American political and social thought resurrected the spirit of thinkers as diverse as Hamilton, Calhoun, and Sumner. But even though the intellectual ideas of laissez-faire and libertarianism were gaining ascendancy during the Cold War years, it would not be until the 1980s and 1990s that a new conception of inequality in American political thought would firmly take hold. There is little question that these ideas that redeemed capitalism and brought its mythic status back to life were also deeply concerned with differentiating the Western, but more specifically American, economic system from communist command economies. If the economic egalitarian tradition in American politics culminated in the formation of the welfare state, it must be remembered that it also spawned a liberal-capitalist consensus that preserved capitalism as an economic system, but with serious political safeguards on its excesses.

REDEFINING AND REORIENTING AMERICAN DEMOCRACY

This renewed ideological orientation merging liberty with markets would have a profound political and cultural impact on American democracy. The reorientation and redefinition of American democracy consisted of the turn away from what John Dewey had referred to as the "social liberalism" that was required for the modern age and back toward the individualistic liberalism that had become intellectually and morally suspect through the Progressive and New Deal Eras. But the new intellectual apparatus that was constructed over the course of the postwar period in the universities would find an elective affinity with the economic and geographical shifts that were overtaking the nation. The intellectual apparatus that had been slowly but definitively forming in the work of Knight, Mises, Hayek, Friedman, and many others soon would come to dominate almost every domain of social-policy debate. It would emerge also as a reified understanding of the American economy, its culture, and its self-consciousness. The reorientation of American democracy away from the expanded conception that was put in place with the New Deal and the social-welfare state and the redefinition of American democracy away from the ideals of economic citizenship and toward a reliance on market processes and the celebration of capitalism would come to pass.

The intellectual ideas developed by those supporting laissez-faire and libertarian economics remained on the periphery of policymaking in the United States until the last two decades of the twentieth century. How these ideas—which were, in effect, highly theoretical and essentially out of step with the culture of the liberal-capitalist consensus that had dominated American political and economic life since the beginning of the New Deal—came to gain primacy and hegemony is one thing; how they nested themselves in the cultural fabric of American politics and political culture is something else. The broad-based support for an ideology of inequality in contemporary America begins with this strand of economic and social thought, and its legacy has been a reorientation of American democracy and political life. The notion that ideas alone were responsible for the various shifts in the discourse on economic inequality throughout American history is patently untrue. New forms of consciousness and political culture arise from changes in institutional arrangements and shifts in economic life. Of course, ideas inform and legitimate these aspects of social and political life, but it is only when a hegemonic system of ideas is melded with new forms of material life that a decisive change in political thought and culture occurs. Ideology is important, but ideas still need to have some kind of material base for them to achieve dominance and influence the direction of social and political life as well as institutions.

With this in mind, it is important to investigate how the transformation of capitalism affected the evolving discourse of economic inequality in American political thought and political culture. With the sudden shocks of deindustrialization in the 1970s, the upward mobility of the traditional, white working class, and the emergence of postindustrial forms of working life, the very culture of work was dissolving traditional forms of class identity. Labor-market segmentation, the explosion of suburbanization, the weakening of labor unions and labor's power to bargain for more equal pay, and the loss of any kind of political control over the market and the workplace, as well as a growing acceptance of consumerism and the depoliticization of the American electorate, all contributed to a general acceptance of economic inequality and its effects. In addition to this, class dissent had also been largely muted because of the rise of the administrative welfare state, which regulated the dissenting interests of the poor and working poor, steering their interests away from political demands for radical social, political, and economic changes.[31]

Indeed, after 1980 the doctrine of economic inequality would become a major feature of American political and social thought as well as American popular consciousness. But this was not the result only of a changed ideological course. The New Deal and social democratic projects that were set in motion in the 1930s and early 1940s were under attack from their inception. Also, thinkers like Mises, Hayek, Friedman, and others saw themselves as part of an intellectual tradition of "philosophical radicalism" that had its beginnings in thinkers such as Bentham, Smith, and Hume, as well as the democrats, classical liberals, and utilitarians in the eighteenth century.[32] More important, they saw their ideas as resting collectively on scientific research into human psychology, market processes, and what they viewed as the pernicious result of collectivism and state intervention. Little was mentioned about the impact that economic inequality had on social cohesion, political democracy, or quality of life. Even less was mentioned about the ways that interests—something that is wholly lacking in the discourse of the defenders of inequality—would affect politics and the distribution of power. And even though the empirical evidence has been clear for decades, the orthodoxy of the libertarian position stubbornly persists even as inequality worsens when economic growth surges.[33]

In another sense, the rise of the new doctrine can be seen as the result of the shift from political to economic preoccupations. Mainstream economics had become, with its methodological modernization and its turn toward a new degree of scientific rigor, a discipline that was no longer concerned with how economic systems distributed power. The economic egalitarian tradition in American political thought had always linked economic power with political power, and it was one of the crucial moves of thinkers such as Mises, Friedman, and Hayek that they shifted discussion of power back onto the state and its monopoly on power and coercion. Perhaps even more remarkable was the way in which they seemingly ignored the growing concentration of monopoly capital as American capitalism continued to centralize and make competition in many industries—such as technology, chemicals, and heavy production—increasingly scarce.[34] But libertarian ideas began to take on ethical primacy while at the same time becoming economic orthodoxy, and this would prove to be a crucial turn in the evolution of the American confrontation with economic inequality.

Shifts in American society, economy, and culture had much to do with forming fertile soil for these intellectual ideas, allowing them to develop into a new variant of the politics of inequality. The economic improvement that American working people experienced during the first two decades after World War II was significant in alleviating the older class antagonisms. Union power was at its peak during those years, and working people were able to extract higher wage rates from capital. The class antagonisms that had plagued American society throughout the previous fifty years began to erode. Inequality was diminishing, and an "affluent society," characterized by consumerism and overall secular economic growth, began to emerge. But despite this, it was becoming painfully clear that urban poverty was a serious social problem and that the inequality between racial groups was acute. This gave rise to new ideological arguments about social mobility. But empirically, it was becoming evident that inequality was more complex than had been previously believed. Differences in skill sets, or human capital, it was said, were key to understanding why certain groups were unable to escape certain income brackets, which led to "dual" or "segmented" labor markets.[35]

In addition, as urbanization trends reversed and suburbs began to expand, the economic and racial divide between urban and suburban regions began to grow.[36] Inequality therefore began to take on spatial and racial overtones. Whereas social stratification throughout the industrial era was fixed and centered largely in urban and industrial centers, today inequality between suburbs—themselves of very different economic resources—and inner-city areas that are, by and large, in economic decline, has created what Douglas Rae calls a "segmented democracy," wherein spatial, racial, and class differences reinforce one another.[37] This in turn has led to what Ian Shapiro calls "physical gulfs" between income groups, where the "segregation of the have-nots from the haves in capitalist democracies is real and increasing."[38] Deindustrialization would have a major impact on the formation of classes in America and transform the way that economic life was perceived by its participants.[39] As industrial society moved toward postindustrialism, breaking down older class and occupational structures and replacing them with high-tech, information, and service jobs, the idea of fluid social mobility looked ever more persuasive.[40]

But even as the actual power that working people had within their places of work began to erode throughout the 1970s and 1980s and economic inequality began to surge, it has remained largely absent from American political discourse. The intellectual project that libertarian thinkers such as Mises, Hayek, and Friedman had set in motion was now fast becoming an acceptable explanation of the trends of American economic life. Their explanations of inequality were, however, deeply flawed. Although it has always been difficult, if not impossible, to deny interpersonal differences, what had actually caused inequalities was a combination of the weakening of labor's power in the market accompanied by the shift from industrial to postindustrial forms of economic organization. The weakening of labor unions and the lack of new forms of worker organization to fill the resulting gap was paramount in giving employers more power to set wages. As industrial jobs dried up and moved overseas, the service-sector jobs that came to take their place were less generous in their wages as well. These were, indeed, the structural elements that led to the new material context for the acceptance of the liberal economic theories laid out during the Cold War.

What the libertarian ideas of the twentieth century did achieve, however, was not only the decontestation of the market as an institution but the decontestation and depoliticization of work and economic life more broadly. And it is here that we can see an important shift in the politics of inequality in American political thought and political culture. The concern with economic inequality in American history did not originate simply with its abstract political implications—as in the discussions of Adams, Hamilton, Madison, and Jefferson, among others—but also with the way that real economic life—how each individual lived everyday life and had to make his living—was a lived experience, a political experience of power relations. The labor radicals of the Jacksonian era who launched the egalitarian critique of capitalism, such as Byllseby and Skidmore, among so many others, saw the problem as—in addition to the older fear of the creation of a new aristocracy—the loss of equality in everyday life, that is, in the workplace itself.[41] The emergence of the system of wage labor in the antebellum period created the foundations for a new kind of relationship between those who worked and those who owned, and this was seen as eroding the political ideas that underpinned America's republican democracy. In fact, throughout the nineteenth century all the critics of inequality saw that inequality was overturning the values of liberty and leading to social dissolution and fragmentation.

These are dimensions of inequality that have been lost from view as economic liberalism has rooted itself within contemporary American political culture. The ideological arguments of laissez-faire capitalism and the libertarian link between free markets and political freedom have meshed with the transformation of American capitalism to provide a new, broad-based justification for economic inequality, severing the links that the long discourse on economic inequality in American political thought had always asserted among inequality, freedom, and democracy itself. Studies focusing on American attitudes toward inequality show a broad consensus even as they differ on details.[42] Inequality is accepted and tolerated largely because of a dominant liberal ideology that has been able to justify the notion that inequality of outcomes is still a result of a fair distribution of opportunity.[43] And the transformation of American capitalism from an industrial to a postindustrial context has seemed to justify this. This has been called the "logic of opportunity syllogism," which states that an inequality of economic outcomes is acceptable since it is broadly perceived that "opportunity for economic advancement based on hard work is plentiful." This dominant ideology—one framed and made more enduring by the intellectual ideas that have linked markets with democracy and justified the logic of markets as inherently fair based on the liberal principle of equality of opportunity—has also made the majority of Americans skeptical of redistributive programs that "are perceived as unnecessary because the stratification system currently presents ample opportunity to better oneself by individual efforts."[44]

The ideology of liberalism therefore succeeded—within the new economic context of postindustrial, service-oriented capitalism—in cementing the notion that equality of opportunity is the only kind of equality that was "fair" in economic terms. Elites who had previously been skeptical of the ability of capitalism and market institutions to create equal conditions and equal opportunities—as in the shadow of the Great Depression and the Keynesian revolution that followed—gave way to a new generation of intellectuals and policymakers who openly embraced more liberal and even libertarian economic ideas.[45] Confidence in markets and capitalism itself were renewed, along with the acceptance and prolifera-

tion among the intellectual defenders of inequality of the subjectivist notion of economic individualism put forth by neoclassical economics generally and more forcefully by thinkers such as Mises, Hayek, and Friedman.
This perspective relativizes the material importance of wealth by arguing
that there is no way to compare the interpersonal utility of wealth, for
example, or inequities of income or property. Since no one can actually
know, let alone measure, the differential in utility between two individuals
of unequal wealth, redistribution becomes even less valid on moral, political, and legal grounds, as Richard Epstein argues in his defense of inequality, "Against Redress":

> Clearly no social ruler (pun intended) lets us know with certainty that
> wealth is worth more in the hands of a poor person than in the hands of
> rich person, so the determined economist can shipwreck the case for wealth
> transfers from the start by denying the possibilities of interpersonal com-
> parisons of utility. I can assert that wealth is worth more to the poor person
> than to the rich person; you can deny that proposition. The rich person
> might use the next dollar to complete work on an invention that will im-
> prove the lives of others. The poor person might squander it on a drinking
> binge. We have no way of knowing if wealth is more useful to a poor than
> a rich person.[46]

Inequality has therefore become a permanent and largely accepted
feature of the social topography of modern American political and social life. Through the ideological changes in the ideas Americans have had
about economic inequality, its sheer existence and magnitude, its causes
and its implications, the liberal economic ethic that had dominated American beliefs about equality has been transformed into a justification for
inequalities of outcomes. It may be that Americans know that inequality
has worsened and that it is, in fact, a bad thing; and they may indeed also
be opposed to the idea that the wealthy pay less than their "fair" share
of the tax burden. But in the end their alienation from broader issues of
public policy and public concerns and material interests—resulting from
an atomized liberalism that emphasizes narrow, misinformed self-interest—tends to weaken political awareness of regressive public policies that
increase inequality.[47] Whereas the notion of an equality of opportunity
was the basis of the liberal economic ethic in the eighteenth century, it
had always been seen that equalities of opportunity would translate into
a rough equality of condition. Differences among skill sets and abilities

would have different economic outcomes, but still it was assumed that equality of opportunity would lead to roughly equal outcomes. It was only with the emergence of capitalism and economic modernity—the decline of autonomous producers and the rise of wage labor and factory production in the early nineteenth century—that it would become clear that equality of opportunity in the face of wage labor and capital would be impossible.

But in modern American economic life, the myth of equality of opportunity has once again made a resurgence. It has changed attitudes toward inequality, making it not only more acceptable overall but legitimizing it as the result of the fair operation of markets. The reaffirmation of a liberal society has also meant the devaluation of the public sphere and the notion of the public or social nature of the individual. Markets can have effects only for individuals; they no longer affect communities. Costs are seen in terms of the individual, not society. Poverty is rarely seen as the result of cumulative causation, but of paucity of effort or laziness. Many Progressive and New Deal theorists and policymakers of the early twentieth century saw that a modern conception of democracy required a transformation of the older, classical liberal theories about society and individualism. This reorientation of democracy moved previous understandings of liberal individualism toward a richer conception of democracy, one that incorporated the economic sphere as an aspect of full democratic citizenship. The return to the framework of classical liberalism in the late twentieth century and the entire program known today as "neoliberalism" have therefore created a barrier to glimpsing the political dimensions of economic inequality.

This renewal of the ethos of classical and libertarian liberalism has been at the core of the redirection of American democracy. Since the degeneration of social liberalism in the 1970s, spurred on by the intellectual project of thinkers such as Hayek and Friedman, American democracy has reverted back to an atomistic conception of liberalism that has decontested the market and led to an overall acceptance, indeed, in many cases a justification of economic inequalities. Indeed, the complexities of economic inequality in America—from its racial or spatial correlates to its effects on quality of life and educational attainment—require attention.[48] The critics of economic inequality, from various political orientations and historical periods, were consistent in linking inequality of economic outcomes with the demise of democratic life and politics; they were consistent in their emphasis on the connection between material inequality and political equality. These notions have been radically reversed. The toleration and acceptance of economic inequality in contemporary America—something that has baffled many political analysts—has been the result of both the persistence of a liberal economic ethic, which has placed emphasis on individual effort and opportunity over structural concerns, and the actual mechanisms of inequality and its transformation. The political dimensions of economic inequality have been masked by this transformation of liberalism. For an aversion to economic inequality to once again enter into the mindset of American politics, its political consequences will need to be made clear. Only by looking back through the egalitarian tradition that was so deeply rooted in American political thought will this new critique ever become possible.

| *Conclusion* | Restating the Case for
            Economic Equality

The confrontation with economic inequality in American political thought
has been complex but enduring. As a political tradition, it put forth an interpretation of inequality that has been delegitimized and forgotten, one
that did not recognize an absolute separation between economic and political power. Rather, it saw the effects of inequality in not only economic
but political terms, emphasizing the loss of freedom that accompanied the
redistribution of social power as a result of economic disparities. This is
the very crux of the tradition, and it grounds a much broader political
project: the elimination of hierarchical forms of social and political power
and the realization that political and social freedom are inherently connected. Politically, the idea of economic inequality was associated with
other forms of inequality and servitude. Economic inequality was therefore not simply an extended discussion about the "fairness" of distribution
as it is so often referred to in contemporary debates; rather it was a distinct
political category that was associated in the minds of most Americans
with dependency, servitude, and unfreedom.

Economic inequality not only challenged the prevailing assumptions
of autonomy, self-sufficiency, and liberty, it also ran counter to the republican themes that emphasized the importance of the free nature of civil

society and the state. Republican institutions had always been character-ized as those that would guarantee that social and political power not be used for the benefit of the few at the expense of the whole and that indi-viduals would be protected from the randomness of power exercised by others. Through an emphasis on the dangers it posed to the "public good," inequality was also seen as having the capacity to distort political power and redirect the activities of the state and society toward the ends desired by smaller factions. If the liberal economic ethic that was so important in the formation of American social and political thought emphasized the centrality of the labor theory of value and property and the negative free-dom of noninterference, then the republican elements of this tradition emphasized the category of citizenship and the rights of a citizen of the political community to be free from the domination and servitude of oth-ers and to rid society of stratified forms of power and hierarchies that had characterized older societies from ancient Egypt through monarchical England. To be sure, this was not a tradition that carried on some abstract political discourse or tradition through the centuries; it was one that con-fronted interests, material forms of social power, and concrete political problems. Most of the critics of inequality in American thought did not seek an absolute or communistic form of egalitarianism but an emphasis on equality as a means to true political freedom and the absence of un-equal power relations within every sphere of life.

It is important to highlight the fact that this tradition was not con-cerned with a crude form of leveling but rather held an antipathy toward social fragmentation and the emergence and solidification of economic and social hierarchy because this frames the calls for equality and the cri-tique of inequality that existed throughout the development of American political thought in a new context. The prevailing conservative view that dominates contemporary discourse is that the concern with equality was always historically a function of the jealousy of the "have-nots" and that it should be seen as little more than a moral pleasantry and, even worse, a social-scientific anachronism. Since the concern of this tradition was rarely, if ever, with utopian ideals of social equality and rather with a rage against the political and social implications of inequality, we are in a better position to argue for the relevance of this tradition for contemporary af-fairs than we might at first realize.

But it is essential to emphasize the political dimensions of economic inequality. What is interesting about the American discourse on economic inequality is the way that the boundaries between political and economic life were in fact not at all firm. Disparities in economic power were interpreted as disparities in social and political power as well. There was no confusing the matter of how social and individual freedom would become endangered: once certain individuals or segments of the community obtained unequal power over others, this would be the beginning of the end of any kind of democratic republicanism and therefore any real sense of political freedom. Feudal institutions were still palpably felt by early American citizens, and their approach to economic inequality was tempered by their opposition to social hierarchy and their hatred of inequality and despotism. But this is precisely the political impulse that has been lost in contemporary American political thought. When applied to the way that economic inequality is now understood and debated, it becomes clear that the split between economics and politics to which American liberalism has always held obfuscates the deeper political significance of economic inequality. This is something that the older critics of economic inequality in America knew all too well, and something that needs to be recovered if a new, critical discourse on economic inequality is to emerge.

This political discourse in American thought was consistent over time in arguing for the elimination of economic disparities and the connection between the effects of unequal wealth and political power. Stemming from both classical and modern sources, the concern with inequality was deeply entwined with the concern for political freedom since the biggest threats to freedom were seen as the emergence of a new aristocracy of wealth, on the one hand, and the loss of any real possibility for economic autonomy, on the other. What informed the early period of the discourse was a dual concern with both liberal and republican themes, and it was the potency of this fusion that had much to do with the early radicalism of the egalitarian tradition. The liberal economic ethic sought self-sufficiency and autonomy in order to fight servitude in economic affairs. It was republican in its characterization of civil society and public institutions, and it privileged public welfare over the interests of the few. Within the context of a preindustrial economy, this would prove a rich ideological source to counter economic inequality in the early republic.

But as capitalism developed and transformed American economic and social life, the political assumptions and arguments that buttressed liberalism began to erode, and it would become—as an economic ethic—a degenerated argument for possessive individualism and inequality. The

economic egalitarian dimension of the liberal tradition has slowly exhausted itself. The reasons were not simply reaction to the welfare state
that became ascendant in the late 1970s and 1980s and that still persists.
There has been a transformation of the political and economic ethic in
American political culture. It is a transformation that has moved popular
ideas about economic and political life away from the radical concerns of
equality and freedom that characterized the egalitarian tradition. It has
reinterpreted liberalism as a purely economic doctrine, replaced concerns for self-sufficiency with self-interest, and castigated the role of the
state in the economy as backward and even authoritarian. The link between economic equality and freedom has also been seriously reworked.
Whereas the backbone of the egalitarian tradition was its emphasis on the
way that economic inequality forged relational networks of servitude and
dependence as well as the corruption of the public welfare, the contemporary discourse on economic inequality—specifically since the 1980s—tells
Americans something quite different: that capitalism and equality of opportunity are essentially the same and that liberty in economic terms is
equivalent to political liberty as well.

It is for this reason that this study focuses on the history of the idea of
economic inequality, on a political tradition as it was articulated in American political thought and social criticism by thinkers who saw the economic system as moving against the imperatives of equality and liberty that
thought lay at the heart of the American political project. My assumption
throughout this analysis has been that ideas inform and legitimize institutions, that they shape the way that political reality is perceived. Ideology
can support or erode the institutional realities of social life, and it is for this
reason that the political tradition of economic egalitarianism, which was
foundational to the understanding of the American political project since
its inception, needs to be reinterpreted and revived. If the implications of
economic inequality were seen in explicitly political terms, it was because
inequality was seen as a threat to republican values—to a harmonious political and social life characterized by the absence of domination and servitude. Economic life was always intertwined with political life—if individuals were dependent upon others, they would, as Jefferson rightly saw,
become subservient to them as well. This is the crucial lesson that must be
drawn from the history that I have sketched in these pages: namely, that
for the contemporary discourse on economic inequality to have any real
impact, it must revive the political interpretation of economic class that

the American egalitarian tradition put forth. It must reconceptualize class divisions as crystallizations of social power and must argue that policies and steps toward economic equality are steps toward a more robust conception of political democracy and the expansion of social and individual freedom.

But history is not a license. The mere existence of a political tradition through time does not bestow upon it any sense of legitimacy. Rather, the past serves as a resource for the present. In this sense, unearthing the economic egalitarian tradition in American political thought can serve to illuminate aspects of economic life that have become hidden. Not unlike Plato's allegory of the cave, the function of this exploration is to render visible what has become largely hidden in American social life: that inequality in economic terms has a corrosive force on political life and democratic culture more broadly. The egalitarian tradition that I have reconstructed here emphasized the links among economic, social, and political power; it connected a project of political liberty and its concern with the elimination of social domination and a political order based on legitimate authority accountable to democratic mechanisms. It was therefore a tradition that sought to privilege politics over economics, the public good over rapacious private interest, and a balance of social power among the members of society. At the heart of this tradition was its ability to see that economic relations were social and political as well; that the expansion of national economic prosperity but was merely a dimension of human liberty. The real essence of political freedom was contained in the absence of domination and dependence and the elimination of social hierarchies that were characteristic of preliberal nonrepublican societies as well as in the insight that only within a social and economic context that prevented such institutions and practices from arising could any kind of actual human liberty be realized.

The American economic egalitarian tradition was inspired by certain republican concepts and the confrontation with a rapidly expanding capitalist economy that made the tradition come alive. It is therefore the mixture of ideas and institutional realities—or more generally, political realities— that serves as the crucial dynamic of political history. The affinity between a set of political ideas and specific social, political, and economic realities is what brings any political tradition alive. When viewed in this way, the importance of history and tradition for the present becomes clear: new insights can be shed on the conditions of the present and new normative ideas can enliven political debate and discourse, thereby affecting political life. The relevance in the modern world of the revival of this tradition and its major insights should be clear enough. In a world marked by an expansion of economic inequality in global as well as national terms, where economic globalization comes at the price of political development and the expansion of vibrant democratic life, the American egalitarian tradition can affirm the aspirations of people to partake fully in political life and resist those social and political forces and interests that seek to pervert political life in the interests of capital rather than broader public concerns. The American economic egalitarian ethos was informed by an overriding desire to eliminate still-present feudal social and political relations. Their concern was therefore fundamentally political in nature, and it was driven by the republican desire to expand and protect political freedom.

The history sketched here therefore serves as a way to rethink and reevaluate the social world of the present. The function of the analysis of history—something known especially to Machiavelli, Hegel, and Weber—has always been to generate new insights into the present. The story that I have laid out in these pages is therefore something more akin to the recovery of a political ethos, one that refuses to allow economic life to become dominant over social and political life. Economic inequality was seen as something not only unjust in moral terms but as an expression of social power. The general argument made throughout the development of the egalitarian tradition was that economic equality was not simply an aspect of political equality but a precondition for all other forms of equality and for any substantive sense of political freedom. To deny this was, for the thinkers in this tradition, to admit the existence of a neo-aristocracy and the institutionalization of a new form of inequality. These points ought not to be lost when thinking about the dynamics of inequality today, especially in the global perspective.

Conservative economists continue to argue the merits of inequality and the actual scope of its economic effects. But, as I have tried to show in this study, it should be clear that the central concern ought to be political rather than economic in nature. The liberal economic ethic that was dominant throughout the eighteenth and early nineteenth centuries has been stripped of its political force. Liberalism as a doctrine no longer possesses an intellectual or political affinity with civic republicanism as it did in the first century of American political thought and culture. The economized conception of liberalism that predominates in American political culture still focuses on the idea of individual liberty, but in negative terms, and its justification for possessive individualism in the context of a market society has led to the justification of inequality. This is why liberalism is insufficient as a foundation for stating the case for economic equality. Liberalism's emphasis on individual freedom and the absence of external constraint made perfect sense for a political project bent on combating feudal social arrangements and preliberal social norms and institutions (everything from racism to sexism and the like). But it has been unable to combat the problem of class and economic inequality simply because liberalism—as an economic ethos—has come to privilege possessive individualism over its previous thrust of economic autonomy. The labor theory of property was a radical one in the context an antifeudal economic context. Its emphasis on individual labor and the freedom to exchange without the interference of the state was an expression of antiauthoritarianism in the face of feudal and mercantilist institutions, assumptions, and ways of life.

As the evolution of the economy moved toward modern capitalism, the political thrust of the liberal economic ethic, once a radical idea that aimed to erode hierarchical divisions of power, would lead toward a reconciliation of capital and labor. To be sure, the radical nature of the egalitarian critics of the early nineteenth century in America rested on an understanding that the new institutions of capitalism would corrupt the ability of the liberal economic ethic to operate properly since capital could only accumulate more of itself by living off of the labor of others. The radical egalitarian critics were unable to stop the transformation and modernization of American capitalism, but their critique still harbors within it a radical message for today: namely, that the lens of liberalism is insufficient for an understanding of economic equality. Liberalism has become a justification for American social stratification simply because capitalism is no longer viewed as the generator of inequality; rather, it is seen that natural distinctions of talent, skill, intelligence, and so on, within the context of a "free" market, are responsible for market outcomes.

This transformation of liberalism, which began with thinkers such as Mises, Hayek, and Friedman, was viewed by them more as a restoration. These thinkers saw their ideas as reinvigorating the authentic tradition of classical liberalism: the minimal state, noninterference with the individual and economic affairs, a firm separation between economy and polity, and, most important, the connection of these attributes with what they saw as "true" liberty. What they achieved was an economization of liberalism that gutted the Lockean-inspired ideas of eighteenth-century and early-nineteenth-century critics of inequality of its political implications. Unlike the critics of inequality during the early republic and Jacksonian periods, the liberal economic ethic now serves to promote and justify inequality rather than critique it. The reason for this has been the transformation of the economic context: whereas an economy based on small-scale production, agrarianism, and localized economic life could utilize the labor theory of value and property as a tool to promote equality, after the industrial period, this kind of economy has been thoroughly replaced by one characterized by wage labor and the unequalizing effects of capital. The older ideal of the liberal economic ethic has turned into a narrow individualism that largely eschews the public good and instead emphasizes economic logic. We are therefore left with a situation where inequality can be justified even by the very people who suffer worst from its consequences.[1]

This transformation of liberalism explains the decline of the egalitarian tradition in American politics. The narrow, libertarian understanding of liberalism—with its emphasis on negative liberty and hedonic utility maximization—has become the staple of a consumerist culture with its postindustrial work relations and an anomic division of labor. The reification of a market society has pushed politics to the periphery of everyday life, and, as a result, the implications of economic inequality become less visible. Of course, the perception of the welfare state from the late 1970s and 1980s persists: an institution that fosters dependence rather than a culture of work, and so on.[2] But it is not simply a reaction against the legacy of New Deal liberalism and the Great Society that we are dealing with, but a deeper transformation of the American liberal tradition itself, its depoliticization and its turning away form the former republican context within which it functioned. Indeed, there should be no mistaking the fact that the civic republican dimensions of American political thought emphasized a different understanding of human and political freedom than is commonly understood today simply because the antipathy to hierarchy and inequality at that time was so intense. The proximity to feudalism and the emergence of modern democratic politics was the reason for this, but it spills over into political culture as well.

Indeed, the way that liberalism was reassessed by the Progressive and New Deal thinkers was crucial for effecting a major reorientation of American democracy. For the first time, the idea that had been in the minds of many during the revolutionary period—that political equality and economic equality were mutually reinforcing concepts—was revived and brought to bear on modern capitalism. The traumatic experience of laissez-faire policies and the brutal effects of industrialism and inequality during the late nineteenth century had taken their toll, and the turn toward the state as the proper arbiter for a complex, developed national economy was seen as obvious. The "social liberalism" of the early twentieth century saw democracy as extending deep into the sphere of economic life. A new sense of public interest was initiated, and the emphasis on politics over the market made sure that economic ends served the public interest and not the interest of capital alone. All of this has been reversed by the libertarian transformation of liberalism. Even though the liberal economic ethic placed primary emphasis on the idea of individual effort as the source of all legitimate wealth and property, it was within an economic context that precluded corporations and the legal protection of accumulated property and profit that was not in fact garnered from one's own labor. In this regard, the production process of modern capitalism was seen for what it was: the theft of labor from laborers for the sake of profit. Inequality was the result of the corruption of the liberal economic ethic, not its realization. By recasting the liberal economic ethic in its libertarian form, liberalism has become little more than an apologia for economic inequality. Inequality is now justified as the outcome of differentials in effort and talent rather than as the result of institutional mechanisms inherent in the production process itself.

It is for this reason that restating the case for economic equality requires transcending the political limitations of modern American liberalism and the kind of political, economic, and cultural ethos that it has unleashed. Whereas in the past, liberalism in America was able to expand political equalities in the face of entrenched irrational traditions and antiliberal doctrines and the institutions of slavery, Jim Crow, and the denial of women's rights, it has shown itself to be consistently ineffectual in maintaining any real, enduring condition of economic equality or making a coherent case for its moral justification in the face of its contemporary detractors. What needs to be reclaimed is the political emphasis on the idea of economic inequality as the starting point for disparities in relations of social and political power. Concern for equality, antipathy toward hierarchies and, most important, concern with the absence of domination informed the critics of economic inequality throughout American political thought, and it is this interpretation of economic inequality that needs to be privileged.[3] Indeed, the earliest American thinkers and writers on the topic also shared this concern, but it was largely a speculative and, indeed, theoretical enterprise. Once the intensification of capitalism began to set in, once individuals began to lose economic autonomy and the reality of class hierarchy became evident, the problem of economic inequality began to evolve as a distinct political discourse within the broader framework of American political thought.

The concern with a republican ethos is important, in this regard, because it provided thinkers with the appropriate normative framework through which to judge the evolving economic divisions and the budding aristocracy of wealth that was emerging. Although its most immediate concerns were with the elimination of patterns of social, economic, and political life such as kinship relations and patronage that were remnants of the older, quasi-feudal social and economic order inherited from Europe, the main thrust of the republican sentiment in American political thought was the thorough elimination of all forms of servitude and domination as the precondition for the realization of a true sense of human equality and freedom.[4] And it is important to note that up until the late nineteenth century, the liberal economic ethic and these republican sentiments were part of the same project. Today, however, liberalism—as applied to the realm of the economy and property—has lost its ability to argue against the effects of capitalism, inequality, and the conditions of the workplace. It is not simply that capitalism has become ascendant, American liberalism has also accepted many of capitalism's effects. Liberalism's emphasis on individual labor and property right and its individualistic conception of liberty have melded with the consumptive ethic of late capitalism. Inequality has therefore ceased to be a social concern, one that touches on the very character of political life; it has become the very result of the liberal economic ethic, a renewed state of nature patterned by the "natural" outcomes of the market. The diminution of inequality as a problem that touches on more than economic concerns is one of the casualties of the modern transformation of liberalism.

Placing the argument against economic inequality in its proper historical context is therefore important. Although early-nineteenth-century critics assailed the emerging institutions of banking and capitalist wage labor, their concern was with economic autonomy: the ability of individuals to be free from the arbitrary exercise of power by owners and employers and to lead a self-sufficient economic life free from dependence and servitude. This was the impulse that informed the critique of inequality, and its political implications still have importance in an age where working people—of all varieties—have less control over their workplace and their economic future. As these radical critics of inequality saw it, there was no simple separation between political and economic equality; they would have rejected the crude distinction because of its implausibility and also because they interpreted economics as a distinct sphere of power, not a neutral mechanism of distribution and production. The emphasis on republican themes is therefore not anachronistic; if liberalism now provides a justification for individualistic economic life, republican themes can shed light on different aspects of social power and inequality. But this must be done with care—the wide array of work that has appeared on republicanism has suffered from abstraction and idealism. On the one hand, the political philosophy of republicanism rests on the notion of civic virtue and the need for citizens to act according to public rather than private ends. The critics of economic inequality and social atomization were wedded to these beliefs. But politically the problem remains that resting any political theory on the vagueness of something like "civic virtue" is to propose a political theory with little actual political power.

Rather, what I think we can glimpse throughout the evolution of America's economic egalitarian tradition is not that civic virtue was in fact the crux of any political idea, but that the elimination of actual social and economic constraints—those that created unequal power relationships—were necessary for any substantive realization of individual liberty or full realization of democracy. But more concretely, what the critique of inequality in American political thought shows is a need to see that individuals do not exist as abstract legal-political entities. Rather, they are part of a material context—a set of economic relations—that can either enhance or erode individual freedom. In other words, it was clear that although each is an individual with individual rights, the nature of the relations of individuals to one another needed to be equally emphasized. The radical egalitarian critique of the early nineteenth century that emphasized the damaging effects that monopoly and gross inequalities of wealth would have on the public good, as well as Walter Weyl's invocation of the idea of a "socialized democracy," both speak to an idea that transcends the narrowness of contemporary liberalism.

The idea of a "republican modernity" would emphasize the need to move beyond a wholly individualized conception of liberty. It does not

dispense with liberalism by wrongly reducing it to possessive individualism. Rather, it seeks a synthesis of individual autonomy and public aims; it
links the interests of individual liberty with broader social institutions; and
it sees that the individual can only attain a sense of real freedom within
the context of a social organization that restrains the excesses of the market and capital and provides where the market is unable to do so. And
unlike many modern interpretations of republicanism that emphasize an
almost exclusive need for "civic virtue," a republican modernity would
maintain ethical and institutional imperatives that are not dependent on
the utopianism of civic virtue.[5] Instead, it would extend the assumptions
and insights that many of the critics within the American egalitarian tradition held or even saw as basic and necessary assumptions. In place of an
emphasis on civic virtue, a republican modernity provides a way to see
modern economic society normatively and bring the political problems of
domination and unfreedom to light. It also delineates those places where
individual autonomy should be emphasized and those places where pubic
aims and goods should be.[6] Republican modernity works off of a set of
assumptions and understandings of political and social life that see "interdependence" and the social context of autonomy as essential to a more
substantive and deeper conception of human freedom.

The modern turn in political theory toward the republican tradition
has rightly emphasized the importance of the normative category of
"nondomination."[7] Indeed, this was the very category that many critics
of inequality in the American egalitarian tradition brought to bear on the
problems of economic inequality and the emergence of capitalism. The
historical account of the discourse on economic inequality in America
sheds light on the particular reasons and rationales that were used against
the disparities of wealth as well as the sociology of the workplace itself.
Implicitly, it glimpsed something that I think has been lost: the insight that
economic inequality creates patterns of domination and dependence that
are concrete and real and that these can only be usefully combated once
the political impulse against hierarchy, domination, subordination, and
lack of material security becomes paramount once again in political and
cultural life.

When applied to the problem of economic inequality, this means rejuvenating the egalitarian tradition and breathing life into the political impulse for a deeper conception of economic rights that is more than simply
an equality of opportunity, as well as extending democratic standards into

the workplace itself. It would be wrong to fault liberalism as a political theory for the problems of contemporary economic inequality and the lack of resistance to it. The concern for the synthesis between personal autonomy and the importance of public goods and aims has an important lineage. Hegel's insight was that absolute freedom would come about through the dialectical sublation of modern individualism into the community or public. He sought this through the institutional power of the state as well as voluntary civic groups (*Korporationen*) that would check that power.[8] But the most immediate intellectual concerns of this synthesis with respect to economic inequality can be found in the American egalitarian tradition itself. Walter Weyl's "socialized democracy" or John Dewey's idea of "social liberalism" rested on the insight that atomistic, laissez-faire individualism was not only sociologically—if not anthropologically—unsound, but that it was, more importantly, politically degenerative as well.[9]

For Dewey—who himself absorbed many Hegelian themes in his social and political thought—the history of liberalism moved from what he termed an "earlier liberalism," which grew out of resistance to oligarchic government beginning with the English revolution of 1688. This evolved into "later liberalism," which was articulated by the demands of a "rising industrial and trading class" that sought to eliminate restrictions on the freedom of private economic enterprise and the burdens of taxation. The problem, as Dewey quite rightly saw it, was that this form of liberalism would come to justify certain forms of society that were in fact against the initial aims that liberalism sought to achieve. This twisting of liberalism Dewey called "pseudo-liberalism": "I call it pseudo-liberalism because it ossifies and narrows generous ideas and aspirations. Even when words remain the same, they mean something very different when they are uttered by a minority struggling against repressive measures and when expressed by a group that, having attained power, then uses ideas that were once weapons of emancipation as instruments for keeping the power and wealth it has attained. Ideas that at one time are means of producing social change assume another guise when they are used as means of preventing further social change."[10]

Dewey suggested that "social liberalism" should take the place of the laissez-faire, atomizing doctrine to which liberalism had given rise. If the core aim was social and political freedom, as well as the humanistic ideal of the ability of each individual to develop him- or herself fully, then the Newtonian conception of liberalism was no longer relevant for the modern age. Instead, it was clear—as it was for Hegel, Weyl, Croly, and many others—that the emphasis had to be on where to privilege the individual and where the community; for Dewey it was clear that the economic sphere was a place where individual liberty was not possible without taking into account the crucial connection between economic life and the rest of political and social life.

> It is absurd to conceive liberty as that of the business entrepreneur and ignore the immense regimentation to which workers are subjected, intellectual as well as manual workers. Moreover, full freedom of the human spirit and of individuality can be achieved only as there is effective opportunity to share in the cultural resources of civilization. No economic state of affairs is merely economic. It has a profound effect upon presence or absence of cultural freedom. Any liberalism that does not make full cultural freedom supreme and that does not see the relation between it and genuine industrial freedom as a way of life is a degenerate and delusive liberalism.[11]

Individual freedom therefore is the product of the context in which the individual belongs. The abstraction of the individual that classical liberalism suggests does into take into account context or class. As such, it can no longer serve as a critical impulse against the prevailing system; it becomes an apologia for the status quo.

The relevance of what I am calling republican modernity for renewing the critique of economic inequality should be obvious once we grasp that inequality and liberalism have a strong affinity with each other. Liberalism—specifically as it has evolved since the nineteenth century and in terms of its emphasis on the institution of free contract—runs into the crucial dilemma of trying to defend individual autonomy in political and economic terms simultaneously. Its emphasis on private property and con-tract has always been at the center of the defense of corporate interests over the interests of the public. It has also—through a process of political and cultural naturalization aided by libertarian and neoconservative social and economic thought—wedded itself to market capitalism. This has had the effect of alienating citizens from the useful role that the state can play in ameliorating inequality, conferring rights on working people, and directing the increasing prosperity of the few toward the needs and substantive prosperity of the public. Republican themes emphasizing the public good and illuminating the economic context within which individuals function are therefore essential; but they cannot be strengthened at the expense of liberal ideas of moral and political autonomy. The tension between these two opposing poles in political thought can be sketched elsewhere; the key here is to see how republican themes can rejuvenate the possibilities for a new, more robust critique of economic inequality and restate the argument for equality in an age so hostile to it.

Shifting the critique of economic inequality to its political valences means shifting attention and concern toward unfreedom, the arbitrary nature of economic constraint, and the possibility of the state enhancing and extending individual freedom rather than acting, according to the libertarian-inspired notion, simply as a constraint on individual liberties. It means drawing attention to the political dimensions of everyday economic life and the workplace and renewing institutions that will ensure economic security. It means seeing the effects of economic inequality on the problems of social fragmentation and the effects this has on creating a disinterested, apolitical public concerned more with the narrow concerns of consumerism and market imperatives. And it also means a strengthening of civic institutions to combat the socially corrosive effects of the market.[12] The need for equality must be emphasized as a path to enhancing democracy in everyday life as well as creating a material context for a richer sense of individualism. If individual liberty cannot be conceived outside of the material and social context in which the individual finds himself, then the need to emphasize economic equality for the purpose of deepening democracy takes on a renewed significance. Republican modernity is both a move toward renewing the balancing of individual autonomy and the recognition of material and economic constraints that stunt social freedom, and a reminder that modern economic life is a core contributor to the lack of political and social freedom of the individual.

These insights find reference in the historical lineage of the American egalitarian tradition. Economic inequality always constituted a transgression of fundamental political principles for most of American political thought in the sense that the common weal was being subordinated to the interests of the few. But this tradition also saw that individuals were caught in a web of economic relations of varying dimensions: at the level of the workplace itself, where employee was subordinate to the employer; at the level of wages since capital and labor reaped unequal rewards from their various inputs of labor; and at the level of society itself since the individual was now caught in an age of limited choice for work and personal and cultural development, with business interests predominating over other social, political, and cultural aims. Many of the early thinkers of America's egalitarian tradition privileged the connection between political principles and economic conditions. They saw that the very conception of citizenship—broadly defined as the participation in the political community and the political rights that it bestowed—was put at risk once the maldistribution of material forms of life worsened. They may not have given voice to the conditions of slavery in the South, and they were indifferent to the inequalities brought about by a gendered division of labor. But their critique of class divisions, the mechanisms of inequality, and the new forms of domination that were rising in everyday life as capitalism developed and deepened its influence bristled with political insight. Stephen Simpson's line from 1831 that America's political and social experiment had discovered that the real ends of government were to "secure the happiness of the many instead of ministering to the benefit of the few" was an expression of this sentiment, but it also spoke to the way that economic inequality would be interpreted as going against the broader ideas of equality that American political thought had at the very core of its being.[13]

The critique of economic inequality was therefore intimately bound up with broader conceptions of social and individual equality and freedom; the ways that working people and their employers related to one another; the various opportunities that were becoming less and less available to them as a distinct social class; and how the ability to live a life of economic autonomy rather than one of servitude, which was becoming the predominant form of economic life. This concern was not liberal in the narrow sense that we understand it precisely because it aimed at more than an ideal of negative liberty, or of noninterference. These thinkers saw—as did the republican theorists throughout Western thought—that noninterference was not equivalent to eliminating forms of domination.[14] This is why the radical critics of the early nineteenth century and the moral critics many decades later saw the problem in institutional terms. The concerns of political freedom (theorized as the lack of domination) were intricately involved with economic inequality.

The liberal-republican critics of economic inequality therefore saw freedom not simply in individual terms, but in social terms as well. They saw the importance of patterning institutions so that inequality would not arise since economic inequality led to dependence and the corruption of the very moral basis behind the politics of America's republican enterprise. This was evident in the concern that the radical critics took in the problem of wage labor and the new institution of capitalism that was emerging during the early nineteenth century. They were concerned not simply with the problem of inequality, but that the institutions of society were generating these inequalities, rendering individual freedom nearly impossible. Although it is certainly true that the fight for legal rights on the part of working people took the form of liberal arguments against what Karen Orren has termed "belated feudalism," it is equally important to see that as a tradition, as a critical political discourse, the critique of economic inequality in American political and social thought was dominated by the republican idea that freedom was not possible in mere individualistic terms; that it required not just an equality of opportunity but also the elimination of institutions that were transforming economic life; that the very social and political context was being remade by the forces of capital. In contrast to the liberal vision, the republican idea of equality and freedom saw political and social freedom more in terms of the elimination of institutions that would interfere with the freedom of individuals and the arrangement of institutions so that domination and interference of individual freedom were eliminated. Even more, they were able to see the political implications of inequality in the ways that perverted power relations would unduly affect the public good, steering democratic institutions away from their universalist ends.

The kind of republicanism that informed the views of the critics of economic inequality throughout the nineteenth century saw such inequality as the result not of merit and reward but of the emerging economic institutions of capitalism. Inequality was produced by a new economic aristocracy, and as inequality grew, the disparity in the relations of power between workers and capitalists would continue to broaden. The emergence of the wage system was particularly problematic not only because it would create a new form of economic servitude—something that the critics of inequality thought the American Revolution had eliminated—but because, as an institution, it was creating an unequal society based on the unequal division of property and wealth rather than one based on merit and reward. There were no illusions about what capital actually was and what its effects would be. The republican themes of this critique were essential because they enabled egalitarian critics to view inequality not as a phenomenon of interpersonal differences but as an institutional phenomenon that was intimately tied to the politics of human liberty.

This is why it is essential to bring the debate about economic inequality back to the very foundations of the egalitarian tradition itself. Even its twentieth-century guises as Weyl's "socialized democracy" and Dewey's "social liberalism" were both modern interpretations of republican themes in the sense that they privileged public interests over individual interests and a conception of the public good over economic hedonism. What they saw as "chaotic individualism" needed to be countered by the institution of the state; the market, the economy, was being revealed for what it was, just as it had been in ancient Athens thousands of years before: an institution that would atomize society and dissolve the cohesiveness of the political community. Even further, they were able to link this to concerns for social justice and a project of deepening democracy itself. It was a project that defined the laissez-faire ideology as antidemocratic and antimodern. The success of the libertarian attack by Hayek and Friedman therefore brought the narrow, "classical" liberal doctrine into ascendance over these republican-inspired themes. The curious balance between or fusion of liberalism and republicanism that characterized American political thought from its inception has become inordinately biased toward liberal ideas of property, accumulation, individualism, and self-interest.

Whereas liberalism was utilized by radicals in the nineteenth century as a means to argue for economic equality, its reliance on the notion of individual labor and the possession of the fruit of one's labor has become the very obstacle to arguing for economic equality in the modern political context. Outside of the agrarian economic framework within which it could exert radical influence, it has become—in its own way—a defense of economic divisions. No longer are CEOs and bankers seen as idlers living off of the labor of working people. Today the reification of the economic system has placed economics over politics; it has collapsed ethics into interest; and it has denatured the idea of public goods to the most menial and insignificant institutions and services. The earlier connection seen between political rights and economic realities has been lost. Liberalism's atomism, its inability to conjure up a notion of political goods as superseding the individualistic economic interests of social actors, has resulted in the fragmentation of the public by economic divisions.

The historical and intellectual arc that I have sketched in this study should be seen in its entirety, as the rise of the American egalitarian tradition, its fruition, and, in the end, its exhaustion and defeat. The concern for economic inequality no longer looms as an important issue in American culture or American political thought. Even among workers and the working poor, on whom the injustices of inequality continue to take their toll, there has been an erosion of the ideas and values that once informed their opposition. And although this study has also sketched an inegalitarian tradition in American political thought—beginning with thinkers like Hamilton and continuing through Sumner, Hayek, and Friedman—it is not so much the victory of this discourse over the egalitarian discourse that, in my view, explains this shift away from concerns with economic equality, as it is the way that liberalism has become predominant over older, republican-inspired themes.

The struggle for economic equality has been weakened by a gradual acceptance of liberal capitalism. The way was paved by the broader turn toward classical liberalism in nineteenth-century American political thought, which served to attenuate the critique of inequality in the sense that it steered American political thought toward being more tolerant of capitalism and its effects. This turn would also give more weight to the antiegalitarian tradition by legitimating an apolitical conception of the market and the economy, a conception that would mature into a broader ideological attack on the modern welfare state and dilute the egalitarian tradition, all but stopping it in its tracks as the twentieth century came to a close.

Apologists for laissez-faire and libertarianism have become very influential in the closing decades of the twentieth century. Their ascendance was not attributable the fact that they appealed to an outright justification of inequality—as Hamilton and Sumner had—but that they emphasized a split between politics and economics. The liberal doctrine that they developed—based on "classical liberalism" and its utilitarian presumptions—articulated a doctrine of an "equal right to be unequal" in the sense that equality was to be restricted to equality before the law, leaving the effects of the market essentially unchecked by any form of political regulation. Even more, they were able to collapse what they referred to as "economic liberty" into political liberty itself. This is a discourse that has not only become influential in the United States but has also gripped much of Europe as well.[15] But perhaps most important of all, it has sunk deep into the fabric of American political culture, serving as a justification for economic divisions and a new economic hierarchy.

Renewing the claim for economic equality therefore requires not a re-invention of liberalism but rather a renewed emphasis on the republican themes that dominated the calls for social equality throughout American social history, most specifically the elimination of institutions that were fostering inequality, such as capital itself. It requires that the emphasis on class hierarchy and its ability to distort democratic politics at multiple lev-els be made apparent and its political effects—perhaps more than its moral implications—be brought to the forefront. There is no question that liber-alism has been able to make serious gains in the areas of race and gender, but the problem of class and economic power persists. And, in many ways, this is the result of the predominance of liberalism over the republican themes that inspired the antihierarchical impulses of the radical critics of economic inequality.

Part of the reason for this is the way that economic institutions have shaped political interests and the way that institutions in America were shaped to protect property rights and the ability to accrue property and wealth at the expense of the broader interests of the political commu-nity. But the other component to this explanatory tale is the realization that American liberalism, with its insistence on the individual and natu-ral rights grounded in property, acts as a consistent counterforce to the more radical impulse toward social equality that served as the intellectual and moral backdrop throughout American egalitarian tradition. Indeed, it should be remembered that the arguments of almost every thinker who worked within the inegalitarian tradition in American political thought were never against political equality and the equal application of the rule of law to all individuals. The problem has always been how to argue for equality in the face of individual claims to property and the vestiges of the liberal labor theory of property. This was, to be sure, something that the egalitarians saw as central to their argument against the rise of economic modernity, but it is also important to see that this persistence of the liberal economic ethic would come into conflict with the republican themes of equality and their emphasis on the abolition of domination, institutional and otherwise.

Contemporary events give evidence to these broad claims. The new in-equality in America has effected a radical change in the course and direc-tion of American democracy. From the spread of regressive tax policies at national and state levels to the deregulation of business and the defunding of social welfare programs, the assault on economic inequality has been pervasive and intense. Economic inequality needs to be seen as more than a moral dilemma over competing conceptions of "fairness." It structures power relations in everyday life; it consigns segments of the population to destitution and servitude; and it enhances the asymmetrical power relations that distort electoral politics and the activity and function of the media, as well as redirecting the goals of social policy toward the interests of business and away from the broader needs and interests of the public. American political thought was characterized by its critique of these themes and a push for a substantive form of social equality. This study has outlined how the ideas of economic inequality and equality were conceptualized, how they were enlisted to criticize the prevailing institutions of various times, and how they were consistently informed by the project of realizing equality. Taking lessons from the insights that this tradition put forth and learning from its political impulse are therefore central to restating the case for equality and reigniting the critique of the "new inequality."

The effects of economic inequality are by no means simple to define—they reach into subtle nuances of everyday life. But there should be no mistake about what the central concern should be: that the failure of the American struggle for economic justice—most obvious in the last quarter century—has been the result of the collapse of the political. Unlike in other areas of social life—from race, gender, and now sexual orientation—political liberalism has been unable to overcome inequalities of class precisely because it has been unable to locate the mechanism of inequality itself: that capitalism and "free" markets generate inequalities from the very nature of the production process and that an "inalienable right" to property—as unequally distributed as it is in modern capitalism—needs to be held accountable to democratic or public ends. Indeed, this was pointed out by the earliest American critics of economic inequality, and it is something that ought not to be lost in contemporary considerations on the subject.

Although the specific fears of social dissolution and tyranny that the Western tradition and early American thinkers possessed may not be on the horizon in the near future in the United States, it should be clear that contemporary inequality, and the transposition of the ideas of liberty and freedom to mean mainly economic freedom and liberty, has led to a society of dependence. The economization of American society has resulted in the forfeiture of political principles to economic ones. American thought has always been based on economics. The political ideas of liberty and equality were fundamentally bound to the material referents of property and labor. These material extensions, if you will, of those concepts buttressed political concepts. But now this situation has been reversed: the political concepts have become subordinate to the economic concepts.

Much of the problem with the liberal assault on economic inequality is that it was never able to grasp the mechanisms of inequality. The focus on redistribution often belonged to the egalitarians. John Pickering advocated a radical redistribution of equal shares of property, and Henry Demarest Lloyd argued a similar program. But even they were unable to see that inequality was not simply the result of privilege or monopoly power. Without question, the anti-aristocratic impulse that stood behind these radical critiques were unable to see that inequality is endemic to market systems and that it is the production process itself that is the engine for inequality. However, the early labor radicals from Langton Byllesby to Orestes Brownson and John Pickering saw capitalism in those terms, and their critique was motivated by what they saw as the corrosive effects of these new economic arrangements on the kind of economic life that, in their view, was constitutive of the political ideals of equality, justice, and liberty. It was motivated by political concerns and not by ideological ends that were imported or derived from non-American sources. And this is significant since it was the political impulses of the American republican tradition that inspired the critique of inequality and sustained the discourse for well over a century as capitalism continued to mature and develop.

The kind of economic individualism that has evolved in contemporary political, economic, and social thought has eroded the foundations of the kind of intellectual, political, and moral assault on economic inequality that marked most of American history. This move has been the result of a certain triumph of economic liberalism. What is curious is that American tradition of criticism has become largely mute. The persistence of inequality is not simply the result of economic factors. The moral critics of inequality knew all too well in the late nineteenth century, although this has been lost on contemporary thinkers, that only a consciousness of the political dimensions of economic divisions can lead us to glimpse the full implications of inequality's effect on political freedom. This was, to be sure, inspired by the requirements of social welfare and the democratic principles of an egalitarian social order that were influenced by Enlightenment ideas countering hierarchy and privilege, but it was also motivated by what we now call the republican themes that emphasized a very different understanding of equality, which was fearful of the fragmentation of public life that would result from economic divisions of power. Restating the case for economic equality therefore requires that we look back to the political dimensions and implications of inequality itself, to resurrect the political project that once pervaded the minds of the American critics of inequality and their radical emphasis on freedom as the absence of inequality. Only then will a renewed egalitarian project become possible, resurrecting the political spirit of the past within the possibilities of the politics of the present.

| Notes |

INTRODUCTION. THE POLITICAL DIMENSIONS OF
ECONOMIC INEQUALITY

1. This interpretation of political history is in stark contrast to the "Cambridge School," which argues that ideas or "political language" alone is the causal factor in explaining the vicissitudes of political history. I will elaborate on this critique more in chapter 2.
2. Rousseau, *Discourse on the Origin of Inequality*, 44.
3. Phillips, *Wealth and Democracy*, xii.
4. See the discussion in Palmer, *The Age of Democratic Revolution*, 1:185–284.
5. For an excellent discussion, see Fink, *The Classical Republic*.
6. Philip Green, *The Pursuit of Inequality*, (New York: Pantheon Books, 1981), 3.
7. See Deere and Welch, "Inequality, Incentives, and Opportunity," 84–109.
8. Freeman, *The New Inequality*, 3.
9. See Freeman and Katz, "Rising Wage Inequality."
10. This is not, however, a problem that is unique to the United States. For a discussion of this phenomenon in Europe, see Atkinson, "Bringing Income Distribution in from the Cold."
11. See James K. Galbraith, *Created Unequal: The Crisis in American Pay*, 133–49.
12. For an excellent discussion of the spatial aspects of economic inequality and the problem of housing segmentation, see Denton and Massey, *American Apartheid*. Also, for the worsening economic conditions of the urban poor, see Wilson, *The Truly Disadvantaged*, and *When Work Disappears*.
13. Wolff, "Racial Wealth Disparities," 7.
14. See Williamson and Lindert, "Long-Term Trends in American Wealth Inequality." One of the more popular explanations for the recent trends in inequality of incomes—and of overall social inequality—has been an emphasis on differentials of skills. This argument claims that when a rise in "skill-biased technical change" sets in, certain groups—i.e., those who possess more highly technical job skills—become more preferred in the

job market and therefore skew the overall income distribution. However, this has been refuted empirically, most recently by Ian Drew-Becker and Robert Gordon, who argue that "the 'economics of superstars,' i.e., the pure rents earned by the top CEOs, sports stars, and entertainment stars . . . combined with the role of deunionization, immigration, and free trade pushing down incomes at the bottom, have led to the wide divergence between the growth rates of productivity, average compensation, and median compensation." See their paper "Where Did the Productivity Growth Go? Inflation Dynamics and the Distribution of Income," http://faculty-web.at.northwestern.edu/economics/gordon/BPEA_Meetingdraft_Complete_051118.pdf (accessed January 5th, 2006), 1.

I. THE CRITIQUE OF ECONOMIC INEQUALITY IN WESTERN POLITICAL THOUGHT

1. The idea that economic relations were also seen as political relations is something somewhat foreign to the contemporary mind. Traditionally, however, the relation between the two was always seen as seamless. As C. B. MacPherson has argued, "since the late nineteenth century, economics has largely turned its attention away from that concern which had made earlier economic thought so congruent with political thought, namely, its concern with the relations of dependence and control in which people are placed by virtue of a given system of production" (*The Rise and Fall of Economic Justice*, 102).

2. Recent work on the origins of the idea of equality in Greek thought has emphasized the issue of political equality over that of economic equality. See Stuurman, "The Voice of Theristes." For a perspective on the historical trajectory of the idea of equality in western thought and the development of modernity, see Dann, *Gleichheit und Gleichberechtigung*. For a more recent discussion of the origins of the critique of unequal property in Greek thought and its implications for republican thought throughout the Western political tradition, see Nelson, *The Greek Tradition in Republican Thought*.

3. As Sanford Lakoff has argued when discussing Judaism and Christianity and the problem of inequality, "in neither of these instances, however, is there an unambiguous and systematic effort to invalidate earthly distinctions except with reference to the ultimate source and destiny of all being, expressed in the belief in the equality of all souls before God" (*Equality in Political Philosophy*, 12).

4. For an important discussion, see McCarthy, *Classical Horizons*, 15–63.

5. Polanyi, *Trade and Market in the Early Empires*, 243.

6. Polanyi, *Primitive, Archaic, and Modern Economies*, 84.

7. Plato, *Republic*, 547 B–C.

8. This interpretation is in sharp contrast to older interpretations of how the Greeks viewed the division of economic classes. M. Rostovtzeff, for example, claims that the Greeks saw the problem of *penia kai ploutos* "not as an important social and economic issue, but as a question of individual morals" (*The Social and Economic History of the Ancient World*, 2:1129). For his broader discussion on the topic, see 2:1115–35. My claim here is that the Greeks were able to see the political dimensions of economic life and therefore that inequlity was an inherently political problem for them since they were able to perceive the dehumanizing effects of poverty and the injustice of its existence next to those possessing wealth.

9. It is important to understand how Greeks themselves would have heard the terms "rich" and "poor." Moses Finley has argued that "the poor embraced all the free men who labored for their livelihood, the peasants who owned their farms as well as the tenants, the landless laborers, the self-employed artisans, the shopkeepers. They were distinguished on the one hand from the 'rich,' who were able to live comfortably on the labor of others, but also from the paupers, the beggars, the idlers" (*Politics in the Ancient World*, 10). Also see Finley's discussion in *The Ancient Economy*, 40–42. For an additional discussion of the way that class was understood by the ancients themselves, see Nippel, *Mischverfassungstheorie und Verfassungsrealität*, 103–5.

10. For a more extended discussion on these two plays of Aristophenes, see Zumbrunnen, "Fantasy, Irony, and Economic Justice in Aristophanes' *Assemblywomen* and *Wealth*."

11. For an excellent discussion of this theme, see Fuks, "Patterns and Types of Social-Economic Revolution in Greece." For more on the importance of utopia in the ancient world, see John Ferguson, *Utopias of the Classical World*. For a more extensive discussion of the problem of class struggle in ancient Greece, see G. E. M. Ste. Croix, *The Class Struggle in the Ancient Greek World*.

12. Plato, *Republic*, 551D.

13. Austin and Vidal-Naquet are clear on this point: "During the fourth century the gulf between rich and poor kept widening. Egalitarian aspirations implicit in the notion of the citizen aggravated tensions, and social inequalities were all the more keenly felt as a result" (*Economic and Social History of Ancient Greece*, 139).

14. Plato, *Republic*, 420B.

15. For an interesting discussion, see Barker, *Greek Political Theory*, 165–80. Also see Vidal-Naquet, *Le chasseur noir*, 317–80.

16. There is also little question that the concept of citizenship itself was an elitist one based on property holding and that class was a fixed notion in Greek political thought. However, this does nothing to diminish the power of the argument that links economic division, egoism, and the breakdown of democratic political institutions and culture.

17. See Pöhlmann, *Geschichte der Sozialen Frage*, 1:227. Also see Austin and Vidal-Naquet's discussion in *Economic and Social History of Ancient Greece*, 130–53.

18. See Fuks, "Patterns and Types of Social-Economic Revolution in Greece," 34–39; Pöhlmann, *Geschichte der Sozialen Frage*, 1:332–48.

19. Isocrates, *Areopagiticus*, §35.

20. It should also be noted that movements for economic equality were based on the notion of land redistribution (*anadasmos gēs*). Such was the case for social reformers in Sparta such as Agis and Cleomenes who sought to establish an absolute equality of shares of property (*isomoiria*). The process of realizing equality (*exisosis*) was therefore seen as a process of an equalization of property. See Fuks, "Agis, Cleomenes, and Equality." For more on egalitarian land reforms in the ancient Greek world, see Fuks, "Redistribution of Land and Houses in Syracuse in 356 B.C., and Its Ideological Aspects"; and Pöhlmann, *Geschichte der Sozialen Frage*, 1:155–169.

21. Raaflaub, "Equalities and Inequalities in Athenian Democracy," 143.

22. Specifically, see Plato, *Laws*, 736e–737b and 739d–e.

23. Wallach, *The Platonic Political Art*, 378.

24. Aristotle, *Nicomachean Ethics*, 5.1.8.

25. This is an important term derived from the phrase *ho pleon echon*, meaning "one who has more than enough" or "a superfluous amount" and that came to simply mean "one who has more than another." In Aristotle's political and ethical theory, the core issue is that of self-sufficiency (*autarkeia*). Hence, taking "more than one's share" is seen as inherently unjust from an ethical point of view, but it is also problematic when it comes to the larger property structure and distribution of land for individuals in the polis, which states that everyone should "command that which is most self-sufficing." See his *Politics*, 5.5.1–2.

26. It should be pointed out that Aristotle's notion of justice as developed in the *Nicomachean Ethics* emphasizes "distributive justice," which Aristotle defines as "accordingly, the just is the proportionate (*analogon*) and the unjust is that which violates proportion (*para to analogon*). The unjust may therefore be either too much or too little" (*Nicomachean Ethics*, 5.3.15). The problem of greed and its relationship to justice is a major theme in the classical world, and Aristotle's ideas are part of a broader

understanding of the immorality of greed. For an excellent discussion, see Balot, *Greed and Injustice in Classical Athens*.

27. McCarthy, *Classical Horizons*, 104.

28. For a discussion, see Leyden, *Aristotle on Equality and Justice*, 1–25.

29. "The adherents of the deviant-form of government (*ta parekbebēkuia*), believing that they alone are right, take it to excess" (Aristotle, *Politics*, 1309b, 22–23). For a discussion of the way that economic inequality becomes the problem of the ambition of a ruling class in Aristotle, see Lintott, *Violence, Civil Strife, and Revolution in the Classical City*, 239–51; also see Ste. Croix, *The Class Struggle in the Ancient Greek World*, 71–80. A broader discussion of these themes can be found in Watson, *Class Struggles in Ancient Greece*.

30. Aristotle, *Politics*, 1302a.9–15.

31. Ibid., 1302a.16.

32. Ibid.

33. Ibid., 1308b.25–31; also 1318a–1318b.5.

34. Aristotle is explicit on this point in his *Politics*: "It is clear then that those constitutions that aim at the common advantage are in effect rightly framed in accordance with absolute justice, while those that aim at the rulers' own advantage are only faulty, and are all of them deviations from the right constitutions; for they have an element of despotism, whereas a *polis* is a community of those who are free (*polis koinonia tōn eleutheriōn estin*)." (1279a.17–20).

35. For a lucid discussion of this distinction between Greek and Roman thought, see Eric Nelson, *The Greek Tradition in Republican Thought*.

36. Cicero, *De officiis*, 2.21.73.

37. Specifically, Philippus is quoted by Cicero as saying: "non esse in civitate duo milia hominum, qui rem haberent" (*De officiis*, 2.21.73).

38. Ibid.

39. "[C]orrupti mores depravatique sunt admiratione divitiarum" after which he follows with the question: "quarum magnitudo quid ad unum quemque nostrum pertinet?" (Ibid, 2.20.71).

40. Cicero, *De re publica*, 1.32 (this quotation is from the translation by Clinton Walker Keyes and slightly modified by the author).

41. Ibid. Cicero goes so far in *De officiis* to maintain that it is also the responsibility of government to make sure that the necessities of life be provided for the public welfare: "Atque etiam omnes, qui rem publicam gubernabunt, consulere debebunt, ut earum rerum copia sit, quae sunt necessariae" (2.21.74).

42. Machiavelli, *Discorsi sopra la prima deca di Tito Livio*, 175. Machiavelli is explicit about the need for any republic to eliminate inequality in terms of

property and the power that results from it. The *gentiluomini*, or those that derive status from property and wealth, are the permanent enemies of republicanism: "Credo che a questa mia opinione, che dove sono gentiluomini non si possa ordinare republica, parrà contraria la esperienza della Republica viniziana, nella quale non possono avere alcuno grado se non coloro che sono gentiluomini" (176). Machiavelli makes a distinction in his republican theory between the *gentiluomini*, on the one hand, and the *ottimati*, or those who hold office or prestige as a result of their personal, ethical, or political virtue, on the other.

43. See Hilton, *Bond Men Made Free*.

44. Luther, "Concerning Christian Liberty," 363.

45. For a discussion of the influence of the humanists on the Reformation and vice versa, see the excellent essay by Spitz, "The Third Generation of German Renaissance Humanists." Spitz points to the young humanists in northern Europe who "were no longer satisfied with criticism, but, following upon the impetus of conversion in many cases, were bent on changing the world" (45).

46. For an excellent historical discussion, see Walker, "Capitalism and the Reformation"; as well as Weber, "Die protestantische Ethik und der Geist des Kapitalismus."

47. Kramnick, *Republicanism and Bourgeois Radicalism*, 1. See Kramnick's broader discussion of liberalism and its opposition to republicanism on pages 163–99. I will discuss this in more detail in chapter 2.

48. For a discussion, see the classic study by MacPherson, *The Political Theory of Possessive Individualism*.

49. James Harrington, *Commonwealth of Oceana*, 127. David Hume would later counter Harrington's argument with respect to the "agrarian law" by arguing that it was "impracticable" since "men will soon learn the art, which was practiced in ancient Rome, of concealing their possessions under other people's name; till at last, the abuse will become so common, that they will throw off even the appearance of restraint" ("Idea of a Perfect Commonwealth," 515).

50. An interesting discussion of Harrington's ideas about republicanism and equal distribution of property can be found in Anna Strumia, *L'immaginazione repubblicana*, 35–48.

51. Montesquieu, *The Spirit of Laws*, 42.

52. Ibid., 45.

53. Hirschman, *Rival Views of Market Society*, 107. For a more developed discussion of this theme of the relation between the market and political thought during the eighteenth century, see Hirschman, *The Passions and the Interests*.

54. Smith, *The Wealth of Nations*, 310. Smith also argues in his *Lectures on Jurisprudence* that economic inequality arises during the transition from the hunting and gathering stage of social development to the herding stage. In the Industrial Age, he argues that poverty is not as big of a problem, but his connection between inequality and politics speaks to a different concern: the possibility of social justice itself. Also see his discussion in *The Wealth of Nations*, 310–11.

55. Ibid., 312.

56. Ibid., 33. For a more detailed analysis of Smith's views of poverty, see Gilbert, "Adam Smith on the Nature and Causes of Poverty." For more on his ideas about the connection between economics and morality and ethics, see Rothschild, *Economic Sentiments*.

57. As economic modernity began to evolve, social inequality emerges as a concern in the literature of the mid-eighteenth century. This is seen in England first, the nation that moved fastest toward capitalism and massive economic and social change. Oliver Goldsmith's poem "The Deserted Village" is an extended lament of the destruction of the English countryside by expanding wealth and privilege. It also critiques the problem of proliferating economic inequality:

Ye friends to truth, ye statesmen, who survey
The rich man's joys increase, the poor's decay,
'Tis yours to judge, how wide the limits stand
Between a splendid and a happy land.
Proud swells the tide with loads of freighted ore,
And shouting Folly hails them from her shore;
Hoards, e'en beyond the miser's wish abound,
And rich men flock from all the world around.
Yet, count our gains. This wealth is but a name
That leaves our useful products still the same.
Not so the loss. The man of wealth and pride
Takes up a space that many poor supplied;
Space for his lake, his park's extended bounds;
Space for his horses, equipage and hounds:
The robe that wraps his limbs in silken sloth,
Has robb'd the neighboring fields of half their growth;
His seat, where solitary sports are seen,
Indignant spurns the cottage from the green;
Around the world each needful product flies,
For all the luxuries the world supplies:—

While thus the land adorn'd for pleasures, all
In barren splendor feebly waits the fall.

| *POETICAL WORKS OF OLIVER GOLDSMITH*, 44–45 |

58. Hume, "Of Commerce," 15.

59. Ibid.

60. For a discussion of these thinkers and their ideas about equality, see Jonathan Israel, *Radical Enlightenment*, 67–71.

61. It should be remarked that even after the French Revolution, the concern with economic inequality did not lessen. Thinkers like Condorcet and Jean Baptiste Say argued for the elimination of poverty and believed that this could be achieved through rational social policies. For an excellent discussion, see Jones, *An End to Poverty?* 16–63 and 111–32.

62. "Je conclus donc que comme le premier devoir du legislateur est de conformer les lois a la volonté générale, la premier regle de l'economie publique est que l'administration soit conforme aux lois" (*Discours sur l'economie politique*, 52). The second law, Rousseau says, is no less important than the first: "Voulez-vous que la volonté générale soit accomplie? Faites que toutes les volontés particulièrs s'y rapportent; et comme la vertu n'est que cette conformite de la volonté particulière a la générale, pour dire la même chose en un mot, faites régner la vertu" (ibid., 53). This is a direct response to the liberal and utilitarian ideas of self-interest that dominated seventeenth- and eighteenth-century discussions about economic life and liberty. For more on the historical and philosophical evolution of self-interest, see Hirschman, *The Passions and the Interests*, 20–66.

63. For an excellent discussion of the relation between Rousseau's ideas and classical Greek themes, see Shklar, *Men and Citizens*. For an interesting discussion of Rousseau's ideas about the relation between property and the notion of *amour-propre*, see Birkhead, "Property and *Amour Propre*."

64. G. W. F. Hegel, *Philosophy of Right*, §49.

65. Ibid.

66. See Franco, *Hegel's Philosophy of Freedom*, 200–207. Another common but incorrect view is that Hegel's views on inequality also led him to a wholly negative view of the problem of those impoverished by economic modernity. See Muller, *The Mind and the Market*, 154–61.

67. Hegel, *Lectures on Natural Right and Political Science*, § 118.

68. It is important to note that, in contrast to Hegel's earlier writings on civil society and the problem of social classes and inequality, in the *Philosophy of Right* he uses the modern term for class (*Klasse*) over the older term (*Stand*), which denotes estate or status as opposed to the economically specific *Klasse*. For an excellent discussion, see Avineri, *Hegel's Theory of*

the Modern State, 147–54. For a historical discussion of the idea of *Stand* as opposed to that of class, see Böröcz, "*Stand* Reconstructed." For another discussion of Hegel's views on poverty, see Paul Diesing, *Hegel's Dialectical Political Economy*, 57–58 and 97–98.

69. Hegel, *Lectures on Natural Right and Political Science*, § 118. Also see the discussion by Neuhouser, *Foundations of Hegel's Social Theory*, 171–74.
70. As Jean Cohen and Andrew Arato have argued:

> It is only what Hegel considers the underside of this process of the emergence of new, nonascriptive status groups that belongs to the socioeconomic level of his analysis. Accordingly, the working class represents a form of inequality produced by civil society in which the absence of inheritance and otherwise unearned income, as well as a specific form of life, makes estate membership inaccessible and exposes individuals to the hazards of economic contingencies beyond their control.
>
> | *CIVIL SOCIETY AND POLITICAL THEORY*, 99 |

71. Hegel's analysis of the problem of inequality shows a concern not simply with the problem of social dissension and strife but also with the moral development of certain segments of society left in poverty: "the subdivision and restriction of particular jobs . . . results in the dependence and distress of the class tied to the work of that sort, and these again entail inability to feel and enjoy the broader freedoms and especially the intellectual benefits of society" (*Philosophy of Right* § 243).
72. Arnold, "Equality," in *The Poetry and Criticism of Matthew Arnold*, 485.
73. Karl Marx, *Economic and Philosophical Manuscripts*, 73.
74. Matthew Arnold, "Equality," 494.
75. Urbinati, *Mill on Democracy*, 191.
76. For an excellent discussion, see McCarthy, *Classical Horizons*, 15–47, 103–10, and 138–47.

2. THE LIBERAL REPUBLIC AND THE EMERGENCE OF CAPITALISM

1. Webster, "An Examination into the Leading Principles of the Federal Constitution," 134.
2. See Wilentz, "America's Lost Egalitarian Tradition," for an excellent discussion of the sources of the egalitarian tradition in American political thought.
3. Tocqueville, *Democracy in America*, 138.
4. I am, of course, referring to Louis Hartz's classic argument for American liberal exceptionalism (see *The Liberal Tradition in America*). Hartz's argu-

2. THE LIBERAL REPUBLIC AND THE EMERGENCE OF CAPITALISM

ment is not wrong, in that liberalism did become an overriding dimension of American political and economic life, but it is important to see how this was separated over time from a broader concern with a civic republican concern for the public good and the search for the proper balance between individual self-interest and liberty, on the one hand, and the duties individuals must have toward the community and the maintenance of the public good, on the other. Even more, Hartz did not consider the extent to which feudal relations—specifically within economic life—persisted well beyond the Revolutionary era.

5. There is a large literature on this subject. Prominent examples include Pocock, *The Machiavellian Moment*, 506–52; Wood, *The Radicalism of the American Revolution*; Dienstag, "Serving God and Mammon"; Kornfeld, "From Republicanism to Liberalism"; and Dworetz, *The Unvarnished Doctrine*. For more recent perspectives on the debate between republican and liberal interpretations of American political thought, see Heideking and Henretta, eds., *Republicanism and Liberalism in America and the German States*.

6. For an important discussion, see Bronner, *Reclaiming the Enlightenment*, 41–60. The argument for a fusion of liberalism and republicanism was made much earlier in Banning, "Republican Ideology and the Triumph of the Constitution," and "Jeffersonian Ideology Revisited." For those who argue not for a synthesis of the two but rather parallels between liberalism and civic republicanism, with an emphasis on liberalism, see Kloppenberg, "The Virtues of Liberalism." Other scholars have questioned the extent to which republicanism displaced liberalism during early American political thought, emphasizing the importance of Lockean liberalism. See Appleby, "Liberalism and the American Revolution," *Capitalism and a New Social Order*, and "Republicanism in Old and New Contexts"; as well as Diggins, *The Lost Soul of American Politics*.

7. Wood, *The Radicalism of the American Revolution*, 172.

8. Several classic examples include MacPherson, *The Political Philosophy of Possessive Individualism*; Laski, *The Rise of Liberalism*; and Strauss, *Natural Right and History*.

9. Kramnick, *Republicanism and Bourgeois Radicalism*, 34.

10. See Kerber, "The Republican Ideology of the Revolutionary Generation."

11. Gordon Wood, among others, makes this argument explicitly: "The great social antagonisms of the American Revolution were not poor vs. rich, workers vs. employers, or even democrats vs. aristocrats. They were patriots vs. courtiers—categories appropriate to the monarchical world in which the colonists had been reared" (*The Radicalism of the American*

Revolution, 175). This point is also famously made by Bernard Bailyn: "The American Revolution was above all else an ideological, constitutional, political struggle and not primarily a controversy between social groups undertaken to force changes in the organization of the society or the economy" (*The Ideological Origins of the American Revolution*, vi). This general argument—also made by J. G. A. Pocock and his circle—seems credible only if we are willing to split the interpretation of social relations from the realities of the economic relations of the period—and this is not a credible interpretive strategy. It is not my contention that the American Revolution was a class revolution in the Marxian sense but rather that the problem of unequal property was seen at the time to be crucially linked with the problem of liberty and the protection of the republic from aristocratic perversion. In this sense, the revolution—and the concept of the republic itself—was not an exclusively ideological event; it was fundamentally tied to issues of property and wealth and the kind of social and political power they engendered in a society that sought to throw off lingering feudal arrangements .

12. In a strange way, this is the antithesis of Louis Hartz's argument of American exceptionalism. Essentially, it is clear that American radicals were deeply opposed to the feudal forms of life that they saw extant in Europe, and this, I think, decisively impacted the object of their radical critique. For an important discussion, see Becker, *The Declaration of Independence*, chap. 2.

13. Freyer, *Producers Versus Capitalists*, 8.

14. For an excellent discussion, see McCoy, *The Elusive Republic*.

15. For an important discussion, see Appleby, "Liberalism and the American Revolution," 1–25. Also see Wood, *The Radicalism of the American Revolution*, 325–347

16. See Wood, *The Radicalism of the American Revolution*.

17. The propertyless were the disenfranchised. As Charles Beard pointed out, "in 1787, we first encounter four groups whose economic status had a definite legal expression: the slaves, the indented servants, the mass of men who could not qualify for voting under the property tests imposed by the state constitutions and laws, and women, disenfranchised and subjected to the discriminations of the common law" (*An Economic Interpretation of the Constitution of the United States*, 24).

18. The literature on economic inequality in early northeastern American cities—where commerce was first taking root—shows a general picture of rising economic disparities between the poor and the wealthy. See Lemon and Nash, "The Distribution of Wealth in Eighteenth-Century America"; Nash, "Urban Wealth and Poverty in Pre-Revolutionary America"; Pencak, "The Social Structure of Revolutionary Boston"; Kulikoff, "The

Progress of Inequality in Revolutionary Boston"; Henretta, "Economic Development and Social Structure in Colonial Boston." For a dissenting view, see Warden, "Inequality and Instability in Eighteenth-Century Boston."

19. For a discussion, see Appleby, *Capitalism and a New Social Order*, 10–15.

20. For an analysis of the economic trends of inequality in this period, see the excellent work of Williamson and Lindert, *American Inequality*, 9–95. Also see Soltow, *Distribution of Wealth and Income in the United States in 1798*, 35–59.

21. See Barbara Clark Smith, "Food Rioters and the American Revolution."

22. For the importance of the discourse of letters on the political atmosphere of the revolutionary period, see Warner, *The Letters of the Republic*.

23. Quoted in Nash, "Urban Wealth and Poverty in Pre-Revolutionary America," 547.

24. *New York Gazette*, July 11, 1765.

25. For an historical discussion, see Becker, *The Declaration of Independence*.

26. For a discussion of leveling in the colonial period and its effect on the discourse on economic inequality, see Ingersoll, "'Riches and Honor Were Rejected by Them as Loathsome Vomit.'"

27. For an excellent discussion of these ideas, see Burke, *The Conundrum of Class*, 1–21.

28. *The Federalist*, no. 51, 339.

29. *The Federalist*, no. 10, 56.

30. Adams, *A Defense of Constitutions of Government of the United States*, 10.

31. For an important discussion, see Howe, *The Changing Political Thought of John Adams*, 133–92. Also see Soltow, *Distribution of Wealth and Income in the United States in 1798*, 18–22; and Dorfman, *The Economic Mind in American Civilization*, 417–33.

32. George Logan, "Five Letters Addressed to the Yeomanry of the United States," quoted in Burke, *The Conundrum of Class*, 39.

33. James Lyon, "To Aristocrats Generally," *National Magazine* 1 (1799): 14–15, quoted in Burke, *The Conundrum of Class*, 40.

34. Noah Webster, "An Examination into the Leading Principles of the Federal Constitution," 132.

35. Ibid., 134.

36. Ibid., 135–36.

37. Millar, *The Origin of the Distinction of Ranks*, 238. Millar's insights echo many of the ideas of the period. His link between commerce and liberty is decidedly liberal in nature: "Where-ever men of inferior condition are enabled to live in affluence by their own industry, and, in procuring their

2. THE LIBERAL REPUBLIC AND THE EMERGENCE OF CAPITALISM

livelihood, have little occasion to court the favour of their superiors, there we may expect that ideas of liberty will be universally diffused" (243).

38. For more on Jefferson's ideas on public and private morality and its Greek and Christian roots, see Sheldon, "Classical and Modern Influences on American Political Thought."

39. Hofstadter, *The Age of Reform*, chap. 1.

40. Jefferson, *Notes on the State of Virginia*, in *The Portable Thomas Jefferson*, 226.

41. Ibid., 217.

42. Ibid.

43. Jefferson, to James Madison, October 28, 1785, in *The Portable Thomas Jefferson*, 396.

44. Jefferson, "First Inaugural Address," in *The Portable Thomas Jefferson*, 293.

45. For an interesting discussion on Jefferson's concept of property and its relation to the ideas of Aristotle, see Jill Frank, "Integrating Public Good and Private Right."

46. Taylor, *An Inquiry into the Principles and Policy of the Government of the United States*, 434.

47. Tocqueville, *Democracy in America*, 582.

48. Ibid., 583.

49. Tocqueville lays this out explicitly: "I think that, taking the whole picture into consideration, one can assert that a slow, progressive rise in wages is one of the general laws characteristic of democratic societies. As conditions become more equal, wages rise; and as wages rise, conditions become more equal" (ibid.).

50. Ibid. Tocqueville was able to see the oppression of early American industrial capitalism quite clearly: "If by common accord they withhold their work, the master, who is rich, can easily wait without ruining himself until necessity brings them back to him. But as for them, they must work every day if they are not to die, for they scarcely have any property beyond their arms. They have long been impoverished by oppression, and increasing poverty makes them easier to oppress. This is the vicious circle from which they cannot escape" (ibid., 584).

51. For a more technical discussion of Quesnay's political economy, see Blaug, *Economic Theory in Retrospect*, 25–29.

52. Conkin, *Prophets of Prosperity*, 264.

53. This is the insight of Karren Orren: "The association of liberalism with market society, however, has created another false impression of rupture with the past. By emphasizing the disintegrating effects of capitalist development on the older institutions of feudalism, and identifying

liberalism as the ideology associated with that process, historical accounts of the rise of market society have tended to eclipse preliberal institutions that survived the transition. The two hyper-histories are mutually re-inforcing: The same institutions allegedly superseded by capitalism are those thought to have graced the United States by their absence" (*Belated Feudalism*, 10). For more on the remnants of feudalism in American labor law and workplace culture, see *Belated Feudalism*, 68–117.

54. For an excellent discussion of the problem of wealth inequality during the antebellum period, see Edward Pessen, *Riches, Class, and Power Before the Civil War* (Lexington, Mass.: D.C. Heath, 1973).

55. Skidmore, *The Rights of Man to Property!* 3–4.

56. Ibid., 5.

57. For an historical discussion, see Schultz, *The Republic of Labor*; and Wilentz, *Chants Democratic*.

58. As J. R. Pole has insightfully argued: "It was growing increasingly clear to the labor radicals of this age, and to the leaders of political and economic labor organizations, that the workers as a class would never enjoy equality of economic opportunity with their capitalist masters, and few of them would escape from their class; but they insisted all the more passionately on equality not because they could hope for more equal rewards but be-cause it was a metaphor for independence, control, and self-respect" (*The Pursuit of Equality in American History*, 167).

59. Fisk, "Capital Against Labor," 2.

60. Simpson, *The Working Man's Manual*, 145.

61. Ibid.

62. For a discussion, see Sellers, *The Market Revolution*.

63. Simpson, *The Working Man's Manual*, 162.

64. Ibid.

65. Byllesby, *Observations on the Sources and Effects of Unequal Wealth*, 24.

66. Ibid., 49.

67. Sedgwick, "What Is a Monopoly?" 222.

68. Henshaw, *Remarks upon the Rights and Powers of Corporations*, 163.

69. Ibid., 165.

70. Gouge, *A Short History of Paper Money*, 184.

71. Ibid.

72. Vethake, "The Doctrine of Anti-Monopoly," 231.

73. Ibid., 217.

74. Brownson, "The Laboring Classes," 49.

75. Pickering, *The Working Man's Political Economy*, 3, 6; emphasis in the original.

76. For an excellent discussion, see Kohl, *The Politics of Individualism*, 186–227; as well as Huston, *Securing the Fruits of Labor*, 259–95.

77. Leggett, "The Inequality of Human Condition," 163.

78. The emphasis on equality of opportunity would move to the forefront of the discourse on inequality later in the nineteenth century, when monopoly power was seen to be its main threat (for a discussion, see chapter 4). But the radicals of the early nineteenth century were more keen, in this regard, since they were able to point to the systemic moment when all forms of economic parity were lost: the move toward wage labor itself. For a discussion of equality of opportunity during the early republic and the early nineteenth century, see Pole, *The Pursuit of Equality in American History*, 150–62.

79. For a discussion of Byllesby and Carey and the historical context of their ideas, see Matson, "Economic Thought and the Early National Economy," 117–36.

80. Brownson, "The Laboring Classes," 52.

1. See Williamson, *Industrialism, Inequality, and Economic Growth*; as well as his *Did British Capitalism Breed Inequality?*.

2. For an excellent discussion, see Kasson, *Civilizing the Machine*, 53–106.

3. Sklar, *The Corporate Reconstruction of American Capitalism, 1890–1916*, 8.

4. See Chandler, "The Organization of Manufacturing and Transportation." Also see Chandler, *The Visible Hand*.

5. Godkin, "The Labor Crisis," 186, 188.

6. See Foner, *Free Soil, Free Labor, Free Men*.

7. For a discussion of the Radical Republicans and their debates on political and economic equality, see Foner, *Reconstruction*, 228–80.

8. See Foner, *Reconstruction*, 235.

9. DuBois, *The Souls of Black Folk*, 43–44.

10. For an important discussion of the differences among various black intellectual ideas of the period, see Wintz, ed., *African American Political Thought, 1890–1930*, 1–18.

11. See Carmichael and Hamilton, *Black Power*, 146–63.

12. DuBois, *Black Reconstruction in America*, 580–636.

13. George, *Progress and Poverty*, 282.

14. Ibid., 545.

15. For important discussions, see Pole, *The Pursuit of Equality in American History*, 254–83; John Thomas, *Alternative America*, 103–31; and Lustig, *Corporate Liberalism*, 57–77.

16. Sorge, "Socialism and the Worker," 207.
17. Most, "The Beast of Property," 213, 215.
18. Lloyd, *Wealth Against Commonwealth*, 1–2.

19. Ibid., 333.
20. The emergence of the "utopian novel" in the last quarter of the nine-teenth century was no mere coincidence. It came about as a direct result of the atomized social effects of early industrialism as well as the emergence of modernity in America. For an interesting discussion, see Forbes, "The Literary Quest for Utopia, 1880–1900."
21. It has also been argued that Bellamy's anti-individualist stance gave rise to a totalitarian impulse because he emphasized a bureaucratic solution—in place of a more social-democratic one—to the problems caused by lais-sez-faire. For this view, see Lipow, *Authoritarian Socialism in America*.
22. In his *Philosophy of Right*, Hegel argues that it is through what he terms the "universal class," or the bureaucracy, that the state will be able to manifest the collective will of society and the objective realization of human freedom vis-à-vis the state (§§ 260, 261). For Hegel, the state was the dialectical culmination of ethical life (*Sittlichkeit*), human freedom, and political modernity. It would overcome the social atomization of "civil society," and it would also strive toward a rational universalism based on the institutions of the state (*objektiver Geist*) and characterized by rational laws grounded in an ethical imperative toward human free-dom. Bellamy spent time in Germany in the winter of 1868–69, where he studied German socialism. The Hegelian themes in *Looking Backward* are certainly not coincidence.
23. Bellamy, *Looking Backward*, 89.
24. Ibid., 65–66.
25. Bellamy, *Equality*, 3.
26. Quoted in Pole, *The Pursuit of Equality in American History*, 266.
27. The classic account of this is Hofstadter, *Social Darwinism in American Thought*, 51–66. For a critical view of the extent to which conservatives during the Gilded Age actually relied upon Darwinian ideas and princi-ples, see Wyllie, *The Self Made Man*; as well as Bannister, "The Survival of the Fittest is Our Doctrine: History or Histrionics?"; and West, "Darwin's Public Policy."
28. For a discussion of this antiegalitarian tradition in early-nineteenth-cen-tury America, see Becker, *The Declaration of Independence*, 234–79.
29. Calhoun, *Disquisition on Government*, 56–57.
30. Calhoun, *Exposition and Protest*, quoted in Hofstadter, *The American Politi-cal Tradition*, 105. Also see the discussion in Ashworth, *Slavery, Capitalism, and Politics in the Antebellum Republic*, 1:201–10.

31. Sumner, *What Social Classes Owe to Each Other*, 29.

32. For a discussion, see Robert McCloskey, *American Conservatism in the Age of Enterprise*, 42–71.

33. Hofstadter, *The American Political Tradition*, 56.

34. Sumner, *What Social Classes Owe to Each Other*, 47.

35. Ibid., 46.

36. Jacoby, "American Exceptionalism Revisited." Also see Voss, *The Making of American Exceptionalism*.

37. Ely, *The Labor Movement in America*, ix–x.

38. Ibid., xi.

39. For a discussion of the expansion of the American state, see Skowronek, *Building a New American State*.

40. For a discussion of the debate on laissez-faire during the early twentieth century, see Barbara Fried, *The Progressive Assault on Laissez Faire*, 1–70.

41. Note the important discussion by Eisenach, *The Lost Promise of Progressivism*, 8–47.

42. For an important discussion of the antiradicalism of American Progressive intellectuals, see Kloppenberg, *Uncertain Victory*.

43. Croly, *The Promise of American Life*, 23.

44. Ibid., 380–81.

45. Weyl, *The New Democracy*, 162; emphasis added.

46. Ibid., 163–164.

47. Ibid., 164.

48. Croly, *The Promise of American Life*, 358–59.

49. See Spargo, *The Socialist*, 34–39 and 71–77.

50. For a discussion of the proletarianization of the American working class and its beginnings in the late nineteenth century, see Gordon, Edwards, and Reich, *Segmented Work, Divided Workers*.

51. Glickman, *A Living Wage*.

52. For a discussion, see Kazin, "The Workers' Party?"

53. Gompers, *Labor and the Common Welfare*.

54. For an interesting discussion of how this deradicalization of labor and capital was carried out in the Progressive and New Deal Eras in the realm of film, see Michael Rogin, "How the Working Class Saved Capitalism."

55. Arnold, *The Symbols of Government*, 259–60.

56. Arnold, *The Folklore of Capitalism*, 203.

57. It should be pointed out that Dewey's ideas about political economy were not particularly sophisticated. He still saw Henry George's ideas as possessing theoretical validity as he argued in one of his radio addresses in 1933 concerning the massive inequality of the day:

|216|

Go to the work of Henry George himself and learn how many of the troubles from which society still suffers, and suffers increasingly, are due to the fact that a few have monopolized the land, and that in consequence they have the power to dictate to others access to the land and to its products—which include waterpower, electricity, coal, iron and all minerals, as well as the foods that sustain life—and that they have the power to appropriate to their private use the values that the industry, the civilized order, the very benefactions, of others produce. This wrong is at the very basis of our present social and economic chaos, and until it is righted, all steps toward economic recovery may be temporarily helpful while in the long run useless.

| "STEPS TO ECONOMIC RECOVERY" |

58. Dewey, *The Public and Its Problems*, 15–16.
59. Dewey, "The Future of Liberalism."
60. Thurman Arnold remarks on this theme: "It is not sufficient to describe social institutions as one describes the organization of an anthill. Ants have no souls and we are writing this book for men who do have souls. Therefore something must be said to point out what men *should* believe in order to make them better, more cooperative, more just, and more comfortable" (*The Folklore of Capitalism*, 332).
61. For a discussion of the various policies enacted by Roosevelt and their impact on income and wealth distribution, see Edsforth, *The New Deal*, 235–52; and Lichtenstein, "From Corporatism to Collective Bargaining," 122–52. These views go against the idea that Roosevelt relied on certain sectors of capital—that is, those that were not labor intensive—to push through his economic reforms. For this view, see Thomas Ferguson, "Industrial Conflict and the Coming of the New Deal," 3–31.
62. For an excellent discussion, see Brinkley, *The End of Reform*, 137–74.
63. Norman Thomas, "Shall Labor Support Roosevelt?" For more extensive comments by Thomas on the New Deal, see *The Choice Before Us*, 83–127.
64. Dewey, "The Economic Basis of the New Society," 430.
65. See Orren, *Belated Feudalism*, 118–208.
66. For a discussion, see Sunstein, *The Second Bill of Rights*, 61–98. Sunstein argues that Roosevelt was not an egalitarian and was concerned with the issue of "security" over that of equality. But this is hard to argue in face of the kind of sweeping power that he gave to labor, and its ability to bargain collectively had a large impact on equalizing income distribution through the 1940s and 1950s.
67. John Bates Clark, "Monopoly and the Struggle of Classes," 141.

4. EMBRACING INEQUALITY

1. Welch, "In Defense of Inequality," 1.
2. For a discussion of the crisis of New Deal liberalism, see Brinkley, *The End of Reform*, 15–30.

3. See Schulman, *The Seventies*. For perspectives on this phenomenon from the point of view of political economy, see Sawyers and Tabb, eds. *Sunbelt/Snowbelt*. Also see Trubowitz, *Defining the National Interest*, 169–234.
4. Phillips, *The Emerging Republican Majority*.
5. John Kenneth Galbraith, *The New Industrial State*, 398.
6. Lizabeth Cohen, *A Consumers' Republic*, 9.
7. Krugman, "For Richer."
8. For a discussion, see Thomas Frank, *One Market Under God*, 1–50; and Bruce J. Schulman, *The Seventies*, 102–20.
9. For an important discussion of Knight's ethical and economic ideas, see Kasper, *The Revival of Laissez-Faire in American Macroeconomic Theory*, 7–28.
10. The evolution of libertarian and laissez-faire ideas within European social and economic thought in the late nineteenth and early twentieth centuries cannot be fully investigated here. For a discussion, see Infantino, *Individualism in Modern Thought*, 100–131.
11. Mises, *Liberalism*, 10.
12. Ibid., 31.
13. Ibid., 32–33.
14. See Finis Welch, "In Defense of Inequality," for an excellent summary of this position in a more contemporary context.
15. Menger, *Principles of Economics*, 121.
16. For a discussion of Hayek's ideas about epistemology, see Gray, *Hayek on Liberty*, 1–26; as well as Kasper, *The Revival of Laissez-Faire*, 46–53.
17. Hayek, *Individualism and Economic Order*, 14.
18. Ibid., 7.
19. Hayek, *The Constitution of Liberty*, 87.
20. For a discussion of Hayek's ideas in this regard, see Hoover, *Economics as Ideology*, 203–18.
21. Hayek, *The Constitution of Liberty*, p. 93.
22. Friedman, *Free to Choose*, 135.
23. Friedman, *Capitalism and Freedom*, 166.
24. For an important discussion, see Bronner, *Ideas in Action*, 55–67.
25. Friedman, *Capitalism and Freedom*, 172.
26. Friedman, *Free to Choose*, 134–35.
27. Friedman, *Capitalism and Freedom*, 29.

28. See Hayek's discussion of liberty in *The Constitution of Liberty*, 11–61.

29. Friedman, *Capitalism and Freedom*, 5.

30. For an important discussion, see Orren, *Belated Feudalism*.

31. The classic analysis of this phenomenon remains Piven and Cloward, *Regulating the Poor*, 248–340.

32. The classic analysis of the ideas from this period is Halévy, *The Growth of Philosophic Radicalism*; for a specific discussion of the utilitarian and liberal theories that thinkers such as Hayek and Friedman invoke, see 120–50.

33. For a discussion, see Noble, *The Collapse of Liberalism*, 14–18.

34. For an important discussion, see Munkirs, *The Transformation of American Capitalism*, 8–50.

35. See Harrison and Sum, "The Theory of 'Dual' or Segmented Labor Markets"; and Moore, *Labor Market Segmentation and Its Implications*.

36. For a discussion, see Lizabeth Cohen, *A Consumers' Republic*, 200–256.

37. Rae, "Democratic Liberty and Tyrannies of Place." Also see Sugrue, "The Structures of Urban Poverty." For more on inequalities within urban areas, see Bobo, ed., *Prismatic Metropolis*; as well as O'Connor, Tilly, and Bobo, eds., *Urban Inequality*.

38. Shapiro, "Why the Poor Don't Soke the Rich.".

39. For recent perspectives on deindustrialization, see Cowie and Heathcott, eds., *Beyond the Ruins*; also Bluestone and Harrison, *The Deindustrialization of America*.

40. For an important discussion, see Aronowitz, *How Class Works*, 23–37; as well as Mills, "The Sociology of Stratification," 305–23. Also see the important analysis by Danziger and Gottschalk, *America Unequal*, 124–50.

41. See the discussion in chapter 3 of the present work.

42. The most important of these studies include: McClosky and Zaller, *The American Ethos*; Verba and Orren, *Equality in America*; Kluegel and Smith, *Beliefs About Inequality*; and Hochschild, *Facing Up to the American Dream*. Also see Glazer, "On Americans and Inequality"; and Samuelson, "Indifferent to Inequality?".

43. See McCloskey and Zaller, *The American Ethos*; as well as Samuelson, "Indifferent to Inequality?"

44. Kluegel and Smith, *Beliefs About Inequality*, 5–6. As Stanley Aronowitz has acutely observed concerning this same theme: "Many Americans take 'equality of opportunity' literally. They believe that being born poor or working class is not economic destiny, that with a combination of luck and hard work . . . they can get rich or at least achieve economic security" (*How Class Works*, 15).

45. For a discussion of this change in macroeconomic thought, see Smithin, *Macroeconomics After Thatcher and Reagan*.

46. Epstein, "Against Redress," 45.

47. Larry Bartels refers to this narrow, misinformed self-interest as "unenlightened self-interest." See his "Homer Gets a Tax Cut."

48. For an important analysis, see McCall, *Complex Inequality*.

CONCLUSION. RESTATING THE CASE FOR ECONOMIC EQUALITY

1. Thomas Frank seeks to analyze this problem as well in *What's the Matter with Kansas?*

2. For a discussion about the turn away from inequality as a concern in modern American politics, see Madrick, "Inequality and Democracy."

3. For a discussion or this aspect of republicanism in early American political thought, see Wood, *The Radicalism of the American Revolution*, 95–145 and 169–89. For a discussion of republican ideas among the early working-class movements, see Wilentz, *Chants Democratic*, as well as Schultz, *The Republic of Labor*.

4. It is important to note that Karren Orren argues that liberal ideas served to attack preliberal institutions in the workplace. See *Belated Feudalism*.

5. For example, see Maynor, *Republicanism in the Modern World*, as well as Viroli, *Republicanism*. For a critical account of both, see Lock, "Review of Maynor and Viroli."

6. Richard Dagger has called this synthesis of autonomy and public good "republican liberalism." See his *Civic Virtues*, 11–25.

7. See Pettit, *Republicanism*, 51–110, as well as Honohan, *Civic Republicanism*, 180–231.

8. Hegel made a distinction between *Moralität*, by which he meant a Kantian, modern form of ethical autonomy, and *Sittlichkeit*, which he defined as a combination of the Aristotelian Greek polis and the secularized version of community derived from Protestantism (as opposed to the otherworldly morality that defined Catholic community in the form of *Heiligkeit*). From Hegel, the idea that rights matter, but within their social and historical *context*, is essential: hence the preservation of individual autonomy and public goods through the institutionalization of the state. For an interesting discussion, see Steven B. Smith, *Hegel's Critique of Liberalism*, 232–46.

9. At about the same time that Dewey was making these arguments, Emile Durkheim was doing the same. See his *Professional Ethics and Civic Morals*, 1–41. Durkheim's emphasis was on the need to prevent modern economic life from ripping apart social cohesion through the amoral logic of the market. "If we follow no rule except that of a clear self-interest, in the occupations that take up nearly the whole of our time, how should we

acquire a taste for any disinterestedness, or selflessness or sacrifice? Let us see, then, how the unleashing of interests has been accompanied by a debasing of public morality" (12). In so doing, he emphasized—not unlike Hegel—the importance of worker "corporations," or the emergence of a "corporate system" that would help in pushing the state to regulate economic life: "A corpus of rules has to be laid down, fixing the stint of work, the pay of the members of staff and their obligations to one another, to the community, and so on" (30–31).

10. Dewey, "The Future of Liberalism," 227–28.

11. Ibid., 230.

12. Mickey Kaus calls for an enhancement of civic institutions as an exclusive way of combating inequality, which he calls "civic liberalism." See *The End of Equality*.

13. Simpson, *The Working Man's Manual*, 138.

14. See Pettit, *Republicanism*, 17–79.

15. See Leydier, "Dimensions of Inequality in French and British Political Discourses."

| Bibliography |

Adams, John. *A Defense of Constitutions of Government of the United States*. In *Complete Works*, vol. 6. Boston: Little, Brown and Co., 1850.

Appleby, Joyce. *Capitalism and a New Social Order: The Republican Vision of the 1790's*. New York: NYU Press, 1983.

——. "Liberalism and the American Revolution." *New England Quarterly* 49 (1976).

——. "Republicanism in Old and New Contexts." *The William and Mary Quarterly* 43 (1986).

Aristotle. *Nicomachean Ethics*. Loeb Classical Library. Cambridge, Mass.: Harvard University Press, 1987.

——. *Politics*. Loeb Classical Library. Cambridge, Mass.: Harvard University Press, 1981.

Arnold, Matthew. *The Poetry and Criticism of Matthew Arnold*. Boston: Houghton Mifflin, 1961.

Arnold, Thurman. *The Folklore of Capitalism*. New Haven, Conn.: Yale University Press, 1937.

——. *The Symbols of Government*. New Haven, Conn.: Yale University Press, 1935.

Aronowitz, Stanley. *How Class Works: Power and Social Movement*. New Haven, Conn.: Yale University Press, 2003.

Ashworth, John. *Slavery, Capitalism, and Politics in the Antebellum Republic*. Vol. 1. New York: Cambridge University Press, 1995.

Atkinson, Anthony B. "Bringing Income Distribution in from the Cold." *Economic Journal* 107 (March 1997).

Austin, Michel, and Pierre Vidal-Naquet. *Economic and Social History of Ancient Greece: An Introduction*. Berkeley: University of California Press, 1977.

Avineri, Shlomo. *Hegel's Theory of the Modern State*. Cambridge: Cambridge University Press, 1972.

——. *The Social and Political Thought of Karl Marx*. Cambridge: Cambridge University Press, 1968.

Bailyn, Bernard. *The Ideological Origins of the American Revolution*. Cambridge, Mass.: Harvard University Press, 1967.

Balot, Ryan. *Greed and Injustice in Classical Athens*. Princeton, N.J.: Princeton University Press, 2001.

Banning, Lance. "Jeffersonian Ideology Revisited: Liberal and Classical Ideas in the New American Republic." *The William and Mary Quarterly* 43 (1986).

———. "Republican Ideology and the Triumph of the Constitution, 1789 to 1793." *The William and Mary Quarterly* 31 (1974).

Bannister, Robert C. "The Survival of the Fittest is Our Doctrine: History or Histrionics?" *Journal of the History of Ideas* 31, no. 3 (1970).

Barker, Ernest. *Greek Political Theory: Plato and His Predecessors*. London: Methuen & Co., 1947.

Bartels, Larry. "Homer Gets a Tax Cut: Inequality and Public Policy in the American Mind." *Perspectives on Politcs* 3, no. 1 (March 2005).

Beard, Charles. *An Economic Interpretation of the Constitution of the United States*. 1913. New York: The Free Press, 1986.

Becker, Carl L. *The Declaration of Independence: A Study in the History of Political Ideas*. New York: Vintage, 1970.

Bellamy, Edward. *Equality*. New York: D. Appleton and Company, 1897.

———. *Looking Backward, 2000–1887*. New York: Penguin Books, 1986.

Birkhead, John Andrew. "Property and *Amour Propre*: Rousseau's Pastoral." Ph.D. diss., Stanford University, 1994.

Blau, Joel, ed. *Social Theories of Jacksonian Democracy*. Cambridge: Hackett Publishers, 2003.

Blaug, Mark. *Economic Theory in Retrospect*. Cambridge: Cambridge University Press, 1979.

Bluestone, Barry, and Bennett Harrison. *The Deindustrialization of America*. New York: Basic Books, 1982.

Bobo, Lawrence. *Prismatic Metropolis: Inequality in Los Angeles*. New York: Russell Sage Foundation, 2000.

Böröcz, Jószef. "*Stand* Reconstructed: Contingent Structure and Institutional Change." *Sociological Theory* 15, no. 3 (November 1997).

Brinkley, Alan. *The End of Reform: New Deal Liberalism in Recession and War*. New York: Vintage Press, 1996.

Bronner, Stephen Eric. *Ideas in Action*. Lanham, Md.: Rowman and Littlefield, 1999.

———. *Reclaiming the Enlightenment: Toward a Politics of Radical Engagement*. New York: Columbia University Press, 2004.

Brownson, Orestes. "The Laboring Classes." In *The Brownson Reader*, ed. Alvan Ryan. New York: P. J. Kennedy & Sons, 1955.

Burke, Martin J. *The Conundrum of Class*. Chicago: University of Chicago Press, 1996.

Byllesby, Langton. *Observations on the Sources and Effects of Unequal Wealth.* 1826. New York: Russell & Russell, 1961.

Calhoun, John C. *Disquisition on Government.* In *Works of John C. Calhoun,* vol. 1. New York: Russell and Russell, 1968.

Carmichael, Stokely, and Charles V. Hamilton. *Black Power: The Politics of Liberation in America.* New York: Random House, 1967.

Chandler, Alfred. "The Organization of Manufacturing and Transportation." In *Economic Change in Civil War Era,* ed. David Gilchrest and W. David Lewis. Greenville, Del.: Eleutherian Mills-Hagley Foundation, 1965.

——. *The Visible Hand: The Managerial Revolution in American Business.* Cambridge, Mass.: Harvard University Press, 1977.

Cicero. *De officiis* Loeb Classical Library. Cambridge, Mass.: Harvard University Press, 1988.

——. *De re publica* Loeb Classical Library. Cambridge, Mass.: Harvard University Press, 1988.

Clark, John Bates. "Monopoly and the Struggle of Classes." In Robert LaFollette, ed., *The Making of America.* 1905. New York: Arno Press, 1969.

Cohen, Jean, and Andrew Arato. *Civil Society and Political Theory.* Cambridge, Mass.: MIT Press, 1992.

Cohen, Lizabeth. *A Consumers' Republic: The Politics of Mass Consumption in Postwar America.* New York: Knopf, 2003.

Conkin, Paul. *Prophets of Prosperity.* Bloomington: Indiana University Press, 1980.

Cowie, Jefferson, and Joseph Heathcott, eds. *Beyond the Ruins: The Meanings of Deindustrialization.* Ithaca, N.Y.: ILR Books, 2003.

Croly, Herbert. *The Promise of American Life.* 1909. New York: Macmillan Co., 1963.

Dagger, Richard. *Civic Virtues: Rights, Citizenship, and Republican Liberalism.* New York: Oxford University Press, 1997.

Dann, Otto. *Gleichheit und Gleichberechtigung: Das Gleichheitspostulat in der alteuropäischen Tradition und in Deutschland bis zum ausgehenden 19. Jahrhundert.* Berlin: Duncker & Humboldt, 1980.

Danziger, Sheldon, and Peter Gottschalk. *America Unequal.* Cambridge, Mass.: Harvard University Press, 1995.

Deere, Donald R., and Finis Welch. "Inequality, Incentives, and Opportunity." In *Should Differences in Income and Wealth Matter?* ed. Ellen Frankel Paul, Fred D. Miller Jr., and Jeffrey Paul. New York: Cambridge University Press, 2002.

Denton, Nancy, and Douglas Massey. *American Apartheid.* Cambridge, Mass.: Harvard University Press, 2001.

Dewey, John. "The Economic Basis of the New Society." In *Intelligence in the Modern World*. New York: Random House, 1939.

——. "The Future of Liberalism." *The Journal of Philosophy* 22, no. 9 (1935).

——. *The Public and Its Problems*. 1927. Athens: Ohio University Press, 1954.

——. "Steps to Economic Recovery." Radio address. WEVD, New York, N.Y., April 28, 1933, 8:45 P.M. Text at: http://www.wealthandwant.com/docs/Dewey_Steps.htm. Accessed December 9, 2006.

Dienstag, Joshua Foa. "Serving God and Mammon: The Lockean Sympathy in Early American Political Thought." *American Political Science Review* 90, no. 3 (1996).

Diesing, Paul. *Hegel's Dialectical Political Economy: A Contemporary Application*. Boulder, Colo.: Westview Press, 1999.

Diggins, John Patrick. *The Lost Soul of American Politics: Virtue, Self-Interest, and the Foundations of Liberalism*. New York: Basic Books, 1984.

Dorfman, Joseph. *The Economic Mind in American Civilization, vol. 1, 1606–1865*. New York: Viking Press, 1946.

DuBois, W. E. B. *Black Reconstruction in America: 1860–1880*. New York: Atheneum, 1962.

——. *The Souls of Black Folk*. New York: The Modern Library, 2003.

Durkheim, Emile. *Professional Ethics and Civic Morals*. Glencoe, Ill.: The Free Press, 1958.

Dworetz, Steven. *The Unvarnished Doctrine: Locke, Liberalism, and the American Revolution*. Durham: Duke University Press, 1990.

Edsforth, Ronald. *The New Deal: America's Response to the Great Depression*. New York: Blackwell, 2000.

Eisenach, Eldon. *The Lost Promise of Progressivism*. Lawrence: University Press of Kansas, 1994.

Ely, Richard T. *The Labor Movement in America*. 1886. New York: Arno Press, 1969.

Epstein, Richard. "Against Redress." *Daedelus* (Winter 2002).

The Federalist. New York: The Modern Library, 1933.

Ferguson, John. *Utopias of the Classical World*. Ithaca, N.Y.: Cornell University Press, 1975.

Ferguson, Thomas. "Industrial Conflict and the Coming of the New Deal: The Triumph of Multinational Liberalism in America." In *The Rise and Fall of the New Deal Order, 1930–1980*, ed. Steve Fraser and Gary Gerstle. Princeton, N.J.: Princeton University Press, 1989.

Fink, Z. S. *The Classical Republic: An Essay on the Recovery of a Pattern of Thought in Seventeenth-Century England*. Evanston, Ill.: Northwestern University Press, 1962.

Finley, Moses. *The Ancient Economy*. Berkeley: University of California Press, 1999.

———. *Politics in the Ancient World*. New York: Cambridge University Press, 1983.

Fisk, Theophilus. "Capital Against Labor: An Address Delivered at Julien Hall Before the Mechanics of Boston on Wednesday Evening, May 20, 1835." *New York Evening Post*, August 6, 1835.

Foner, Eric. *Free Soil, Free Labor, Free Men: The Ideology of the Republican Party Before the Civil War*. New York: Oxford University Press, 1995.

———. *Reconstruction: America's Unfinished Revolution, 1863–1877*. New York: Perennial Classics, 1989.

Forbes, Allyn B. "The Literary Quest for Utopia, 1880–1900." *Social Forces* 6, no. 2 (1983).

Franco, Paul. *Hegel's Philosophy of Freedom*. New Haven, Conn.: Yale University Press, 2000.

Frank, Jill. "Integrating Public Good and Private Right: The Virtue of Property." In *Aristotle and Modern Politics: The Persistence of Political Philosophy*, ed. Aristide Tessitore. South Bend, Ind.: University of Notre Dame Press, 2002.

Frank, Thomas. *One Market Under God: Extreme Capitalism, Market Populism, and the End of Economic Democracy*. New York: Doubleday, 2000.

———. *What's the Matter with Kansas?* New York: Metropolitan Books, 2004.

Fraser, Steve, and Gary Gerstle, eds. *The Rise and Fall of the New Deal Order, 1930–1980*. Princeton, N.J.: Princeton University Press, 1989.

Freeman, Richard B. *The New Inequality: Creating Solutions for Poor America*. Boston: Beacon Press, 1999.

Freeman, Richard B., and Lawrence Katz. "Rising Wage Inequality: The United States Versus Other Advanced Countries." In *Working Under Different Rules*, ed. Richard B. Freeman. New York: Russell Sage Foundation, 1993.

Freyer, Tony. *Producers Versus Capitalists: Constitutional Conflict in Antebellum America*. Charlottesville: University Press of Virginia, 1994.

Fried, Albert, ed. *Socialism in America: From the Shakers to the Third International*. New York: Columbia University Press, 1992.

Fried, Barbara. *The Progressive Assault on Laissez Faire: Robert Hale and the First Law and Economics Movement*. Cambridge, Mass.: Harvard University Press, 1998.

Friedman, Milton. *Capitalism and Freedom*. Chicago: University of Chicago Press, 1982.

———. *Free to Choose*. New York: Harcourt Brace Jovanovich, 1979.

Fuks, Alexander. "Agis, Cleomenes, and Equality." *Classical Philology* 57, no. 3 (1962).

——. "Patterns and Types of Social-Economic Revolution in Greece from the Fourth to the Second Century B.C." *Ancient Society* 5 (1974).

——. "Redistribution of Land and Houses in Syracuse in 356 B.C., and Its Ideological Aspects." *The Classical Quarterly* 18, no. 2 (1968).

Fukuyama, Francis. *The End of History and the Last Man.* New York: The Free Press, 1992.

Galbraith, James K. *Created Unequal: The Crisis in American Pay.* New York: The Free Press, 1998.

Galbraith, John Kenneth. *The New Industrial State.* Boston: Houghton Mifflin, 1967.

George, Henry. *Progress and Poverty.* New York: Robert Schalkenbach Foundation, 1938.

Gilbert, Geoffrey. "Adam Smith on the Nature and Causes of Poverty." *Review of Social Economy* (Fall 1997).

Glazer, Nathan. "On Americans and Inequality." *Daedelus* 132 (2003).

Glickman, Lawrence B. *A Living Wage: American Workers and the Making of Consumer Society.* Ithaca, N.Y.: Cornell University Press, 1997.

Godkin, E. L. "The Labor Crisis." *North American Review* 105 (July 1867).

Goldsmith, Oliver. *Poetical Works of Oliver Goldsmith.* London: William Pickering, 1851.

Gompers, Samuel. *Labor and the Common Welfare.* New York: E. P. Dutton & Company, 1919.

Gordon, David M., Richard Edwards, and Michael Reich. *Segmented Work, Divided Workers: The Historical Transformation of Labor in the United States.* Cambridge: Cambridge University Press, 1982.

Gouge, William. *A Short History of Paper Money and Banking in the United States.* In *Social Theories of Jacksonian Democracy,* ed. Joel Blau. Cambridge: Hackett Publishers, 2003.

Gray, John. *Hayek on Liberty.* Oxford: Blackwell, 1985.

Green, Philip. *The Pursuit of Inequality.* New York: Pantheon Books, 1981.

Halévy, Elie. *The Growth of Philosophic Radicalism.* Boston: Beacon Press, 1960.

Harrington, James. *Commonwealth of Oceana.* New York: Cambridge University Press, 1992.

Harrison, Bennett, and Andrew Sum. "The Theory of 'Dual' or Segmented Labor Markets." *Journal of Economic Issues* 13, no. 3 (1979).

Hartz, Louis. *The Liberal Tradition in America.* New York: Harcourt, 1991.

Hayek, Friedrich. *The Constitution of Liberty.* Chicago: University of Chicago Press, 1960.

——. *Individualism and Economic Order*. Chicago: University of Chicago Press, 1948.

Hegel, G. W. F. *Lectures on Natural Right and Political Science*. Berkeley: University of California Press, 1995.

——. *Philosophy of Right*. New York: Prometheus Books, 1996.

Heideking, Jürgen, and James Henretta, eds. *Republicanism and Liberalism in America and the German States, 1750–1850*. New York: Cambridge University Press, 2002.

Henretta, James. "Economic Development and Social Structure in Colonial Boston." *The William and Mary Quarterly* 22 (1965).

Henshaw, David. *Remarks upon the Rights and Powers of Corporations, and of the Rights, Powers, and Duties of the Legislature Toward Them*. In *Social Theories of Jacksonian Democracy*, ed. Joel Blau. Cambridge: Hackett Publishers, 2003.

Hilton, Rodney. *Bond Men Made Free: Medieval Peasant Movements and the English Rising of 1381*. London: 1973.

Hirschman, Albert. *The Passions and the Interests: Political Arguments for Capitalism before its Triumph*. Princeton, N.J.: Princeton University Press, 1972.

——. *Rival Views of Market Society*. Cambridge, Mass.: Harvard University Press, 1992.

Hochschild, Jennifer. *Facing Up to the American Dream: Race, Class, and the Soul of the Nation*. Princeton, N.J.: Princeton University Press, 1995.

Hofstadter, Richard. *The Age of Reform*. New York: Vintage, 1955.

——. *The American Political Tradition and the Men Who Made It*. New York: Vintage Press, 1989.

——. *Social Darwinism in American Thought*. New York: George Braziller, Inc., 1965.

Honohan, Iseult. *Civic Republicanism*. London: Routledge, 2002.

Hoover, Kenneth R. *Economics as Ideology*. Lanham, Md.: Rowman and Littlefield, 2003.

Howe, John R. Jr. *The Changing Political Thought of John Adams*. Princeton, N.J.: Princeton University Press, 1966.

Hume, David. "Idea of a Perfect Commonwealth." In *David Hume: Essays Moral, Political, and Literary*. Indianapolis: The Liberty Fund, 1985.

——. "Of Commerce." In *David Hume: Writings on Economics*, ed. Eugene Rotwein. Madison: University of Wisconsin Press, 1970.

Huston, James L. *Securing the Fruits of Labor*. Baton Rouge: Louisiana State University Press, 1998.

Infantino, Lorenzo. *Individualism in Modern Thought: From Adam Smith to Hayek*. London: Routledge, 1998.

Ingersoll, Thomas. "'Riches and Honor Were Rejected by Them as Loathsome Vomit': The Fear of Levelling in New England." In *Inequality in Early America*, ed. Carla Gardina Pestana and Sharon V. Salinger. Hanover: University Press of New England, 1999.

Isocrates. *Areopagiticus*. Loeb Classical Library. Cambridge, Mass.: Harvard University Press, 1986.

Israel, Jonathan. *Radical Enlightenment*. New York: Oxford University Press, 2001.

Jacoby, Sanford. "American Exceptionalism Revisited: The Importance of Management." In *Masters to Managers: Historical and Comparative Perspectives on American Employers*, ed. Sanford M. Jacoby. New York: Columbia University Press, 1991.

Jefferson, Thomas. *The Portable Thomas Jefferson*. Ed. Merrill Peterson. New York: Viking Press, 1975.

Jones, Gareth Stedman. *An End to Poverty? A Historical Debate*. London: Profile Books, 2004.

Kasper, Sherryl Davis. *The Revival of Laissez-Faire in American Macroeconomic Theory: A Case Study of the Pioneers*. Cheltenham, U.K.: Edward Elgar, 2002.

Kasson, John. *Civilizing the Machine: Technology and Republican Values in America, 1776–1900*. New York: Penguin Books, 1976.

Katz, Michael B., ed., *The Underclass Debate*. Princeton, N.J.: Princeton University Press, 1993.

Kaus, Mickey. *The End of Equality*. New York: Basic Books, 1992.

Kazin, Michael. "The Workers' Party?" *New York Times*, October 19, 1995.

Kerber, Linda. "The Republican Ideology of the Revolutionary Generation." *American Quarterly* 37, no. 4 (1985).

Kloppenberg, James T. *Uncertain Victory: Social Democracy and Progressivism in European and American Thought*. New York: Oxford University Press, 1986.

——. "The Virtues of Liberalism: Christianity, Republicanism, and Ethics in Early American Political Discourse." *Journal of American History*, no. 74 (1987).

Kluegel, James, and Eliot Smith. *Beliefs About Inequality: Americans' Views of What Is and What Ought to Be*. New York: Aldine de Gruyter, 1986.

Kohl, Lawrence Frederick. *The Politics of Individualism*. New York: Oxford University Press, 1989.

Kornfeld, Eve. "From Republicanism to Liberalism: The Intellectual Journey of David Ramsay." *Journal of the Early Republic* 9 (1989).

Kramnick, Isaac. *Republicanism and Bourgeois Radicalism: Political Ideology in Late-Eighteenth-Century England and America*. Ithaca, N.Y.: Cornell University Press, 1990.

Krugman, Paul. "For Richer: How the Permissive Capitalism of the Boom Destroyed American Equality." *New York Times Magazine*, October 20, 2002.

Kulikoff, Allan. "The Progress of Inequality in Revolutionary Boston." *The William and Mary Quarterly* 28, no. 3 (1971).

———. "The Transition to Capitalism in Rural America." *The William and Mary Quarterly* 46, no. 1 (1989).

LaFollette, Robert, ed. *The Making of America*. 1905. New York: Arno Press, 1969.

Lakoff, Sanford. *Equality in Political Philosophy*. Cambridge, Mass.: Harvard University Press, 1964.

Laski, Harold. *The Rise of Liberalism: The Philosophy of a Business Civilization*. New York: Harper and Brothers, 1936.

Leggett, William. "The Inequality of Human Condition." In *A Collection of the Political Writings of William Leggett*. Vol. 2. New York: Taylor & Todd, 1840.

Lemon, James, and Gary Nash. "The Distribution of Wealth in Eighteenth-Century America: A Century of Changes in Chester County Pennsylvania, 1693–1802." *Journal of Social History* 2, no. 1 (1968).

Leyden, Wolfgang von. *Aristotle on Equality and Justice: His Political Argument*. New York: St. Martin's Press, 1985.

Leydier, Gilles. "Dimensions of Inequality in French and British Political Discourses Since the Early 80s." In *Discourse on Inequality in France and Britain*, ed. John Edwards and Jean-Paul Révauger. Aldershot, U.K.: Ashgate, 1998.

Lichtenstein, Nelson. "From Corporatism to Collective Bargaining: Organized Labor and the Eclipse of Social Democracy in the Postwar Era." In *The Rise and Fall of the New Deal Order, 1930–1980*, ed. Steve Fraser and Gary Gerstle. Princeton, N.J.: Princeton University Press, 1989.

Lintott, Andrew. *Violence, Civil Strife, and Revolution in the Classical City*. London: Croom Helm, 1982.

Lipow, Arthur. *Authoritarian Socialism in America: Edward Bellamy and the Nationalist Movement*. Berkeley: University of California Press, 1982.

Lloyd, Henry Demarest. *Wealth Against Commonwealth*. Washington, D.C.: National Home Library Foundation, 1936.

Lock, Grahame. "Review of Maynor and Viroli." *Acta Politica* 40 (2005).

Lustig, Jeffrey. *Corporate Liberalism: The Origins of Modern American Political Theory, 1890–1920*. Berkeley: University of California Press, 1982.

Luther, Martin. "Concerning Christian Liberty." Trans. R. S. Grignon. In *Harvard Classics*, ed. Charles W. Eliot, vol. 36, 336–78. New York: P. F. Collier & Son, 1910.

Machiavelli, Niccolò. *Discorsi sopra la prima deca di Tito Livio*. Milan: Biblioteca Universale Rizzoli, 2000.

MacPherson, C. B. *The Political Theory of Possessive Individualism*. Oxford: Oxford University Press, 1964.

——. *The Rise and Fall of Economic Justice and Other Essays*. New York: Oxford University Press, 1987.

Madrick, Jeff. "Inequality and Democracy." In *The Fight Is for Democracy*, ed. George Packer. New York: Harper Perennial, 2003.

Marx, Karl. *Economic and Philosophical Manuscripts*. In *The Marx-Engels Reader*, ed. Robert Tucker. New York: W. W. Norton & Co., 1978.

Matson, Cathy D. "Economic Thought and the Early National Economy." In *Wages of Independence: Capitalism in the Early American Republic*, ed. Paul A Gilje. Madison, Wis.: Madison House, 1997.

Maynor, John. *Republicanism in the Modern World*. Cambridge: Polity Press, 2003.

McCall, Leslie. *Complex Inequality: Gender, Class, and Race in the New Economy*. New York: Routledge, 2001.

McCarthy, George E. *Classical Horizons: The Origins of Sociology in Ancient Greece*. Albany: SUNY Press, 2003.

McCloskey, Robert Green. *American Conservatism in the Age of Enterprise, 1865–1910*. New York: Harpers Torchbooks, 1964.

McClosky, Herbert, and John Zaller. *The American Ethos: Public Attitudes Toward Capitalism and Democracy*. Cambridge, Mass.: Harvard University Press, 1984.

McCoy, Drew. *The Elusive Republic: Political Economy in Jeffersonian America*. New York: W. W. Norton, 1982.

Menger, Carl. *Principles of Economics*. New York: New York Univeristy Press, 1950.

Millar, John. *Origin of the Distinction of Ranks*. 1771. Indianapolis: Liberty Fund, 2006.

Mills, C. Wright. "The Sociology of Stratification." In *Power, Politics, and People: The Collected Essays of C. Wright Mills*, ed. Irving Louis Horowitz. London: Oxford University Press, 1967.

Mises, Ludwig von. *Liberalism: A Socio-Economic Exposition*. 1927. Kansas City, Mo.: Sheed Andrews and McMeel, 1978.

Montesquieu. *The Spirit of Laws*. Trans. Thomas Nugent. New York: Hafner Press, 1975.

Moore, Dahlia. *Labor Market Segmentation and Its Implications: Inequality, Deprivation, and Entitlement*. New York: Garland Publishers, 1992.

Most, Johann. "The Beast of Property." In *Socialism in America: From the Shakers to the Third International*, ed. Albert Fried. New York: Columbia University Press, 1992.

Muller, Jerry Z. *The Mind and the Market: Capitalism in Western Thought*. New York: Anchor Books, 2002.

Munkirs, John R. *The Transformation of American Capitalism*. Armonk, N.Y.: M. E. Sharpe, 1985.

Nash, Gary. "Urban Wealth and Poverty in Pre-Revolutionary America." *Journal of Interdisciplinary History* 6, no. 4 (1976).

Nelson, Eric. *The Greek Tradition in Republican Thought*. New York: Cambridge University Press, 2004.

Neuhouser, Frederick. *Foundations of Hegel's Social Theory: Actualizing Freedom*. Cambridge, Mass.: Harvard University Press, 2000.

Nippel, Wilfried. *Mischverfassungstheorie und Verfassungsrealität in Antike und früher Neuzeit*. Stuttgart: Klett-Cotta, 1980.

Noble, Charles. *The Collapse of Liberalism*. Lanham, Md.: Rowman and Littlefield, 2004.

O'Connor, Alice, Chris Tilly, and Lawrence Bobo, eds. *Urban Inequality: Evidence from Four Cities*. New York: Russell Sage Foundation, 2001.

Orren, Karen. *Belated Feudalism: Labor, Law, and Liberal Development in the United States*. New York: Cambridge University Press, 1991.

Palmer, R. R. *The Age of Democratic Revolution: A Political History of Europe and America, 1760–1800*. Vol. 1. Princeton, N.J.: Princeton University Press, 1959.

Pencak, William. "The Social Structure of Revolutionary Boston: Evidence From the Great Fire of 1760." *Journal of Interdisciplinary History* 10, no. 2 (1979).

Pessen, Edward. *Riches, Class, and Power Before the Civil War*. Lexington, Mass.: D. C. Heath, 1973.

Pettit, Philip. *Republicanism: A Theory of Freedom and Government*. New York: Oxford University Press 1997.

Phillips, Kevin. *The Emerging Republican Majority*. New Rochelle, N.Y.: Arlington House, 1969.

——. *Wealth and Democracy: A Political History of the American Rich*. New York: Broadway Books, 2002.

Pickering, John. *The Working Man's Political Economy*. 1847. New York: Arno Press, 1971.

Piven, Frances Fox, and Richard Cloward. *Regulating the Poor: The Functions of Public Welfare*. New York: Pantheon Press, 1971.

Plato. *Laws*. Loeb Classical Library. Cambridge, Mass.: Harvard University Press, 1988.

———. *Republic*. Loeb Classical Library. Cambridge, Mass.: Harvard University Press, 1988.

Pocock, J. G. A. *The Machiavellian Moment: Florentine Political Thought and the Atlantic Republican Tradition*. Princeton, N.J.: Princeton University Press, 1975.

Pöhlmann, Robert von. *Geschichte der Sozialen Frage und des Sozialismus in der Antiken Welt*. Vol. 1. Munich: C. H. Beck'sche Verlagsbuchhandlung, 1925.

Polanyi, Karl. *Primitive, Archaic, and Modern Economies: Essays of Karl Polanyi*. Garden City, N.Y.: Anchor Books, 1968.

———. *Trade and Market in the Early Empires*. New York: The Free Press, 1957.

Pole, J. R. *The Pursuit of Equality in American History*. Berkeley: University of California Press, 1993.

Raaflaub, Kurt. "Equalities and Inequalities in Athenian Democracy." In *Dēmokratia: A Conversation on Democracies, Ancient and Modern*, ed. Josiah Ober and Charles Hedrick. Princeton, N.J.: Princeton University Press, 1996.

Rae, Douglas. "Democratic Liberty and Tyrannies of Place." In *Democracy's Edges*, ed. Ian Shapiro and Casiano Hacker-Cordón. New York: Cambridge University Press, 1999.

Rogin, Michael. "How the Working Class Saved Capitalism: The New Labor History and *The Devil and Miss Jones*." *The Journal of American History* 89, no. 1.

Rostovtzeff, M. *The Social and Economic History of the Ancient World*. 2 vols. Oxford: Oxford University Press, 1941.

Rothschild, Emma. *Economic Sentiments*. Cambridge, Mass.: Harvard University Press, 2002.

Rousseau, Jean-Jacques. *Discourse on the Origin of Inequality*. Indianapolis: Hackett Publishers, 1992.

———. *Discours sur l'economie politique*. Paris: Librarie Philosophique J. Vrin, 2002.

Samuelson, Robert J. "Indifferent to Inequality?" *Newsweek*, May 7, 2001.

Sawyers, Larry, and William Tabb. *Sunbelt/Snowbelt: Urban Development and Regional Restructuring*. New York: Oxford University Press, 1984.

Schulman, Bruce. *The Seventies: The Great Shift in American Culture, Society, and Politics*. Cambridge, Mass.: Da Capo Press, 2001.

Schultz, Ronald. *The Republic of Labor: Philadelphia Artisans and the Politics of Class, 1788–1830*. New York: Oxford University Press, 1993.

Sedgwick, Theodore, Jr. "What Is a Monopoly?" In *Social Theories of Jacksonian Democracy*, ed. Joel Blau. Cambridge: Hackett Publishers, 2003.

Sellers, Charles. *The Market Revolution: Jacksonian America, 1815–1846*. New York: Oxford University Press, 1991.

Shapiro, Ian. "Why the Poor Don't Soke the Rich." *Daedelus* (Winter 2002).

Shapiro, Ian, and Casiano Hacker-Cordón, eds. *Democracy's Edges*. New York: Cambridge University Press, 1999.

Sheldon, Garrett Ward. "Classical and Modern Influences on American Political Thought: The Political Theories of Thomas Jefferson." Ph.D. diss., Rutgers University, 1983.

Shklar, Judith. *Men and Citizens: A Study of Rousseau's Social Theory*. New York: Cambridge University Press, 1969.

Simpson, Stephen. *The Working Man's Manual: A New Theory of Political Economy, on the Principle of Production the Source of Wealth*. In *Social Theories of Jacksonian Democracy*, ed. Joel Blau. Cambridge: Hackett Publishers, 2003.

Skidmore, Thomas. *The Rights of Man to Property!* New York: Burt Franklin, 1829.

Sklar, Martin. *The Corporate Reconstruction of American Capitalism, 1890–1916*. New York: Cambridge University Press, 1988.

Skowronek, Stephen. *Building a New American State: The Expansion of National Administrative Capacities, 1877–1920*. Cambridge: Cambridge University Press, 1982.

Smith, Adam. *The Wealth of Nations*. Chicago: University of Chicago Press, 1952.

Smith, Barbara Clark. "Food Rioters and the American Revolution." *The William and Mary Quarterly* 51, no. 1 (1994).

Smith, Steven B. *Hegel's Critique of Liberalism: Rights in Context*. Chicago: University of Chicago Press, 1989.

Smithin, John H. *Macroeconomics After Thatcher and Reagan: The Conservative Policy Revolution in Retrospect*. Aldershot, U.K.: Edward Elgar, 1990.

Soltow, Lee. *Distribution of Wealth and Income in the United States in 1798*. Pittsburgh: University of Pittsburgh Press, 1989.

Sorge, Friedrich. "Socialism and the Worker." In *Socialism in America: From the Shakers to the Third International*, ed. Albert Fried. New York: Columbia University Press, 1992.

Spargo, John. *The Socialists: Who They Are and What They Want*. Chicago: Charles H. Kerr & Co., 1910.

Spitz, Lewis, ed. *The Reformation: Basic Interpretations*. Lexington, Mass.: D. C. Heath and Company, 1972.

——. "The Third Generation of German Renaissance Humanists." In *The Reformation: Basic Interpretations*, ed. Lewis Spitz, 44–59. Lexington, Mass.: D. C. Heath and Company, 1972.

|234| Ste. Croix, G. E. M. *The Class Struggle in the Ancient Greek World: From the Archaic Age to the Arab Conquests*. Ithaca, N.Y.: Cornell University Press, 1981.

Strauss, Leo. *Natural Right and History*. Chicago: University of Chicago Press, 1953.

Strumia, Anna. *L'immaginazione repubblicana: Sparta e Israele nel dibattito filosofico-politico dell'età di Cromwell*. Florence: Casa Editrice Le Lettere, 1991.

Stuurman, Siep. "The Voice of Theristes: Reflections on the Origins of the Idea of Equality." *Journal of the History of Ideas* 65, no. 2 (2004).

Sugrue, Thomas. "The Structures of Urban Poverty: The Reorganization of Work and Space in Three Periods of American History." In *The Underclass Debate*, ed. Michael B. Katz. Princeton, N.J.: Princeton University Press, 1993.

Sumner, William Graham. *What Social Classes Owe to Each Other*. 1883. Caldwell, Idaho: Caxton Press, 2003.

Sunstein, Cass. *The Second Bill of Rights*. New York: Basic Books, 2004.

Taylor, John. *An Inquiry Into the Principles and Policy of the Government of the United States*. New Haven, Conn.: Yale University Press, 1950.

Thomas, John L. *Alternative America*. Cambridge, Mass.: Harvard University Press, 1983.

Thomas, Norman. *The Choice Before Us: Mankind at the Crossroads*. New York: Macmillan Co., 1934.

——. "Shall Labor Support Roosevelt?" New York: Socialist Party, 1936.

Tocqueville, Alexis de. *Democracy in America*. New York: Harper Perennial, 1969.

Trubowitz, Peter. *Defining the National Interest: Conflicts and Change in American Foreign Policy*. Chicago: University Press of Chicago, 1998.

Urbinati, Nadia. *Mill on Democracy: From the Athenian Polis to Representative Government*. Chicago: University of Chicago Press, 2002.

Verba, Sydney, and Gary Orren. *Equality in America: The View from the Top*. Cambridge, Mass.: Harvard University Press, 1985.

Vethake, John. "The Doctrine of Anti-Monopoly." In *Social Theories of Jacksonian Democracy*, ed. Joel Blau. Cambridge: Hackett Publishers, 2003.

Vidal-Naquet, Pierre. *Le chasseur noir: Formes de pensée et formes de société dans le monde grec*. Paris: Francois Maspero, 1981.

Viroli, Maurizio. *Republicanism*. New York: Hill and Wang, 2001.

Voss, Kim. *The Making of American Exceptionalism: The Knights of Labor and Class Formation in the Nineteenth Century*. Ithaca, N.Y.: Cornell University Press, 1993.

Walker, P. C. Gordon. "Capitalism and the Reformation." In *The Reformation: Basic Interpretations*, ed. Lewis Spitz, 60–74. Lexington, Mass.: D. C. Heath and Company, 1972.

Wallach, John. *The Platonic Political Art: A Study of Critical Reason and Democracy*. University Park: Penn State Press, 2001.

Warden, G. B. "Inequality and Instability in Eighteenth-Century Boston: A Reappraisal." *Journal of Interdisciplinary History* 6, no. 4 (1976).

Warner, Michael. *The Letters of the Republic: Publication and the Public Sphere in Eighteenth-Century America*. Cambridge, Mass.: Harvard University Press, 1990.

Watson, Margaret. *Class Struggles in Ancient Greece*. New York: Howard Fertig, 1973.

Weber, Max. "Die protestantische Ethik und der Geist des Kapitalismus." In *Gesammelte Aufsätze zur Religionssoziologie*. Tübingen: J. C. B. Mohr / Paul Siebeck, 1972.

——. *From Max Weber: Essays in Sociology*. New York: Oxford University Press, 1958.

——. *Weber: Selections in Translation* W. G. Runciman, ed.,. New York: Cambridge University Press, 1978.

Webster, Noah. "An Examination into the Leading Principles of the Federal Constitution." In *The Essential Federalist and Anti-Federalist Papers*, ed. David Wootton. Cambridge, Mass.: Hackett Publishers, 2003.

Welch, Finis. "In Defense of Inequality." *American Economic Review* 89, no. 2 (May 1999).

West, John G. "Darwin's Public Policy: Nineteenth-Century Science and the Rise of the American Welfare State." In *The Progressive Revolution in Politics and Political Science: Transforming the American Regime*. ed. John Marini and Ken Masugi. Lanham, Md.: Rowman and Littelfield, 2005.

Weyl, Walter. *The New Democracy: An Essay on Certain Political and Economic Tendencies in the United States*. New York: Macmillan Co., 1912.

Wilentz, Sean. "America's Lost Egalitarian Tradition." *Daedelus* (Winter 2002).

——. *Chants Democratic: New York City and the Rise of the Working Class, 1788–1850*. New York: Oxford University Press, 1984.

Williamson, Jeffrey G. *Did British Capitalism Breed Inequality?* Boston: Allen & Unwin, 1985.

——. *Industrialism, Inequality, and Economic Growth.* Cheltenham, U.K.: Edward Elgar, 1997.

Williamson, Jeffrey G., and Peter Lindert. *American Inequality: A Macroeconomic History.* New York: Academic Press, 1980.

——. "Long-Term Trends in American Wealth Inequality." In *Modeling the Distribution and Intergenerational Transmission of Wealth,* ed. James D. Smith. Chicago: University of Chicago Press, 1980.

Wilson, William Julius. *The Truly Disadvantaged.* Chicago: University of Chicago Press, 1987.

——. *When Work Disappears: The World of the New Urban Poor.* New York: Knopf, 1996.

Wintz, Cary D. *African American Political Thought, 1890–1930.* Armonk, N.Y.: M. E. Sharpe, 1996.

Wolff, Edward N. "Racial Wealth Disparities." *Jerome Levy Institute of Economics Public Policy Brief,* no. 66 (2001).

——. *Top Heavy: The Increasing Inequality of Wealth in America and What Can Be Done About It.* New York: The New Press, 2002.

Wood, Gordon. *The Radicalism of the American Revolution.* New York: Vintage, 1993.

Wyllie, Irving. *The Self Made Man.* New Brunswick: Rutgers University Press, 1954.

Zumbrunnen, John. "Fantasy, Irony, and Economic Justice in Aristophanes' *Assemblywomen* and *Wealth.*" *American Political Science Review* 100, no. 3 (2006).

| Index |